Prefaces to Shakespeare

10

Prefaces to Shakespeare

HARLEY GRANVILLE-BARKER

VOLUME II

King Lear
Cymbeline
Julius Caesar

Introduction, illustrations and notes
by M. St. Clare Byrne

B. T. BATSFORD LTD LONDON

PRINTED AND BOUND IN THE NETHERLANDS BY
THE HOOIBERG PRINTING COMPANY, EPE, FOR THE PUBLISHERS
B. T. BATSFORD LTD
4 FITZHARDINGE STREET, PORTMAN SQUARE, LONDON W. I.

Contents

List of Illustrations

Acknowledgments

As in Volume I a number of the illustrations have been reproduced from the originals I collected for the Arts Council of Great Britain exhibition of *The History of Shakespearian Production in England*, and I again gratefully acknowledge permission to draw upon this material. My thanks are due to the following for permission to reproduce illustrations: the Committee of the Garrick Club, No. 24; the London County Council, Fig. F; the Old Vic and the Royal Shakespeare Theatre, Stratford-upon-Avon for all photographs of their productions; Common Ground (1951) Ltd. for permission to quote freely from my film-strip *Shakespearian Production in England, 1700–1800* (CGA : B411), and to Miss Joan Beard of Common Ground for photographic work, old and new; the Victoria and Albert Museum, Nos. 2, 4, 9; Messrs. Raymond Mander and Joe Mitchenson, No. 12 (photo by Tunbridge); *The Observer*, No. 21 (photo, David Sim); *The Stage*, Nos. 37, 38; Mr. W. Bridges Adams and Mr. J. B. Charlesworth, Nos. 39 and 40; Mr. Ernst Stern, Nos. 29, 30, Figs. C, D, and the British Drama League for permission to photograph these items from their copy of *The Players' Shakespeare*; and to the following photographers for the use of copyright photographs: Angus McBean, Nos. 8, 13–16, 19, 26, 33, 34, 41, 42; John Vickers, Nos. 17, 18; Bryan Heseltine, No. 20; Desmond Tripp, Nos. 43–45; The Canadian Postcard Co. Ltd., Toronto, No. 46.

I am greatly indebted to Sir John Gielgud for permission to quote personal letters written to him by Granville-Barker, and to the following for personal help, loans, information, etc.: Sir Laurence Olivier, Sir Michael Redgrave, Mr. Glen Byam Shaw; Miss Anne Bolton of the Old Vic Theatre, Mr. Vincent Pearmain of the Royal Shakespeare Theatre; Mr. George Nash of the Enthoven Collection and his assistants, Miss M. Johnson and Mr. E. Lovelock; Miss Mary Garnham, Librarian of the British Drama League; Miss Eileen Robinson, Librarian of the Royal Shakespeare Theatre; Miss Ann Kahn. I also gratefully acknowledge permission to quote comments and extracts from the following: Miss Audrey Williamson and Barrie and Rockliff (Barrie Books, Ltd.), *Old Vic Drama;* Mr. Christopher Hassall, *The Timeless Quest*; Mr. T. C. Worsley and *The New Statesman*; the Public Trustee and The Society of Authors, *Our Theatres in the Nineties* (originally, *Dramatic Opinions and Essays*) and Preface to *Plays Unpleasant;* The Stratford Festival, Canada, and Clarke, Irwin and Co. Ltd., Toronto, *Thrice the Brinded Cat Hath Mew'd;* Mrs. Herbert Farjeon, *The Shakespearean Scene* by Herbert Farjeon; Jonathan Cape Ltd. *Brief Chronicles* by James Agate; Macdonald & Co. (Publishers) Ltd., *Old Vic Saga* by Harcourt Williams; Sir Tyrone Guthrie and Hamish Hamilton, *My Life in the Theatre*.

M.S.B.

Introduction to the Illustrations

Fig. A   Benjamin Webster's Haymarket production of
The Taming of the Shrew, 1844
(from *The Illustrated London News*)

In the English theatre the story of the search for Shakespeare's
stage begins in 1844. Scholarship, in the person of Edmund
Malone, had started serious investigation of that lost Elizabethan theatre and its stagecraft in 1790. In March 1844 *The
Illustrated London News*, under the heading "Good News
for the Admirers of Shakespeare", announced that Benjamin
Webster, the famous actor and manager of the Haymarket,
was to revive *The Taming of the Shrew* "in its original form",
or, as the theatre's advertisement says, "from the original
text as acted divers times at the Globe and Blackfriars Play-
houses, 1606." For nearly a hundred years it had been practically superseded by Garrick's abridged version, *Katharine and*

Petruchio. Webster restored the full text, including the Induction, "and though the play lasted three hours and a half, the attention of the house never failed" *(The Times*, 17 March). He also reproduced the original conditions in which scholarship was then saying it must have been staged, and "the audience did not in the least seem to feel the absence of scenery."

The Illustrated London News (23 March), impressed by the success of this "hazardous experiment", gave a drawing of the scene (Fig. A). Having originally questioned the wisdom of choosing one of the least popular plays, it had allowed that "after the cruel manner in which the poet has been treated of late, it will be interesting to observe what the actors are capable of doing . . . with the language and characters involved in the original work." In the event, its verdict was unqualified: "As to the 'getting up' of the piece, nothing could have been better," and "the general effect produced by some excellent acting" more than compensated for the absence of scenery.

The Athenaeum (23 March) took a sour view of this "pedantic affectation of accuracy", opined that its only purpose was to give "a feature of novelty", and objected to the mixture of styles: the Induction had "all the modern accessories of scenery",

> Christopher Sly is ejected from a scenic alehouse, and installed in the "lord's" chamber, with a substantial bed and pictured splendour. This being the place where the comedy is supposed to be acted, a couple of screens and a curtain, divided in the middle, form a veil to hide the actors off the stage, and labels affixed to the curtain denote the changes of scene; Sly being present as a spectator during the whole time.

The Times, however, reported that the announcement of its repetition for every evening was received with enthusiastic applause, and commented that, although "the whole dramatic apparatus" was only "two screens and a pair of curtains",

> this arrangement, far from being flat and ineffective, tended to give closeness to the action, and by constantly

allowing a great deal of stage room, afforded a sort of freedom to all the parties engaged ... The greatest credit is due to Mr. Webster for reviving the play in the shape in which we find it in Shakespeare's work and for producing it in a style so unique that this revival is really one of the most remarkable incidents of the modern theatre.

It seems a far cry from Benjamin Webster in 1844 to William Poel in 1881 and Granville-Barker at the Savoy in 1912, and in the years between much happened abroad, especially in the German theatre, which was to affect the ideas of twentieth-century English producers. But Webster's 'hazardous experiment' points with uncanny accuracy to the specifically English characteristics of the work of Poel and Barker. There is first the avowed and publicized care for the text – "the manager being desirous of producing the play in its original form and not in the modern shape of a three-act drama which is scarcely to be recognized as 'from the text of Shakespeare'." Almost equally remarkable, in a theatre steadily growing in mechanic mastery of scenic illusion and splendour, there was already this quite surprising knowledge of the stage conditions for which the plays were originally designed, and an eagerness to discover what could be gained by trying to reproduce them. Finally, there is the emphasis upon speech and acting, and, in the critical response, a recognition of the value of continuity in the action and of the effectiveness gained for Shakespeare "by constantly allowing a great deal of stage room" for freedom of movement. All this, be it noted, nearly fifty years before anyone had heard of the now-famous Swan drawing – the only pictorial representation of the interior of a sixteenth century English theatre which we possess (Vol. I, Fig. A).

In Germany, as *The Times* critic who reviewed Webster's 1844 production pointed out, Ludwig Tieck, the best of the German translators of Shakespeare, had already suggested that the plays should be revived on the stage of the period, and in 1843 at Potsdam had given a performance of *A Midsummer Night's Dream*, acted on different stage levels connected by

Fig. B Karl Immermann's design for a Shakespearian Stage

steps, with no scenery save curtained pillars.[1] In 1852, in
pursuit of Tieck's ideas, Karl Immermann, dramatist and producer, presented *Twelfth Night* at Dusseldorf on what pur-
ported to be a reconstruction of the Shakespearian stage but
was, in fact, much nearer to the Renaissance version of the
classical stage, equipped with six entrances and a small inner
stage which could be curtained off and set while the action
on the main stage proceeded (Fig. B). Through the side and
rear arches glimpses of appropriate outdoor settings could be
given. This experiment, like Webster's, was not followed-up in
its own time; but comparison with Figs. C and D, and with
Julius Klein's Munich Court Theatre stage (Vol. I, 31), suggests that it was not without influence upon the simplified
German settings of the present century which influenced Barker's ideas and also Barry Jackson's.

In 1889, at the Munich Court Theatre, under the direction
of the Freiherr von Perfall, the Hungarian producer Savits
staged *King Lear* in a setting which aimed at providing,

1 *Shakespeare Survey 12* has an interesting reproduction of Tieck's
stage, redrawn from an 1936 sketch based on the Fortune playhouse. It
suggests a dignified and aesthetically pleasing background, and its affinities
are with Walter Hodges' conjecture, (Vol. I, Fig. B), rather than the half-
timbered reconstructions of earlier research.

within the frame of the proscenium arch, the main structural facilities of the Elizabethan stage, establishing something of the original intimacy between actors and audience by a fore-stage built out well beyond the front curtain, with steps leading down into the orchestra pit as at Stratford or the Old Vic today (5). With its painted settings it was admittedly a compromise between Shakespeare's unlocalised stage and the nineteenth century stage of illusion; but this experiment, and also a literal attempt by Max Krüger to reproduce the conditions suggested by the Swan drawing, both failed, like Tieck's and Immerman's, to establish themselves in professional theatre practice. There do not appear to have been any further experiments with antiquarian reconstructions.

Like Webster and Tieck, William Poel began his experiments in Elizabethan staging before Karl Gaedertz's discovery of the Swan drawing in 1888. He gave his first performance in 1881. The full story of what he did for the reform of English methods of Shakespearian production has been brilliantly told by Robert Speaight, who was one of his actors, in *William Poel and the Elizabethan Revival* (1954), – a book which no reader of these *Prefaces* can afford to neglect if he wishes to understand the theatre as Poel and Barker knew it in the last years of the nineteenth century and the first decade of this. He inspired with his own ideals such famous professional players as Edith Evans, Lillah McCarthy, Sara Allgood, Lewis Casson, Robert Loraine, Esmé Percy, and also others of a younger generation; he influenced the work of Granville-Barker and Nugent Monck as producers, and won the respect of the scholars. In 1896 Bernard Shaw, who as critic of *The Saturday Review* was busily attacking the vices of spectacular Shakespeare and our acting traditions, wrote that the more he saw of the work of Poel's Elizabethan Stage Society, the more he was convinced that not only was Poel's method the right one for Elizabethan drama but that "any play performed on a platform amidst the audience gets closer home to its hearers than when it is presented as a picture framed by a proscenium." When in 1913 a *Daily Chronicle* interviewer asked him why he had founded the Society, Poel explained that he was not really an archaeologist but a modernist:

> My original aim was just to find out some means of acting Shakespeare naturally and appealingly from the full text as in a modern drama. I found that for this the platform stage was necessary and also some suggestion of the spirit and manners of the time.

He could not have summarized more succinctly the nature of the reforming impulse, as manifested in his own work and in Barker's. They were both Shakespearians in search of authenticity – the "authentic Swan of Avon" that Shaw greeted with acclaim whenever it unexpectedly turned up in the theatre, as in Forbes Robertson's *Hamlet* (see *Note* 33–36, Vol. I).

The only Elizabethan feature of Poel's reconstruction which Barker adopted was the forestage he built out over the orchestra pit – 12 ft. deep in the centre and 11 ft. at the sides – which gave actor-audience intimacy and allowed for quick, lively speech. Otherwise, as E. A. Baughan wrote at the time, "Mr. Barker's ideas do not pretend to be Elizabethan at all", and he thought it "quite evident" that the "eccentric scene" and the "baroque dresses" of *The Winter's Tale* "were not the expression of any sincere artistic need on the part of Mr. Barker, except inasmuch as he had come to the general conclusion that old-fashioned, realistic scenery hampers rather than helps Shakespeare." In lay-out his stage was very similar to the stages of the 'new movement' in the German theatre, which under the influence of Appia, Gordon Craig and Fuchs was abandoning scenic realism, pictorial backgrounds and painted perspective for permanent architectural units, the cyclorama and simplicity; and in some instances, as at the Munich Künstlertheater, was using for Shakespeare an almost Elizabethan arrangement of forestage, middle and inner acting areas. Barker fixed a false proscenium behind the arch, reducing the stage proper not, indeed, to Elizabethan inner-stage dimensions but to a smaller acting area for set, furnished scenes. It could be divided by decorative curtains from the wide, shallow, middle area beneath the arch, which could be similarly divided from the forestage. The rear stage was raised four steps above the middle area, which was raised two steps above the forestage. This incidentally, was to prove the most widely adopted feature of his stage lay-out in this country.[1] Proscenium doorways gave entry to the two forward areas. Footlights were abolished: lighting was from above and from the front of the circle and the stage boxes. There is a distinct resemblance in lay-out to Julius Klein's stage and to the *Julius Caesar* setting by the German designer, Ernst Stern, Figs. C and D.

ACT I, SCENE I. ROME: A STREET

Fig. C   Stage setting by Ernst Stern for *Julius Caesar*
(*The Players' Shakespeare*, 1925)

In 1912 Poel's opinion of the English theatre was that "in the interpretation of Shakespeare's characters and in the intelligent reading of his text there seems to be no progress made and no individuality shown." The challenge was taken up when in that same year Barker rescued such characters as Malvolio, Maria, Sir Toby and Sir Andrew from conventional characterization, and such scenes as Act V Sc. ii of *The Winter's Tale* from the producer's blue pencil. While Barker's *Twelfth Night* was still running at the Savoy, Barry Jackson opened the Birmingham Repertory Theatre in February 1913 with the same

[1] cf. the Immermann and Klein stages; and see for examples Vol. I, 7, 19 and 32, 22 and 24, 30; Vol. III, 31–32, 46; Vol. IV, 6, 27, 59, 60, 61.

ACT V, SCENE I. THE PLAINS OF PHILIPPI

Fig. D   Stage setting by Ernst Stern for *Julius Caesar*
(The Players' Shakespeare, 1925)

play, and gave four more Shakespeare productions in his first
season. By 1923 he had presented seventeen altogether. *The
Stage Year Book* for 1914 described his method as "somewhat similar to that adopted by Mr. Granville-Barker at the
Savoy, though there has been no copying." He used, and continued to use, a permanent set, with a fore-stage and an inner
stage with its own proscenium, but his main stage was given
more space and more importance in the action. Like Barker's,
his inner stage was raised by two or more steps, and its proscenium gave the dominant 'period' note of the production—
in *Macbeth*, for example, a heavy Norman arch on short,
thick pillars. Access to the central acting area was by two
proscenium doors. His front-of-house lighting had the advantage over the Savoy's, however, as he had equipped the theatre
with the Fortuny lighting system, and therefore had a true
'sky-dome' to give "great charm of colour and atmosphere"
to outdoor scenes.

The Old Vic opened for Shakespearian performances in
1914 and kept open throughout the First World War. From
1920 to 1925 Robert Atkins presented the plays with at most

one or two set scenes, combined with curtains, to give the necessary speed and continuity for what were virtually un-abridged texts, with only verbal or linear cuts and no trans-posing of scenes. "Comparatively judged", by that enthusi-astic Shakespearian and avowed 'Poel-ite', Herbert Farjeon,[1] the work was admirable: if there was too much inexperienced and inferior acting, there were also individual performances of high merit; and good production enabled him in 1922, for example, for the first time in his experience, to enjoy *Othello* as a whole play, "with all its magnificent proportions and overwhelming catastrophies unimpaired". But judged "abso-lutely", the performances in that year had "not really more than a faint smell of the real Shakespeare". They were not good enough, could not expect to be, with a new production roughly every fortnight. In 1919 Bridges-Adams became di-rector at Stratford, and though the Old Vic's team-work and acting were generally better, here, too, speedy playing and unabridged texts carried on the Poel-Barker reforms. His settings, mostly of his own design, were admirably suggestive and often of great pictorial beauty, and were devised, as he has said, "to combine the spaciousness, intimacy and con-tinuity of the Elizabethan stage with as much scenic effect as seemed desirable."

The immediate post-war period saw a decline and then a revival of Shakespearian acting.[2] It was probably inevitable, in the circumstances, and it was by no means a disservice to Shakespeare to get the play rather than the star-player well and truly established as the thing the audience went to see. And then, gradually, the names began to come back. In 1923 Sybil Thorndike and Lewis Casson put on *Cymbeline* in the West End, followed by *Henry VIII* and *Macbeth* in 1925 and 1926, in handsomely mounted productions. For Christmas 1924 Basil Dean staged *A Midsummer Night's Dream* at Drury Lane, with one of the starriest casts ever assembled, spectacle to

[1] *The Shakespearean Scene: Dramatic Criticism* (1949).

[2] See the present writer's "Fifty Years of Shakespearian Production", *Shakespeare Survey 2*, (1949).

rival the Tree tradition, and the inevitable sacrifice of the text to Mendelssohn and machinery. Edith Evans went to the Old Vic for the 1925–26 season and played half-a-dozen of the great roles – "Ye gods and little West Enders!" wrote Farjeon, "what dramatic history is now unfolding itself in the Waterloo Road!" And to round off the twenties, in 1929 John Gielgud went to the Old Vic to essay, in two seasons, no less than eleven of the greatest roles, and emerge in 1931 with the reputation of the best young Shakespearian actor of his time. Judging by Drury Lane's *Dream*, however, and the Hammersmith Lyric's famous *Merry Wives* of 1923, there had been some danger in the early twenties of a reversion to spectacle, scenery and mauled texts, if we were to rise above the inevitable limitations of uncommercial repertory for Shakespeare. The play-going public loves its scenery and has never been very particular about texts. Farjeon described the *Merry Wives* as "resolutely reactionary" in production, "with picture scenery of the most undistinguished type" and "cuts, perversions of the text, misrepresentations of the text, even additions to the text". But James Agate described it as "a gorgeous success" – which it was, and deservedly so, by reason of the superb acting of Edith Evans and Dorothy Green as the Wives and Roy Byford and Randle Ayrton as Falstaff and Ford. And in the same year, when reviewing another *Dream* at the Kingsway, where "there was not enough of feasting for the eye", this same critic asked, "Is it possible that simplified scenery is being overdone? . . . Is it too reactionary to suggest that bad realistic scenery were better?"

It was fortunate, therefore, that 1925, which saw the Drury Lane 'full treatment', and also Sybil Thorndike as Queen Katharine in one of the finest performances of her career, was the year in which Barry Jackson's modern-dress *Hamlet* at the Kingsway made us recognise more clearly than any other Shakespearian theatrical event since Barker's Savoy seasons the function of the producer as interpreter. *Hamlet* in contemporary costume was not 'new' to the theatre, (cf. Vol. I, *Notes*); but in 1925 it was a novelty, as Barker's productions had been. It was important because it stressed the obligation

Barker lays upon the producer to "gain Shakespeare's effects" and to discern for himself what these are by making a fresh, informed and intellectual approach to the author's own text. It was doubly important that it should have happened to be produced at that moment, so that the return of outstanding players to Shakespearian work was matched by this encouragement to producers who believed in the text and dramatic values and were not prepared to throw in their lot with 'reactionary production'.

What the modern-dress *Hamlet* did for most people was to make them realise that never before had they seen it *as a play* – a closely-knit, clear and exciting drama, full of vigorously conceived and varied individuals. They had only seen star actors using it as a vehicle for the interpretation of a single character. Now, in the wholeness of statement intended by the author, it was seen to be an extraordinarily good play. As early as 1908, in a remarkable essay on *Shakespearian Representation,* Percy Fitzgerald had criticised the "maimed characters" and the "hashed-up selection of the more telling portions of the play" which "the stage-managers" had been exhibiting for generations as *Hamlet*, turning Claudius, for example, into "an unmeaning cardboard figure, a patient foil for his nephew, instead of being an intriguing crafty fellow", with Polonius as "an old butt or buffoon, a tedious dodderer, with much white wool on his head and carrying a white wand", when "in our day he would be a Sir Peter Polonius, K.C.B., late envoy" and a "capable, commanding figure, a skilled man of the world". In 1925 Bromley Davenport's handling of the character, very much along these lines, was a revelation[1] (Vol. 1, 39), as was the good-looking, vigorous Claudius, urbane and keen-witted, created by Frank Vosper, who wrote at the time,

> The traditional robes, the farouche beard and moustaches, the improbable-looking crown (usually a size too

[1] cf. Shaw's comment in 1899 (Preface: *Plays for Puritans*) that Benson's 'entirety' made the numerous critics whom he accuses of never having read the play "remark with naive surprise that Polonius is a complete and interesting character."

large or too small) have swamped the poor fellow to the point of extinction. I play him clean-shaven, silver-haired at the temples, and, – I hope – fairly *soigné*. (Vol. I, 32)

He was right to say Claudius had never such a chance before: one reviewer even thought that his modern clothes and the excellent performance gave the King altogether too good an innings; but nobody could be surprised at Gertrude's re-marriage or wonder why this man in the prime of life had successfully "popped in between th'election" and the hopes of the Wittenberg undergraduate. And the whole play was as freshly imagined as if it were being staged for the first time. In the years between 1925 and Poel's challenge of 1912 progress had been made. But repertory conditions were still responsible for too much 'dull' Shakespeare, and it was, therefore, a really exciting experience to encounter another experiment with Barker's end in view – vitality and authenticity. At which point it is not irrelevant to remind the reader who did not live in those stirring times of the concurrent stimulus to interpretation that was being provided by Granville-Barker's *Introduction*, his 1924 British Academy lecture "From *Henry V* to *Hamlet*", and the original Players' Shakespeare *Prefaces* – all flowing in a steady stream from the press between 1923 and 1925, and in this last year reaching their sixth volume: eight commentaries in two years, to demonstrate just what a producer's intensive study and "intelligent reading" of the author's text really involved.

The final link between Shakespeare in the theatre today and the Shakespearian revolution of 1912 that was 'Barker at the Savoy' was forged in 1929 when Harcourt Williams took over production at the Old Vic. It was the psychological moment for a refresher course in the Poel-Barker reforms and methods, for actors, audiences and producers; and Harcourt Williams was the right man for the job. As John Gielgud says of him, "he combined the new ideals of Poel, Craig and Granville-Barker with the best traditions of the theatre that preceded them – the theatre of Irving, Tree and Alexander – and so linked in his work the most valuable lessons of both generations." He was two years younger than Barker, had been in a number of his productions, had begun his acting career in F. R. Benson's company in 1897, and had played in a wide range of modern plays as well as Shakespeare. He came to his first rehearsal fresh from a week-end with Granville-Barker, and in his *Old Vic Saga* he wrote,

> I have never found a producer to surpass Granville-Barker. He had an intimate knowledge of the play he was working on, down to the least significant comma in each part. He never allowed you to slide down the easiest path; he never gave you intonations and accents but the reason why and where the emphasis should be made . . . Roughly one might say that Barker worked from the inside to the outside. He had an exceptional instinct for what was theatrically effective but never got it by theatrical means. It had to be won by mental clarity and emotional truth.

His first concern, like Barker's, was the fresh approach to the genuine text. He went back to the Folio because it helped him to grasp the continuity, and ignored all cut acting-versions. He was determined to get rid of any traditional business that still slowed down the action, of "unnecessary and meaningless gesture", and of the last traces of slow, declamatory speech and what he called "the absurd convention of the Shakespearian voice". His first two productions were a *Romeo and Juliet* with no waits and only one interval, and a *Julius Caesar* in its entirety. His most daring experiment was a Renaissance *Antony and Cleopatra* (Vol. III, 17, 18), staged according to Barker's ideas, which won from Gordon Craig the praise that it was his best production to date, and "A I at that" and "all of a piece – not clever – good."

His leading man was the twenty-five year old John Gielgud, for whom these two Old Vic seasons came at a critical moment in his career, after what he calls "a drifting, unsatisfactory time", when he had felt he was "not gathering much strength in the West End theatre". Aware in himself of that real passion for the theatre which he had recognised as the driving force in the producers he most admired – notably, Granville-Barker and Komisarjevsky – he found in the then 'revolutionary' methods of Harcourt Williams the right kind of stimulus to give direction to his endeavours, converting a vague unwillingness to become "nothing but a leading man" into a positive determination to devote his energies to working for the theatre in every way that might lie open to him. He was encouraged "to contribute ideas to the productions" and "began to work at directing with even greater enthusiasm than at acting"[1]; and under the man who "never found a producer to surpass Granville-Barker" and was directly and continuously influenced by him in those years, he gained, as he says, "confidence in myself and a new respect for integrity and teamwork".

"Mr. John Gielgud has fairly gingered up *The Merchant of Venice*" was the opening of Farjeon's notice of his first professional Shakespeare production. He himself records that he was "accused of fantasticating the story too much, and of overloading it with dancing, music and elaborate decorations". Balancing the good ideas against the bad, Farjeon found it so full of both that it was "continuously interesting", and a welcome relief after years of "unenterprising representations" that had made the play seem "distinctly musty". He praised the "strong speed with which the story is unfolded", found the words "more intelligently spoken than usual", and approved of "the single, nondescript set" which enabled the play to be

> disencumbered of those drawings and withdrawings of the curtain that cut Shakespeare up as badly as any blue pencil. This is what Shakespeare meant. And what Shakespeare meant is what matters. Mr. Gielgud has done an important thing in finally proving the fallacy of the contention that Shakespeare without scenery becomes *ipso facto* dull. Nothing could be less dull than this production.

What he has singled out for praise shows how clearly the new young producer was committed to the Barker creed – the good speaking, fidelity to the author's intention, a setting that helped pace and continuity, and the fresh approach which kept

1 See his autobiography, *Early Stages* (1939, revised 1948, enlarged 1953); also Hallam Fordham's pictorial biography of 1952.

the play "continually interesting".

This was in December 1932. Three months later Gielgud had soared into West End star-dom with *Richard of Bordeaux,* his first great success as actor-producer; and in November 1934, with the experience of eight productions behind him, including a highly-successful *Romeo and Juliet* at Oxford for the O.U.D.S., he challenged his fate as Hamlet in his own production in the West End. Its success made it a landmark in his career; and it re-defined and re-affirmed the Barker tradition in terms of the nineteen-thirties. Experience had brought his ideas and enthusiasm under discriminating artistic control; and he still believes that, as a team, his first-rate cast was the finest he has assembled for any of his *Hamlet* productions. In this particular he established a pattern and set a standard, not only for his own future productions but for Shakespeare and the classics generally in our time.

The moment of opportunity is not inevitably matched by the man of the right calibre. Twice in the recent history of Shakespearian production Granville-Barker had been the man to seize upon such moments – in 1912, when notice of boredom and dismissal had already been served upon spectacular Shakespeare,[1] and in the nineteen-twenties when the theatre and scholarship drew together in the *Prefaces*. At the end of the twenties, 'producer's Shakespeare' was upon us, vouched for by the genuinely interpretative power of the modern dress *Hamlet* and encouraged by experimental work, English and foreign. Gordon Craig, writing to Harcourt Williams, had prophesied, "The Producers are going to save the English stage and have already begun". But just as that aspect of Barker's productions which had 'sold' reformed Shakespeare to the West End dinner-tables had been suspect to a critic of E. A. Baughan's acumen and integrity, so to Harold Child, at the beginning of the thirties, the producer's theatre seemed mainly concerned with finding "some way of playing Shakespeare that has never been tried before". In

[1] Perhaps never more wittily and devastatingly than in *The Times* notice of Tree's *Macbeth* (6 Sept. 1911): for extracts see "Fifty Years of Shakespearian Production" cited p. xix.

search of 'stunts' – the 'novelty' of which Webster had been accused in 1844 – producers were playing tricks with "the construction and tone of plays every whit as daring as those of Tate and Cibber". He instanced "Shakespeare acted in modern dress; all in black and white; on a stage that is all staircase; so lighted that no face can be seen."[1] The 1928 modern dress *Macbeth* and *The Shrew*, which had done nothing to reveal any unguessed-at richness in either and had merely cheapened them, and such eccentricities as Terence Gray's Cambridge Festival productions of Shakespeare had made his comments fair and well-timed. It was to this theatre, adventurous but over-excited by its own cleverness and the possibilities of the theatrical, that Gielgud was to devote that passion for 'theatre' which had taken him to the Old Vic; and fortunately for Shakespeare, what it gained at this critical moment was a young man in whom the star and the producer, the vitality of the older acting tradition and the reforms of the new dispensation, had come to terms – already in 1934 an outstanding figure in his profession, who by inclination and experience was sealed of the tribe of Barker and as deeply imbued as this producer he most admired with a respect for dramatic values and verities.

One important problem that faced him was still the same as Barker's in 1912 – to find his own "new hieroglyphic language of scenery". This was *Hamlet* for the West End and the audiences that had made *Richard of Bordeaux* the success of the season: it must acknowledge West End standards of presentation, as well as of casting, as Barker's productions had done. He had often discussed the ideal setting with his clever young designers, the firm of Motley, who had been responsible for his *Merchant of Venice* and *Richard* and two other plays. Their solution was a non-representational setting, of a kind familiar on the continent, inspired originally by the ideas of Craig and Appia. The elements were simple – a cyclorama, richly-coloured patterned curtains and a large rostrum on a

[1] See his chapter on the history of Shakespearian Production in *A Companion to Shakespearean Studies*, edited by Granville-Barker and G. B. Harrison, 1934.

turntable, built-up into a three-dimensional unit, composed of platforms of varying sizes and levels connected by inclines and flights of steps, which provided for variations of scenic effect as well as speedy playing and continuity. Height and dignity were given by the long flowing lines of the curtains, with their heavy, opulent swags and curves balancing the solidity, the mass and the horizontal lines of the central structure. Combined with the rich, glowing colour and the almost decadent exuberance of the Cranach costumes, the setting created the atmosphere of a corrupt and sensual Court – as if the very air hung heavy with intrigue, oppressing and stifling the "free spirit" of the young Prince; until, in the final scene, the sense of space given by the cyclorama lifted the tragedy above the toil and fret to "where th'eternal are".[1]

Superficially there was nothing to recall the Barker settings or those of his followers. There was no forestage, no inner proscenium. Admittedly, in 1910, Barker had recommended the "revolve" as the device which could "quite revolutionize the playing of many-scened Elizabethan classics",[2] though he did not use it himself. He and others had used curtains combined with architectural units such as pillars and archways, and stepped stages for varied levels; but their effects, though formalized, were realistic in comparison to this organization of planes and rectangular and cubic forms and the reliance upon pure form, line and colour to create mood and atmosphere. Nevertheless, history was repeating itself, in that Gielgud drew for ideas and inspiration upon established continental practice and upon the same master, Gordon Craig.[3] Craig's influence was apparent in the use of line and mass which gave importance to the figure of the actor and the grouping, and upon which light and shadow could play with great dramatic effect. And thanks to Barker's lead twenty years earlier and the subsequent work of his followers, Gielgud had inherited a prepared position. Shock treatment was no longer necessary: there was no need to "out-Poel

[1] See Vol. I, 42, 43.
[2] When reporting the Berlin Theatre Exhibition in *The Times*, 7 Nov. 1910.
[3] cf. Vol. I, p. x.

Poel and out-Tree Tree in a single superb gesture" to sell a reformation to the public, no need to startle and provoke. The Old Vic had a permanent abstract set and at least two architecturally conceived settings for this play had already attracted attention.[1] But these had not been West End experiments, and that was what Gielgud, like Barker before him, was out to conquer for the classics, to bring reformed Shakespeare with simplified functional staging into the commercial theatre, now that the new approach to the text and the acting had proved generally acceptable. To compare the staging of a tragedy with Barker's treatment of three middle-weight plays would be unprofitable; the live tradition he had established was the need for experiment to determine the right kind of staging for the particular play:

> as a new formula, a new convention has to be found, the audience must learn to see, even as we learn to work in it.[2]

The end in view was the same. Like Barker, Gielgud was concerned to create a functional equivalent with Elizabethan facilities – a setting aesthetically pleasing, theatrically simple and undistracting, harmonizing with the mood of the play and providing for speed and continuity and significant movement and grouping. That it was open to some minor criticisms he himself was as quick as anyone to realise. But that he, like Barker, had succeeded and won this West End foothold back again is a matter of theatre history. *Hamlet* in the new manner ran for a hundred and fifty-five performances – its longest run since Irving's, sixty years earlier.

His next attack on the scenic problem, again with Motley, came in the following year with *Romeo and Juliet*. Barker spoke warmly of the production:

> I liked it much. I could have made reservations, but I'd do that of a performance of archangels. But it was *far* the best bit of Shakespeare I'd seen in years.[3]

[1] cf. pp. xxix-xxx; also Vol. I, Note 37, for J. B. Fagan's O.U.D.S. production in 1924.

[2] "The Golden Thoughts of Granville Barker". *Play Pictorial*, XXI, No. 126.

[3] In a personal letter tot John Gielgud, 16 June 1937.

The set was a bold and largely successful attempt to provide a permanent background structure for the balcony and bedchamber 'above', while meeting the play's other specific demands for the Capulet vault, the Friar's cell and the Apothecary's shop, and leaving enough stage room for the street scenes, the fighting and the Capulet ball, (Vol. IV, 28–31, and *Notes*). Like the *Hamlet* rostrum, this permanent structure was used in conjunction with curtains – in this case, black velvet. Its Elizabethan facilities enabled the action to move swiftly, with no breaks in the continuity, from one area to another, and gave great animation to the movements and groupings of the actors. Again there was no indebtedness to Barker's staging, but the same insistence upon the essentials for the effects of the particular play; and just as Barker had taken hints for striking colour and costumes from the Russian Ballet – then the latest thing in contemporary art – so Gielgud and his designers reflected in their multiple setting an affinity with current theatrical experiment, which had given us in 1931 the three-, four- and five-roomed, two-storey settings of *Three Flats, Desire under the Elms* and *Late Night Final,* and, earlier in 1935, the effective three-roomed set with different levels, designed by Motley, which he had used for his own production of *The Old Ladies*. It had its practical drawbacks, to which some reference is made in the *Note*s, but it was an advance on the compromise Elizabethan setting of Barry Jackson's *Romeo and Juliet* at the Regent in 1924, in which Gielgud as Romeo had played his first London Shakespearian lead, and it was an ambitious exploration of the scenic problem in a mode totally different from the *Hamlet* experiment.

Gielgud and Motley were not the only experimenters in equivalent facilities. London had seen the 1924 *Romeo and Juliet* and Barry Jackson's characteristic staging in the 1925 *Hamlet*, and it had known the Elizabethanism of Robert Atkins and Harcourt Williams at the Old Vic. In 1930, Peter Godfrey had put on a production of *Hamlet*, with Esmé Percy, at the Court Theatre, in a setting which James Agate described as

> a nice compromise between the exiguous Elizabethan

stage – platform, balcony, and cubby-hole – and the columnar jigsaw arrangements beloved of Mr. Gordon Craig.

He commented:

> The best argument for the simplified setting of Shakespeare is the saving of time and the preservation of continuity. But it is hard to believe that the revolving-stage, which a National Theatre would presumably possess, would hurt the play of *Hamlet* more than the consent wrung forcibly from us that Ophelia shall be buried in the middle of Gertrude's closet. Given the occasional revival of Shakespeare's plays by private, limited enterprise, there can be no doubt that the method adopted by Mr. Godfrey is the best. It asks a good deal, but then the practised Shakespearean playgoer is prepared to give a good deal.

At the Old Vic in 1933 Tyrone Guthrie had a permanent abstract set designed by Wells Coates "to provide the necessary facilities and avoid any precise suggestion of period" and to serve for any of the plays. He himself considered it "distinctly handsome", but found that, in practice, it looked "almost impertinently modern" and "wildly obtrusive"; and when "painted pinky-grey for *Twelfth Night* ... completely dominated the evening and suggested not Illyria but a fancy dress ball on a pink battleship". Instead of being merely a functional background, it proved "a powerful, stridently irrelevant competitor for the audiences' attention".[1] Farjeon, in his *Twelfth Night* notice, remarked,

> The permanent architectural unscenic stage, which would otherwise be excellent, is cluttered with steps. The characters can't take more than a few paces in any direction without going up or down. But this can and should be remedied.

Gielgud's two sets, however, were the most original and artistically pleasing experiments that the West End had seen since Barker's time. Coupled as they were with first-class

[1] See Chap. 9, *A Life in the Theatre*, in which he describes his plans for staging Shakespeare according to the principles of Poel and Barker.

production and acting, they were important pronouncements against scenic realism, in favour of a decorative and architecturally-functional concept; and the genuinely creative part played by Motley in working out possible answers to the demands of a stage for Shakespeare which could accommodate itself to ordinary theatres has not always received the pioneer credit it deserves. Another practical attempt to solve the special problems of a particular play was their design for Glen Byam Shaw's 1946 production of *Antony and Cleopatra*, with Edith Evans and Godfrey Tearle at the Piccadilly, (Vol. III, 24–27). It was harshly criticised, with facetious chaff about the Battersea Power Station and the lifts at Selfridges, because it was too 'modern' in its architectural associations, like the Wells Coates Old Vic set. But in spite of what was wrong and the things people disliked, it gave the death-blow to realistic pictorial scenery for this play, and the kind of mistake it made pointed the way to the right solution.

The nineteenth century regarded it as *the* play for elaborate pictorial treatment. Even Phelps mounted it more splendidly than any of his previous productions; Benson's first Stratford production, in 1898, was described at the time as "the costliest ever seen there"; and Tree's in 1906 was as spectacular as anything he afterwards achieved, (Vol. III, 19–22). This tradition died hard. In 1925 Agate wrote of a "rather meagrely put on" Old Vic production, "If ever a Shakespearian play calls for music, processions, and Tadema-like excesses in bathroom marble, *Antony and Cleopatra* is that play"; and in 1935 all the grand scenery and 'correct' costumes were hailed with relief by Stratford audiences which had not relished the departure from tradition when, in 1931, Bridges-Adams followed the example of Harcourt Williams at the Old Vic and staged it as Barker recommends – after Paolo Veronese, with Cleopatra in a farthingale, (Vol. III, 17–18). What had rung a bell in the imaginations of those concerned in the 1946 production, however, was the opening sentence of Barker's *Preface* – "Here is the most spacious of the plays." The first quality a production must have is this sense of space. Their design made their aim apparent, so that the failure to achieve it in theatrical terms drew attention to the quality itself: the essential was apprehended and seen to be missing.[1] The spaciousness achieved with a cyclorama depends upon the magnification which its well-calculated use gives to actual stage space: if the amount of stage room available in front of any necessary practicable structure is small in proportion to the number of players and their deployment in groups and movement, the effect will be lost. To overcome the problem of sight-lines with a proscenium only 22 ft. high and no forestage,[1] the set had to be too far down stage: there was not enough room for manoeuvre, and consequently the stage seemed cramped and cluttered and the set itself heavy. More than any of the plays it asks open-stage freedom for its many scenes and quick changes of locality. The set's equivalent facilities provided technically for speed and continuity, but denied to the play's imaginative spatial range the equivalent impression of stage space which its own theatre gave. They had the right line on the play, however, as the next three productions show (Vol. III, 28–34). Their second attempt, at Stratford in 1953, was entirely successful: the setting was as essentially simple as T. C. Kemp's description –"a pillared open space with steps to varying levels, a place of free air and a wide sky," (Vol. III, 32 and *Note* 33–34). But the 1946 project had been an instructive experiment and ranks with the two Gielgud-Motley productions as one of the most illuminating explorations of the problem before Tanya Moiseiwitsch's permanent sets for *Henry VIII* in 1929 and the 1951 history cycle at Stratford.

Further tracing of the development of practicable 'equivalent' settings should not be necessary. A continuity of idea, from Barker to Gielgud, is clearly indicated, though as was said of Barry Jackson's methods in 1914, "there has been no copying". Functionalism has become a first charge on the

---

[1] The photographs (26, 27) show that the design, as such, could have given the required effect. Its failure is not obvious from them.

[2] At the New Theatre for *Romeo and Juliet* they had 27 ft. 6 in. Barker, with only 23 ft. 6 in. at the Savoy, had a forestage and no upper stage, except for the narrow 5 ft. rostrum for the play in *A Midsummer's Night's Dream*.

designer's ingenuity, although formal 'decoration' has by no means ousted the pictorial setting. Formality and simplicity have tended to distinguish the best productions of the tragedies, and the *Antony and Cleopatra* lesson has probably helped to alert us to the desirability of creating that sense of Shakespearian space which is part of the imaginative impact of the great plays and physically the birthright of any play written for the original open-air stage.

Alongside of experiments with structural facilities akin to the Elizabethan, experiment with Elizabethan reconstruction continued, but, with one exception, outside the professional theatre. Poel gave his last performance in 1932; and in 1952, Nugent Monck, who for some thirty years had been running the Norwich Maddermarket, the only Elizabethan theatre in this country, was still prepared to say,

> We do not really know anything about the Elizabethan theatre. It is all very carefully worked-out supposition ... My guess is as good as anyone else's, and so my theatre upsets those people who expect to find there this, that, or the other thing.

Monck was a disciple of Poel and had been one of his stage-managers; but when Poel came to see it, "He hated it!", Monck reports, and he himself would cheerfully refer to his own stage as "bogus" (Fig. E). It had neither proscenium arch nor curtain, but it was no more an Elizabethan open stage than any platform that stretches across the end of a hall from one side to the other. Secure in the knowledge that the smallness of his theatre, seating just over two hundred, gave the necessary intimacy for quick, natural speech, and that his Elizabethan performances captured the essentials, he could afford his joke. He achieved absolute continuity, and his productions were notable for their speed and pace and liveliness. But having presented the whole of the canon in the Elizabethan manner he found that "after six productions of *Twelfth Night* the audience got nearly as bored with it as I did", and so began to experiment with some suggestions of scenery, such as a woodland backcloth for the *Dream* or a billowing gauze for waves in *The Tempest*.

Stratford's experience of Elizabethanism in the thirties, under Iden Payne, yielded similar results. His aim was "continuity of performance, contact with the audience, and simplification of scenic investiture". Continuity and simplicity were achieved, but the size and remoteness of the new theatre's stage made real 'contact' impossible. His Elizabethan costumes were extremely fine, but his permanent background, closely resembling Poel's, had "an air of pedantry". Norwich and Stratford both found that, once the 'novelty' had worn off, the ordinary theatre audience was bored by the externals of Elizabethanism – as if, without the open-ness of the genuine platform stage, they blurred the "intensely alive" quality that Barker demanded and the intensely contemporary impact of the characters that the modern-dress *Hamlet* had revealed. By 1936 Guthrie was convinced, as he tells us in his autobiography, that open-ness – with the reciprocal actor-

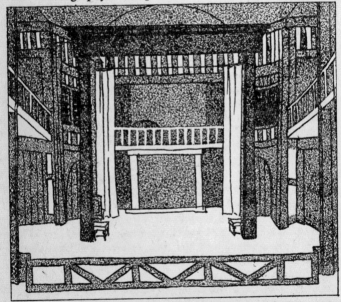

Fig. E   The Maddermarket Theatre, Norwich

audience, audience-actor excitement it engenders – was the real clue for the living theatre to follow, and that there could be no radical improvement in Shakespearian production until we achieved two things:

> first, to set the actors against a background with no concessions whatever to pictorial realism, the sort of background which the Elizabethan stage provided ... secondly, to arrange the actors in choreographic patterns, in the sort of relation both to one another and to the audience which the Elizabethan stage demanded and the picture-frame stage forbids.

The trouble is that you cannot have the genuine open stage until you rebuild your theatre and its auditorium. Shakespeare's stage, as Farjeon wrote in 1930, in a spasm of disgust at a reactionary West End production of *Othello,*

> thrust out its long, rude tongue into the auditorium, so that it was surrounded on three sides by spectators, in whose very midst the players, as large as life and twice as dramatic, declaimed the mighty lines and bodied forth the mighty passions bestowed upon them ... When Othello raged round the boards, he raged not in two dimensions, but in three. When he fell into his trance, his position, relative to the spectators, was very much that of a boxer taking the count. Propinquity, which disenchants the view, put him on his histrionic mettle. It also helped him to take fire from his audience, and his audience to take fire from him.

For Guthrie, the secret of the Elizabethan playhouse can be summed up in two words – "intimacy and magnitude". As he points out, closely packed together, and brought by the design of the building into this close proximity with the players, "the audience surrounded and hung over the cockpit where the play took place"; and instead of being isolated individuals became, in unanimity of feeling, "one single, massive, composite beast". Imagine that "rude tongue" thrust out into the stalls to a depth of nearly thirty feet in the crowded auditorium shown in Plate 37, Volume III, and we get some idea of what Elizabethan conditions may have been like. No forestages such as we have known since Barker's time – now back in favour again – can hope to reproduce the intimacy of the real open stage or generate this crowd-excitement; and it is this stimulating, intimate contact between player and audience that is stressed today by its advocates, together with the nearness to the stage of every spectator, that enables the actor, as Guthrie says,

> to use the full range of his voice from a shout to a whisper; to speak, when necessary, as fast as ever he can, and to mime the action with the subtlety and delicacy which it deserves.

By not campaigning against the proscenium arch and by not espousing the cause of the Elizabethan theatre or the open stage or his own experimental stage, Granville-Barker did the theatre a great service. By examining the dramatic values of individual, representative plays in the *Prefaces*, and showing what essentials of the author's stagecraft have to be provided for if those values are to be theatrically realised, in whatever theatre or upon whatever kind of stage his work is presented, he gave producers and actors the fundamental task of studying the texts to discover the author's intentions, instead of giving them a new toy to play with, before they were ready for it or it for them. Thanks to the direction he had already given to Shakespearian experiment, the new approach to the text and the acting was not thrust upon them simultaneously with the demands of an entirely new technique, for a stage of which no one then had any real professional experience – except, perhaps, as Barker says, "the modern music-hall comedian getting on terms with his audience."

Though he does not set them forth as so many arguments against a reconstruction for the stage for Shakespeare, Barker's insistence – in the *Introduction* and the *Preface* to *Cymbeline* – that there was no one Elizabethan theatre and that the buildings and their stages were changing during Shakespeare's lifetime, provides the commonsense theatrical argument against it. Build the Globe or the Fortune indoors – supposing you can get sufficient agreement as to how this should be done – and you lose the effect of free air, open sky and daylight, which all count for something and the last for a great deal. Rebuild the Blackfriars (Fig. F)[1], which was an indoors theatre, and you will have a theatre which must be carefully considered when we stage *Cymbeline*, "if for no other reason than that here was a theatre far liker to our own than the open-air Globe". Reminding us that the later plays "had to serve for both theatres", he discusses the relative sizes of the two stages and the effect the smaller one would have on the writer's stage-craft, the plotting, the style of the writing and of the speaking and acting, (pp. 248–52). The Globe stage is generally thought to have been about 41–43 ft. wide and some 29 ft. in depth. He suggests for the Blackfriars a practicable main stage of roughly 26 ft. wide and 12 ft. deep –"cramped acting space, after the Globe" – with a sizeable inner stage, for which Dr. Armstrong's examination of plays performed there lends solid support.

"The Globe had been the breeding ground of the greater work", the great tragedies, "and their force and simplicity were cardinal virtues", enhanced by the theatre's every condition, "the daylight and the actors on their patform, making point-blank unvarnished appeal". At the Blackfriars, he concludes, "it was Shakespeare with a difference": as a result of using this indoors private theatre, "the old Elizabethan freedom very slowly, almost imperceptibly contracted". The drawing, Fig. F, is to some extent conjectural, as we do not know that the stage extended right across the full width of the hall (46 ft.), like the stages of the Maddermarket and the third Mermaid Theatre. It may have projected into the auditorium, like the Fortune stage in its rectangular theatre (Vol. IV, Fig. A): it could have been tapered, as Cranford Adams considers the Globe stage to have been (Vol. I, 11). But if it actually extended from side to side, then already, within

[1] For an account of this reconstruction by the late J. H. Farrar of the Architect's Department of the London County Council, see W. A. Armstrong, *The Elizabethan Private Theatres*, (Society for Theatre Research, Pamphlet Series, No. 6, 1958). There is no evidence for the use of footlights on any English stage before 1670, so this detail should be disregarded. The capacity of the Blackfriars is thought to have been about six to seven hundred persons. 10 ft. on each side of the stage, Barker suggests, would be taken up by those who sat on stools (p. 100).

Shakespeare's lifetime, the theatre that is generally thought to have been the model for the best of the other private play-houses had lost the true open stage.

In 1936–37 Robert Atkins gave three genuine open-stage productions at the Blackfriars' Ring, a former boxing stadium. The audience sat round three-quarters of its not very large circle and the open platform was backed by a reasonable imitation of the tiring-house, with an inner stage and balcony. *The New Statesman* noted that the stage served the war scenes and the love scene of *Henry V* equally well. *The Times* singled

Fig. F The Second Blackfriars Theatre, 1596–1642
A reconstruction, drawn by J. H. Farrar (1921)
(Reproduced by courtesy of the London County Council)

out Jack Hawkins as Benedick in *Much Ado* for his "art in playing all round the stage at once", taking first one section of the audience into his confidence and then another, "but in reality embracing the whole ring of spectators"; and admired the way Atkins produced *The Merry Wives* "as to the manner born", with great liveliness and pace "and a rare measure of intimacy". The actors gave their services, so performances could only be given on Sundays, but it was an exciting demonstration of the virtues of the real thing and roused much enthusiasm. In the nineteen-forties Ronald Watkins, in the annual Shakespeare performance at Harrow School, introduced a select audience to an Elizabethan stage of full dimensions, with inner and upper stages and the whole of the open platform area surrounded by the spectators. Throughout the fifties, these performances and the two books in which he illustrated from his experience the practical application of open-stage methods, were a great stimulus to general interest and helped us to visualize the possibilities of the large open platform and to estimate the value of a reconstruction in line with modern knowledge. Appropriately, however, the crucial experiment which seriously directed professional attention to the claims of the open stage was Tyrone Guthrie's production of *The Three Estates* in the Assembly Hall at the 1948 Edinburgh Festival, upon what its creator describes as "a first sketch for the sort of Elizabethan stage I had long hoped, somehow and somewhere, to establish" – a platform built for the occasion, with steps around three sides, and a gallery with a recess beneath it on the fourth side. So complete was its success that the play was staged for three successive festivals.[1]

The profession took up the challenge in the early fifties with the first Mermaid Theatre (Vol. I, Fig. C), the second Mermaid at the Royal Exchange, and the performances given by Ann Jellicoe at the Cockpit Theatre, Westminster, where the audiences were crowded right up to the stage and surrounded it completely on three sides. Considerable attention was also called to the whole question of Elizabethan and modern open staging during 1952, Poel's centenary year, when among

[1] There is a good photograph in his autobiography.

authoritative and encouraging statements from leading Shake-spearians such as Guthrie and Lewis Casson, John Gielgud in a lecture at Oxford, speaking of the drawbacks of the Strat-ford theatre, advocated a more or less Elizabethan design where the essential actor-audience contact could be established; where one could know that, "once the playhouse had been seen and accepted for the first time, neither critics nor public would expect anything *except the play*"; and where, con-sequently, the hectic search for novelty in staging "would no longer be possible, nor even matter any more".

Once the essential working of a smooth flow of action had been accepted and worked out, using fore and back stage, apron and upper balcony – all the players would need to be given would be handsome costumes and properties and, I think, artificial light, though probably in a simpler form with many less subtleties than in the average picture-stage productions – for I have found my-self that too many changes of lighting can be as distract-ing to the text as changes of scenery – and the play would speak – and speak well, one hopes, for itself.

Barker does not deal in general terms with the subject of lighting for the stage for Shakespeare, but that he was sensitive to the anti-illusionist quality and value of the daylight of the open-air theatres is clear, not only from his remarks on con-trasting conditions at the Globe and the Blackfriars but also from the lighting of his own Shakespeare productions. The general effect in all three was of a clear, white light – "a hygienic light", Bridges Adams calls it, "the sort of light that shines upon an operating table", as if he wanted "to let fresh air and day-light into Shakespeare, because they were whole-some things"; and in *The Winter's Tale* and *Twelfth Night,* "he swept shadows from the stage as if they harboured germs." Today, Guthrie speaking for the open stage and Ronald Watkins for the reconstructed Globe stage, both insist that the aim should be to create an effect equivalent to ordinary daylight. The former, in his 1949 *Henry VIII,* used uncoloured light throughout, unaltered except for a number of imperceptible light cues that varied its emphasis; and at

Stratford, Ontario, in the first season, he allowed "no illusionary effects of light save for an unobtrusive 'dim' where
it seemed appropriate". Watkins recommends "a steady light
representing daylight", because "it is half the battle to have
the audience sitting in the same light as the players; the actor's
courage will be rewarded by the astonishing intimacy thus
created between himself and his audience."

Open-stage insistence upon daylight equivalence has a value
perhaps greater than we have yet fully realised for the classics,
which depend on the 'word over all' – Farjeon's phrase. Its
quality of essential truthfulness, and the basic steadiness and
reality it provides, helps both concentration and continuity by
not calling attention to itself with the modern, production-
conscious audience, as I realised for the first time with
Guthrie's *Henry VIII*. It is possible that dramatic effect, as
provided by the author's words and the acting, can be greater
without theatrical assistance from lighting coloured for mood.
The comments on the cold, harsh brilliance of Barker's lighting must have made students wonder why he used overhead
and front-of-circle arcs, mostly white, with a few described as
'flame'. But when *The Times* critic, a quarter of a century
later, notes how in the open-stage *Much Ado* produced by
Robert Atkins at the Ring, his glaring arcs catch each glint of
expression on the actors' faces, so that "every flicker of an
eyelid tells", it is reasonable to guess that Barker, aiming at
naturalness and intimacy in acting and speech, also wanted
the dramatic flicker of the eyelid as well as fresh air and daylight, and knew how to get it. The more one sets his practice
and precepts beside our latest innovations, the more deep and
instinctive his understanding of the demands of a stage for
Shakespeare becomes.

As already explained, one main purpose of the illustrations
is to provide – more especially for younger students – a
'background to Barker', to show how the best Shakespearian
work of the last fifty years is definitely related to his practice
and influence. The point urged in the *Foreword* was that

Barker's productions set the theatre on the right path at a crucial moment, so that what it has pursued in these fifty years is not Shakespeare's stage but stages for Shakespeare.

Considerable stress has been laid upon scenic history because Barker himself insisted on the importance of this problem, warning us in 1912 that "realistic scenery won't do", but that "we shall not save our souls by being Elizabethan". The theatre has followed this lead in its rejection of Elizabethan reconstructions; and the determining factor in its acceptance of his directives has been his compromise with the conditions imposed by the proscenium arch, for which his doctrine of essentials and equivalence provides the practical answer. It looks as if we have found some pleasing and serviceable conventions such as he bade us seek – as if, for example, 'an open space with pillars and curtains and varying levels' is basic material for *Hamlet* or *Antony and Cleopatra* and will provide for other plays, not necessarily the tragedies only. It would seem that in the cyclorama we have something which is even less distracting than the tiring-house facade and creates the atmosphere of Shakespearian space in the proscenium arch theatre – an asset which is perhaps as valuable as the fluidity of movement which the open stage achieves, and which appears at present to give us something which open stages and theatre in the round both lack. The Elizabethan method of localization by properties, so admirably handled by Guthrie in picture-frame theatres and superbly demonstrated in Peter Hall's *Troilus and Cressida*, is certainly one of the most exciting of the more recent conventions now accepted in the commercial theatre.

Apart from his immediate influence on his own contemporaries in the theatre, there is, after his virtual retirement from it, a direct link in the inter-war years between Barker and Harcourt Williams, and Williams and Gielgud, a further direct link between Barker and Gielgud[1], and between Gielgud and the actors and producers of his own generation and notably Glen Byam Shaw, who acted in so many of his productions and in some cases co-produced with him. Barker himself paid

1 cf. *Notes*, 33–36, 35.

tribute in 1939 to Gielgud's "dominant position in the acting of Shakespeare and therefore in the theatre generally"[1] and Gielgud still affirms that Barker remains the strongest influence he has encountered in the theatre. T. C. Worsley wrote in 1954:

> the revival of our theatre from the trough of triviality into which it had fallen in the post-Du Maurier days is very largely due to Sir John, who between the wars successfully challenged the assumption that the classics, produced and acted in the new manner, could not compete on commercial terms with light comedy.

We have followed the line of descent and the continuity of idea. Whether we call it the new manner or the modern tradition, the acting reforms, the demand for authentic texts and for the same fresh and alert interpretation of the classics as would be accorded to a modern play constitute the tradition for which Poel and Barker were responsible.

In an essay *On Cutting Shakespeare*[2] in which he attacked the mutilated texts of "the commercial managements", Shaw wrote,

> The only workable plan is Mr. Barker's plan, which makes Shakespeare and not the producer the ultimate authority.

This was Barker of the Savoy – the producer who saw his part as interpreter between author and player, and who once warned us, when speaking of Reinhardt, that "too great creative power is a dangerous attribute in a producer of plays"[3]. And Barker the producer was one man with the writer of the *Prefaces*, in which he gives us, as Ivor Brown says, "Shakespeare, in his habit, as he worked". The way had been prepared for him by Poel, by such productions as Forbes Robertson's *Hamlet* (Vol. I, *Note* 35) and Benson's 'entirety' version in 1899 and 1900, so that as early as 1898 Shaw had written in his Preface to *Plays Unpleasant*:

> some of our younger actor-managers have been struck with the idea, quite novel in their profession, of perform-

[1] In a personal letter to John Gielgud, 15 Sept. 1939.
[2] *The Fortnightly Review*, August 1919.
[3] *The Times* 19 Nov. 1910, in a review of the Berlin Theatre Exhibition.

ing Shakespeare's plays as he wrote them, instead of using them as a cuckoo uses a sparrow's nest.

The preparation had been sufficient, in spite of the war and Barker's withdrawal from the theatre, to make the combined impact of his three productions and the earlier *Prefaces* decisive, so that in 1925 Shaw could rebuke John Barrymore for a *Hamlet* text "cut to ribbons" and tell him that his methods were out of date and that he had obviously not followed the course of English Shakespearian production closely enough in the last fifteen years.[1]

The centenary of Poel's birth was celebrated in 1952: in fourteen years' time we shall be celebrating Barker's. The *Prefaces* were begun over forty years ago. They remain unique, though by means of what he modestly calls "some research into Shakespeare's stagecraft," and the treatment of each play as "a score waiting performance" they have encouraged all producers, scholars and critics to consider more deeply the relationship between the author's dramatic intentions and their theatrical realization. He does not claim for him "impeccability as a playwright. His work abounds in improvisations of technique" and is "never more skilful than when he is in a difficulty." But as he says at the beginning of the original version of the *Lear* Preface,

if we fling ourselves at the task, as Burbage and the rest had to do when he brought them a new manuscript, with something of the faith they must have had in him as a playwright, for all his disturbing genius – it may be we shall not do so badly. But to this faith must be added something which the company from the Globe had also gained, a knowledge of his playwright's craft.

By these *Prefaces* we may still continue to guide our endeavours in that theatre for Shakespeare – today's or tomorrow's – towards which his three productions directed our experiments. How often, when we hail with delight some fresh and faithful rendering of one of Shakespeare's effects do we not find that Barker has anticipated us in a sentence. It was Zeffirelli who by general acclaim gave us in 1960 a *Romeo and Juliet*

[1] Printed in Barrymore's *Confessions of an Actor*, 1926: personal letter.

with an accent on youth hitherto unachieved. But it was Barker in 1930 who wrote, "This is a tragedy of youth, as youth sees it". Where will the player find, in such brief compass, a more complete characterization of Juliet's "blissfully unregenerate" Nurse than in Barker's account of this "triumphant and complete achievement"? "Shakespeare has had her pent up in his imagination; and out she gushes. He will give us nothing completer till he gives us Falstaff." We may cut the Ventidius scene in *Antony and Cleopatra* but we shall know we use the blue pencil at our peril if we read Barker on its structural and theatrical value and follow this most cunning of fellow-craftsmen in his detailed study of the play's admirable construction to the conclusion that, in spite of its multiplicity of short, swiftly-changing scenes, its

> scheme is plain and ordered enough once we grasp its purpose, and – the essential thing – once we relate it to the theatre of its nativity.

As R. A. Scott James wrote of the *Prefaces* in 1936, in them Barker had

> put all his experience and intuitive understanding at the service of those whose task it may be to interpret Shakespeare on the stage or who may simply wish to appreciate performances. After Mr. Granville-Barker there will never again be the same excuse for misinterpretation.[1]

[1] *London Mercury,* editorial notes; Dec. 1936.

King Lear

"Lear is essentially impossible to be represented on a stage" – and later critics have been mostly of Charles Lamb's opinion. My chief business in this Preface will be to justify, if I can, its title there.

Shakespeare meant it to be acted, and he was a very practical playwright. So that should count for something. Acted it was, and with success enough for it to be presented before the king at Whitehall. (Whatever his faults, James I seems to have had a liking for good drama.) And Burbage's performance of King Lear remained a vivid memory. At the Restoration it was one of the nine plays selected by Davenant for his theatre. He had in mind, doubtless, its "reforming and making fit" – all of them except *Hamlet* and *Othello* were to suffer heavily from that. But Downes, his prompter, tells us that it was "... *Acted* exactly as Mr *Shakespeare wrote it ...*" – several times apparently – before Nahum Tate produced his version in 1681. This hotchpotch held the stage for the next hundred and fifty years and more, though from Garrick's time onwards it would generally be somewhat re-Shakespeareanized.[1] One cannot prove Shakespearean stage-worthiness by citing Tate, but how far is it not Tate rather than Shakespeare that Lamb condemns? He has Shakespeare's play in mind, but he had never seen it acted. Part of his complaint is that "... Tate has put his hook in the nostrils of this Leviathan, for Garrick and his followers, the showmen of the scene, to draw the mighty beast about more easily". And he never considers Shakespeare's play in relation to Shakespeare's stage. He came near to doing so; for, later in the essay, with *The Tempest* for theme, he speaks of "... the elaborate and anxious provision of scenery, which the luxury of the age demands ..." which "... works a quite contrary effect to what is intended. That which in comedy, or plays of familiar life, adds so much to the life of the imitation, in plays which appeal to the higher

---

[1] Elliston and Kean, after a little hesitation, went so far as to restore the tragic ending. Then, in 1838, Macready acted Shakespeare's play again. But even he tampered with its structure, and – by much omission – with its text.

1

faculties positively destroys the illusion which it is introduced to aid". Had he followed out this argument with *King Lear* for an example, giving credit to Shakespeare the playwright as well as to Shakespeare the poet – I do not say that he would have reached a different conclusion, for there is still the plea to be met that here, for once, Shakespeare the playwright did overreach himself, but he must at least have recognized another side to the question. Lamb's essay should be read, of course, as a whole. He loved the drama; the theatre alternately delighted and exasperated him. The orotund acting of his day, its conventional tricks, can have been but a continual offence to his sensitive ear and nicety of taste. He here takes his revenge – and it is an ample one – for many evenings of such suffering. He never stopped to consider whether there might not be more even to the actor's despised art than that.

A profounder and a more searching indictment of the play's stage-worthiness comes from A. C. Bradley in the (for me) most remarkable of those remarkable lectures on Shakespearean Tragedy. To him it seems ". . . Shakespeare's greatest achievement, but . . . *not* his best play". The entire argument should be read; but this, I think, sums it up not unfairly. He says that "The stage is the test of strictly dramatic quality, and *King Lear* is too huge for the stage . . . . It has scenes immensely effective in the theatre; three of them – the two between Lear and Goneril and between Lear, Goneril and Regan, and the ineffably beautiful scene in the Fourth Act between Lear and Cordelia – lose in the theatre very little of the spell they have for imagination; and the gradual interweaving of the two plots is almost as masterly as in *Much Ado*. But (not to speak of defects due to mere carelessness) that and *King Lear* is too huge for the stage. . . . It has scenes immense scope of the work; the mass and variety of intense experience which it contains; the interpenetration of sublime imagination, piercing pathos, and humour almost as moving as the pathos; the vastness of the convulsion both of nature and of human passion; the vagueness of the scene where the action takes place, and of the movements of the figures which cross this scene; the strange atmosphere, cold and dark, which

2

strikes on us as we enter this scene, enfolding those figures and magnifying their dim outlines like a winter mist; the half-realised suggestions of vast universal powers working in the world of individual fears and passions, all this interferes with dramatic clearness even when the play is read, and in the theatre not only refuses to reveal itself fully through the sense but seems to be almost in contradiction with their reports". And later: "The temptation of Othello and the scene of Duncan's murder may lose upon the stage, but they do not lose their *essence,* and they gain as well as lose. The Storm-scenes in *King Lear* gain nothing, and their very *essence* is destroyed." For this essence is poetry, and, he concludes, ". . . such poetry as cannot be transferred to the space behind the foot-lights, but has its being only in imagination. Here then is Shakespeare at his very greatest, but not the mere dramatist Shakespeare".

Notice, first of all, how widely Bradley's standpoint is removed from that – we may venture to surmise it – of "the mere dramatist Shakespeare" and his fellows the actors. To say of certain scenes that they were "immensely effective in the theatre" and add that they *lost* there "very little of the spell they have for imagination", to argue that "the temptation of Othello and the scene of Duncan's murder may lose upon the stage, but they do not lose their *essence,* and they gain as well as lose" – it would have sounded to them queer commendation. For in whatever Shakespeare wrote was the implied promise that in the theatre it would *gain*. Bradley passes easily to: "The Storm-scenes in *King Lear* gain nothing, and their very *essence* is destroyed." But the dramatist, on his defence, would rightly refuse to follow him; for the premises to the argument are not the same.

Bradley and Lamb may be right in their conclusions. It is possible that this most practical and loyal of dramatists did for once – despite himself, driven to it by his unpremeditating genius – break his promise and betray his trust by presenting to his fellows a play, the capital parts of which they simply could not act. Happily for them, they and their audiences never found him out. But if Bradley is right, not the most perfect performance can be a fulfilment, can be aught but a betrayal of *King Lear*. There is the issue. The thing is, of course, incapable of proof. The best that imperfect human actors can give must come short of perfection, and the critic can always retort to their best that his imagination betters it. Bradley's argument is weighty. Yet – with all deference to a great critic – I protest that, as it stands, it is not valid. He is contending that a practical and practised dramatist has here written a largely impracticable play. Before condemning these "Storm-scenes" he should surely consider their stagecraft – their mere stagecraft. For may not "the mere dramatist" have his answer hidden there? But this – starting from his standpoint of imaginative reader – he quite neglects to do.

Ought we, moreover, to assume – as Bradley seems to – that a play must necessarily make all its points and its full effect, point by point, clearly and completely, scene by scene, as the performance goes along? Not every play, I think. For the appreciation of such a work as *King Lear* one might even demand the second or third hearing of the whole, which the alertest critic would need to give to (say) a piece of music of like calibre. But leave that aside. No condoning of an ultimate obscurity is involved. And comedy, it can be admitted, demands an immediate clarity. Nor is the dramatist ever to be dispensed from making his story currently clear and at least provisionally significant. But he has so much more than that to do. He must produce a constant illusion of life. To do this he must, among other things, win us to something of a fellow-feeling with his characters; and even, at the play's critical moments, to identifying their emotions with our own.

Now the *significance* of their emotions may well not be clear to the characters themselves for the moment, their only certainty be of the intensity of the emotions themselves. There are devices enough by which, if the dramatist wishes, this significance can be kept currently clear to the audience. There is the Greek chorus; the earlier Elizabethans turned Prologue and Presenters to account; the *raisonneur* of nineteenth-century comedy has a respectable ancestry. Shakespeare uses the *raisonneur* in varying guises. In this very play we detect him in the Fool, and in Edgar turned Poor Tom. But note

4

that both they and their "reasoning" are blended not only into the action but into the moral scheme, and are never allowed to lower its emtional temperature by didactics – indeed they stimulate it. For here will be the difficulty in preserving that "dramatic clearness" which Bradley demands; it would cost – and repeatedly be costing – dramatist and actors their emotional, their illusionary, hold upon their audience. Lear's progress – dramatic and spiritual – lies through a dissipation of egoism; submission to the cruelty of an indifferent Nature, less cruel to him than are his own kin; to ultimate loss of himself in madness. Consider the effect of this – of the battling of storm without and storm within, of the final breaking of that Titan spirit – if Shakespeare merely let us look on, critically observant. From such a standpoint, Lear is an intolerable tyrant, and Regan and Goneril have a case against him. We should not side with them; but our onlooker's sympathy might hardly be warmer than, say, the kindly Albany's.[2] And Shakespeare needs to give us more than sympathy with Lear, and something deeper than understanding. If the verity of his ordeal is really to be brought home to us, we must, in as full a sense as may be, pass through it with him, must make the experience and its overwhelming emotions momentarily our own.

Shakespeare may (it can be argued) have set himself an impossible task; but if he is to succeed it will only be by these means. In this mid-crisis of the play he must never relax his emotional hold on us. And all these things of which Bradley complains, the confusion of pathos, humour and sublime imagination, the vastness of the convulsion, the vagueness of the scene and the movements of the characters, the strange atmosphere and the half-realized suggestions – all this he needs as material for Lear's experience, and ours. Personally, I do not find quite so much vagueness and confusion. To whatever metaphysical heights Lear himself may rise, some character (Kent and Gloucester through the storm and in the hovel, Edgar for the meeting with the blinded Gloucester), some

[2] Whom Shakespeare carefully keeps out of the angry scenes which lead to Lear's self-banishment to the wild and the storm.

circumstance, or a few salient and explicit phrases will always be found pointing the action on its way. And if we become so at one with Lear in his agony that for the time its full significance escapes us, may not memory still make this clear? For that is very often true of our own emotional experiences. We are in confusion of suffering or joy at the time; only later do we realize, as we say, "what it all meant to us". It is, I suggest, this natural bent which Shakespeare turns to his account in these larger passages of *King Lear*. In the acting they move us profoundly. The impression they make remains. And when the play is over they, with the rest of it, should cohere in the memory, and clarify; and the meaning of the whole should be plain. Shakespeare, I protest, has not failed; he has – to the degree of his endeavour – triumphantly succeeded. But to appreciate the success and give effect to it in the play's performance we must master and conform to the stagecraft on which it depends.

In this hardest of tasks – the showing of Lear's agony, his spiritual death and resurrection – we find Shakespeare relying very naturally upon his strongest weapon, which by experiment and practice he has now, indeed, forged to an extraordinary strength, and to a suppleness besides: the weapon of dramatic poetry. He has, truly, few others of any account. In the storm-scenes the shaking of a thunder-sheet will not greatly stir us. A modern playwright might seek help in music – but the music of Shakespeare's day is not of that sort; in impressive scenery – he has none. He has, in compensation, the fluidity of movement which the negative background of his stage allows him. For the rest, he has his actors, their acting and the power of their speech. It is not a mere rhetorical power, nor are the characters lifted from the commonplace simply by being given verse to speak instead of conversational prose. All method of expression apart, they are *poetically conceived;* they exist in those dimensions, in that freedom, and are endowed with that peculiar power. They are dramatic poetry incarnate.

Thus it is that Shakespeare can make such calls upon them as here he must. In the storm-scenes they not only carry forward the story, revealing and developing themselves as they

6

do so, they must – in default of other means – create the storm besides. Not be detachedly describing it; if they "lose themselves" in its description, they will for that while lose something of their own hold on us. The storm is not in itself, moreover, dramatically important, only in its effect upon Lear. How, then, to give it enough magnificence to impress him, yet keep it from rivalling him? Why, by identifying the storm with him, setting the actor to impersonate both Lear and – reflected in Lear – the storm. That, approximately, is the effect made when – the Fool cowering, drenched and pitiful, at his side – he launches into the tremendous:

> Blow, winds, and crack your cheeks! rage! blow!
> You cataracts and hurricanoes, spout
> Till you have drench'd our steeples, drown'd the cocks!
> You sulphurous and thought-executing fires,
> Vaunt-couriers of oak-cleaving thunder-bolts,
> Singe my white head! And thou, all-shaking thunder,
> Strike flat the thick rotundity of the world!
> Crack nature's moulds, all germens spill at once
> That make ungrateful man.

This is no mere description of a storm, but in music and imaginative suggestion a dramatic creating of the storm itself; and there is Lear – and here are we, if we yield ourselves – in the midst of it, almost a part of it. Yet Lear himself, in his Promethean defiance, still dominates the scene.

But clearly the effect cannot be made by Lamb's "old man tottering about the stage with a walking-stick"; and by any such competitive machinery for thunder and lightning as Bradley quite needlessly assumes to be an inevitable part of the play's staging it will be largely spoiled. What actor in his senses, however, would attempt to act the scene "realistically"? (I much doubt if any one of Lamb's detested barn-stormers ever did.) And as to the thunder and lightning, Shakespeare uses the modicum to his hand; but it is of no dramatic consequence, and his stagecraft takes no account of it.[3] Yet

[3] Bradley argues in a footnote that *because* Shakespeare's "means of

if the human Lear seems lost for a moment in the symbolic figure, here is the Fool to remind us of him:

> O nuncle, court holy water in a dry house is better than this rainwater out o' door. Good nuncle, in, ask thy daughters' blessing; here's a night pities neither wise men nor fools.

– and to keep the scene in touch with reality. Yet note that the fantasy of the Fool only *mitigates* the contrast, and the spell is held unbroken. It is not till later – when Lear's defiant rage, having painted us the raging of the storm, has subsided – that Kent's sound, most "realistic" common sense, persuading him to the shelter of the hovel, is admitted.

But Shakespeare has other means of keeping the human and the apocalyptic Lear at one. Though the storm is being painted for us still–

> Rumble thy bellyful! spit, fire! spout, rain!
> Nor rain, wind, thunder, fire are my daughters:
> I tax not you, you elements, with unkindness;
> I never gave you kingdom, call'd you children,
> You owe me no subscription: then let fall
> Your horrible pleasure; here I stand, your slave;
> A poor, infirm, weak and despis'd old man

– both in the sense of the words and the easier cadence of the verse the human Lear is emerging, and emerges fully upon the sudden simplicity of

> here I stand, your slave;
> A poor, infirm, weak and despis'd old man.

But the actor is not meant, therefore, suddenly to drop from

imitating a storm were so greatly inferior to ours" he could not have "had the stage-performance only or chiefly in view in composing these scenes". But this is, surely, to view Shakespeare's theatre and its craft with modern eyes. The contemporary critic would have found it easier to agree that just *because* your imitation storm was such a poor affair you must somehow make your stage effect *without* relying on it.

trenchant speech to commonplace, present us a pathological likeness of poverty, infirmity and the rest, divest himself of all poetic power, become, in fact, the old man with a walking-stick. For if he does he will incontinently and quite fatally cease to be the Lear that Shakespeare has, as we said, conceived and embodied in poetry. In poetry; not, one must again insist, necessarily or simply in verse. And it is no more, now or later, a mere question of a method of speaking than of form in the writing. Verse, prose, and doggerel rhyme, in those strenuous scenes, each has its use, each asks an appropriate beauty of treatment, and the three in harmony are, by dramatic title, poetry.

The actor has then, not simply or chiefly to speak poetically, but, for the while, somehow to incarnate this poetry in himself. He can do so – paradoxically – by virtue of an exceptional self-sacrifice. Physically, Shakespeare's Lear must surrender to *him*; he makes himself in return an intellectual and emotional instrument for its expression. That is the way of all honest acting. If the actor's personality is the richer, a character will be absorbed in it. In a play of familiar human commerce actor and character may collaborate, so to say, upon equal terms. But give the character the transcendent quality of poetry, the actor can no longer bring it within the realistic limits of his personality. He may – obtusely – try to decompose it into a realism of impersonation, decorated by "poetic" speech. It is such a treatment of Lear which produces Lamb's old man with a walking-stick, and, for Bradley, dissipates the poetic atmosphere. But what Shakespeare asks of his actor is to surrender as much of himself as he can – much must remain; all that is physical – to this metaphysical power.

The thing is easier to do than to analyse. Children, set to act Shakespeare, will fling themselves innocently at the greatest of the plays; and, just because they do not comprehend and so cannot subdue the characters to their own likeness, they let us see them – though diminished and feeble – as through a clear glass. For the matured actor it is not quite so easy. He must comprehend the character, identify himself with it, and then – forget himself in it. Yet in this play and these

9

very scenes he will find the example of Lear's own relation to the storm; in the reflection of its grandeur upon him, and the force lent by his fellowship with it to the storm devouring his mind. One must not push the comparison too far, nor is the psychology of acting a subject to be compassed in a sentence or two. But very much as the storm's strength is added to Lear's when he abandons himself to its apprehension, so may the Lear of Shakespeare's poetic and dramatic art be embodied in the actor if he will but do the same. And *there* should be the Lear of Lamb's demand, great "not in corporal dimension but in intellectual". Upon a "realistic" stage the thing cannot well be done. With Shakespeare made to delegate half his privileges to scene-painter and property-man a like dissociation will be forced upon the actor. And it is not only that the apparently real heath and hovel and the all but real thunder and lightning will reduce the characters which move among them to mere matter of fact also, but that by the dissociation itself, the appeal to our imagination – upon which all depends – is compromised. For the strength of this lies in its unity and concentration. It is the unity of the appeal that allows Shakespeare to bring so much within its scope. And, with time, place and circumstance, night, storm and desolation, and man's capacity to match them in despair all caught into a few lines of poetry, it should not be so hard to absorb besides – he willing – the ego of the actor who speaks them. Then he will stand before us not physically ridiculous by comparison with them, but invested with their dynamic quality.

Shakespeare contrives within this harmony the full range of the effects he needs. There are not two Lears – the Titan integrating the storm and the old man breaking under it. In the accommodating realm of dramatic poetry they can remain one. Those contrasted aspects of them are shown in the swift descent we noted from magniloquence to simplicity, from rivalry with the elements to the confession of

> here I stand, your slave;
> A poor, infirm, weak and despis'd old man.

10

Or, we may say, there are the two Lears in one: the old man pathetic by contrast with the elements, yet terribly great in our immediate sense of his identity with them.

At best, of course, the actor can be but a token of the ideal Lear; and (thanking him) some of us may still feel that in the rarefied spaces of our imagination without his aid we come nearer to Shakespeare's imaginings – though what have we after all but a token of words upon paper to measure these by? But does the actor only remove us a stage farther from our source? I think not. He gives the words objectivity and life. Shakespeare has provided for his intervention. He can at least be a true token.

The Main Lines of Construction

King Lear, alone among the great tragedies, adds to its plot a subplot fully developed. And it suffers somewhat under the burden. After a few preliminary lines – Shakespeare had come to prefer this to the grand opening, and in this instance they are made introductory to plot and subplot too – we have a full and almost formal statement of the play's main theme and a show of the characters that are to develop it, followed by a scene which sets out the subplot as fully. The two scenes together form a sort of double dramatic prologue; and they might, by modern custom, count as a first act, for after them falls the only clearly indicated time-division in the play. The Folio, however, adds the quarrel with Goneril before an act pause is allowed: then – whatever its authority, but according to its usual plan – sets out four more acts, the second allotted to the parallel quarrel with Regan, the third to the climax of the main theme; the fourth we may call a picture of the wreck of both Lear and Gloucester, and in it subplot and main plot are blended, and the fifth act is given to the final and rather complex catastrophe. This division, then, has thus much dramatic validity, and a producer may legitimately choose to abide by it. On the other hand, one may contend, the play's action flows unchecked throughout (but for the one check which does not coincide with the act-division of the Folio). Still it is not to be supposed that a Jacobean audience

11

did, or a modern audience would, sit through a performance without pause. Yet again, it does not follow that the Folio's act-divisions were observed as intervals in which the audience dispersed and by which the continuity of dramatic effect was altogether broken. A producer must, I think, exercise his own judgment. There may be something to be said for more "breathing-spaces", but I should myself incline to one definite interval only, to fall after Act III. To this point the play is carried by one great impetus of inspiration, and there will be great gain in its acting being as unchecked. If the strain on actors or audience seems to be too great, I should choose a breathing-space after Act I, Scene ii, for all the Folio's authority to the contrary. But the strain should not be excessive upon either audience or actors. Shakespeare's stagecraft – his interweaving of contrasted characters and scenes – provides against this, as does the unity of impression and rapidity of action, which his unlocalized staging makes possible.[4]

The scene in which Lear divides his kingdom is a magnificent statement of a magnificent theme. It has a proper formality, and there is a certain megalithic grandeur about it, Lear dominating it, that we associate with Greek tragedy. Its probabilities are neither here nor there. A dramatist may postulate any situation he has the means to interpret, if he will abide by the logic of it after. The producer should observe and even see stressed the scene's characteristics; Lear's two or three passages of such an eloquence as we rather expect at a play's climax than its opening, the strength of such single lines as

The bow is bent and drawn, make from the shaft

with its hammering monosyllables; and the hard-bitten

4 Modern scenic productions, even at their simplest, not only destroy this unity of impression, but lengthen the performance of the plays considerably, and the acting habits they have engendered lengthen them still more. Mr Nugent Monck has produced *King Lear* at the Maddermarket Theatre, Norwich, upon an unlocalized stage. He cut approximately 50 of the 3340 lines of text (the Folio will give authority for the cutting of some 200), allowed a ten minutes' interval, did not play overrapidly, and the whole performance only lasted two hours and a half.

together with the loosening of the tension in changes to rhymed couplets, and the final drop into prose by that business-like couple, Goneril and Regan. Then follows, with a lift into lively verse for a start, as a contrast and as the right medium for Edmund's sanguine conceit, the development of the Gloucester theme. Shakespeare does this at his ease, allows himself diversion and time. He has now both the plot of the ungrateful daughters and the subplot of the treacherous son under way.

But the phenomenon for which Shakespeareans learn to look has not yet occurred, that inexplicable "springing to life" —a springing, it almost seems, into a life of its own — of character or theme. Very soon it does occur; Lear's entrance, disburdened from the care of state, is its natural signal. On his throne, rightly enough, he showed formal and self-contained. Now he springs away; and now the whole play in its relation to him takes on a liveliness and variety; nor will the energy be checked or weakened, or, if checked, only that the next stroke may be intenser, till the climax is past, till his riven and exhausted nature is granted the oblivion of sleep. This is the master-movement of the play, which enshrines the very soul of the play — and in the acting, as I have suggested, there should be no break allowed. To read and give full imaginative value to those fifteen hundred lines at a stretch is certainly exhausting; if they were written at one stretch of inspiration the marvel is that Shakespeare, with his Lear, did not collapse under the strain, yet the exactions of his performance he tempers with all his skill. Lear is surrounded by characters, which each in a different way take a share of the burden from him. Kent, the Fool, and Edgar as Poor Tom are a complement of dramatic strength; and the interweaving of the scenes concerning Oswald, Edmund and Gloucester saves the actor's energy for the scenes of the rejection and the storm.[5]

[5] Therefore the producer who will for the sake of his scenery (as has been the pleasant picture-stage custom) run two or three of the storm-scenes into one, presents himself and his Lear with failure.

As the Lear theme expanded under his hand Shakespeare had begun, and perforce, to economize his treatment of the Gloucester-Edgar-Edmund story. Edgar himself is indeed dismissed from the second scene upon no more allowance of speech than

> I'm sure on't, not a word

– with which the best of actors may find it hard to make his presence felt; and at our one view of him before he had been left negative enough. Edmund is then brought rapidly into relation with the main plot, and the blending of main plot and subplot begins.[6] Edgar also is drawn into Lear's orbit;

---

[6] We find, too, at this point, some signs that the emphasis of the play's whole scheme was altered.

> Have you heard of no likely wars toward,
> 'Twixt the Dukes of Cornwall and Albany?

Curan asks Edmund, who answers "Not a word". Edmund, with admirable promptitude, turns the notion to the further confusing of the so easily confused Edgar, but the wars themselves come to nothing. Kent, in an involved speech in Act III (for him most uncharacteristically involved), suggests that it is the threat of them which is bringing the French army to England. But the vagueness is suspicious. It looks a little as if Shakespeare had thought of making the hypocrite inheritors of Cordelia's portion fall out over it (an obvious nemesis) and had changed his mind. There are slight signs indeed that greed of possessions was to have been the axis for the whole play to turn upon. It begins with the parting of the realm; and

> Legitimate Edgar, I must have your land

is the coping point of Edmund's first soliloquy. Did the discovery of deeper spiritual issues in Lear's own character and fate give us the present play? Another and a later change in the plot can be divined. The King of France comes armed with Cordelia to Lear's rescue, as is natural. Then, by virtue of the clumsiest few lines in the play, he is sent back again. Did Shakespeare originally mean Cordelia to restore her father to his throne as in the old play; but would a French victory in England not have done? It may be; though I cannot think he ever intended Lear to survive. On the other hand, Cordelia herself is not a figure predoomed to death. This catastrophe, though the moral violence of the play may aesthetically justify it, and though it is needed dramatically, as a final blow to Lear (see p. 44 for the fuller argument of this), always seems to me a wrench from his first plan. This decided on, though, he would certainly have to get rid of France. The point for the producer is that the Folio cuts the clumsy explanation, as if on the principle – and it is an excellent one in the theatre – of: "Never explain, never apologize."

(cont.)

14

and, for the time, to the complete sacrifice of his own interests in the play. "Poor Tom" is in effect an embodiment of Lear's frenzy, the disguise no part of Edgar's own development.

As we have seen, while Act III is at the height of its argument, Shakespeare is careful to keep alive the lower-pitched theme of Edmund's treachery, his new turn to the betrayal of his father. He affords it two scenes, of twenty-five lines each, wedged between the three dominant scenes of the storm and Lear's refuge from it. They are sufficient and no more for their own purpose; in their sordidness they stand as valuable contrast to the spiritual exaltation of the others. The supreme moment for Lear himself, the turning point, therefore, of the play's main theme, is reached in the second of the three storm-scenes, when the proud old king kneels humbly and alone in his wretchedness to pray. This is the argument's absolute height; and from now on we may feel (as far as Lear is concerned) the tension relax, through the first grim passage of his madness, slackening still through the fantastic scene of the arraignment of the joint-stools before that queer bench of justices, to the moment of his falling asleep and his conveyance away – his conveyance, we find it to be, out of the main stream of the play's action. Shakespeare then deals the dreadful blow to Gloucester. The very violence and horror of this finds its dramatic justification in the need to match in another sort – since he could not hope to match it in spiritual intensity – the catastrophe to Lear. And now we may imagine him, if we please, stopping to consider where he was. Anticlimax, after this, is all but inevitable. Let the producer

In fact it cuts the whole scene, which later contains as dramatically feeble an excuse for the delay in handing Lear over to his daughter's care, though it gives none for the devoted Kent letting the distracted old man out of his sight to roam the fields crowned with wild flowers. I think on the whole that the Folio gives a producer a good lead. Yet another slight change of plan may be guessed at; it would effect some economy in the working-out of the subplot. Edmund says to Gloucester about Edgar:

If your honour judge it meet, I will place you where you shall hear us confer of this ... and that without any further delay than this very evening.

But he never does. Shakespeare may have remembered, besides, that he had lately used this none too fresh device in *Othello*.

15

take careful note how Shakespeare sets out to avoid the worst dangers of it.[7]

Had the play been written upon the single subject of Lear and his daughters, we should now be in sight of its end. But the wealth of material Shakespeare has posited asks for use, and his own imagination, we may suppose, is still teeming. But by the very nature of the material (save Cordelia) left for development the rest of the play must be pitched in a lower key. Shakespeare marshals the action by which the wheel of Gloucester's weakness and Edmund's treachery is brought full circle with extraordinary skill and even more extraordinary economy. Yet for all this, except in a fine flash or two, the thing stays by comparison pedestrian. He is only on the wing again when Lear and Cordelia are his concern; in the scenes of their reconciliation and of the detached tragedy of Lear's death with the dead Cordelia in his arms, as in the still more detached and – as far as the mere march of the action is concerned – wholly unjustifiable scene of Lear mad and fantastically crowned with wild flowers. We must add, though, to the inspired passages the immediately preceding fantasy of Gloucester's imaginary suicide, an apt offset to the realistic horror of his blinding, and occasion for some inimitable verse. The chief fact to face, then, is that for the rest of the play, the best will be incidental and not a necessary part of the story.[8] The producer therefore must give his own best attention to Albany, Goneril and Regan and their close packed contests, and to the nice means by which Edgar is shaped into a hero; and in general must see that this purpose-

[7] It is worth remarking here upon the fact that Edgar's two soliloquies – the one which ends Act III, Scen vi, and the one which begins Act IV – the Folio omits the first. They are somewhat redundant in mood if not in matter. The interesting thing is that the Folio omission is of a speech ending a scene and moralizing upon the event; it forms a "considering point". Without it the catastrophe to Gloucester is linked more closely to Lear's misfortunes, and the long due development of Edgar's character then begins – and importantly – the fourth act. For further argument upon this point, see pp. 68 and 81.

[8] The meeting of mad Lear and blind Gloucester (I give the scene more attention on p. 39), is, of course, most germane to the play's *idea* – a more important thing to Shakespeare than the mere story – but it does check the march of the story.

ful disciplined necessary stuff is given fullness and, as far as may be, spontaneity of life in its interpretation. If he will take care of this the marvellous moments will tend to take care of him.

Shakespeare strengthens the action at once with the fresh interest of the Edmund-Goneril-Regan intrigue, daring as it is to launch into this with the short time left him for its development and resolving. He is, indeed, driven to heroic compressions, to implications, effects by "business", action "off", almost to "love-making by reference only", Goneril's first approach to Edmund (or his to her; but we may credit the lady, I think, with the throwing of the handkerchief) is only clearly marked out for the actors by Regan's reference to it five scenes later, when she tells us that at Goneril's

> late being here
> She gave strange œilliads and most speaking looks
> To noble Edmund.

(Regan credits her with what, if we prefer our Shakespeare modernized, we might literally translate into "giving the glad eye".) But this silent business of the earlier scene is important and must be duly marked if the arrival of the two together and Edmund's turning back to avoid meeting Albany, the "mild husband", is to have its full effect. For the first and last of their spoken lovemaking, excellently characteristic as it is, consists of Goneril's

> Our wishes on the way
> May prove effects. . . .
> This trusty servant
> Shall pass between us: ere long you are like to hear,
> If you dare venture in your own behalf,
> A mistress's command. Wear this; spare speech;
> Decline your head: this kiss, if it durst speak,
> Would stretch thy spirits up into the air.
> Conceive, and fare thee well

17

and Edmund's ("Spare speech," indeed!)

> Yours in the ranks of death!

– all spoken in Oswald's presence too. It is, of course, not only excellent but sufficient. The regal impudency of the woman, the falsely chivalrous flourish of the man's response – pages of dialogue might not tell us more of their relations; and, of these relations, is there much more that is dramatically worth knowing? The point for the producer is that no jot of such a constricted dramatic opportunity must be missed.

For the whole working-out of this lower issue of the play the same warning stands true; an exact and unblurred value must be given to each significant thing. The interaction of circumstance and character is close-knit and complex, but it is clear. Keep it clear and it can be made effective to any audience that will listen, and is not distracted from listening. Let us underline this last phrase and now make the warning twofold. In working out a theme so full of incident and of contending characters Shakespeare allows for no distraction of attention at all, certainly not for the breaking of continuity which the constant shifting of realistically localized scenery must involve. The action, moreover, of these later scenes is exceptionally dependent upon to-ings and fro-ings. Given continuity of performance and no more insistence upon whereabouts than the action itself will indicate, the impression produced by the constant busy movement into our sight and out again of purposeful, passionate or distracted figures, is in itself of great dramatic value, and most congruous to the plot and counterplot of the play's ending. The order for Lear's and Cordelia's murder, the quarrel over Edmund's precedence, Albany's sudden self-assertion, Regan's sickness, Edgar's appearance, the fight, his discovery of himself, Goneril's discomfiture, the telling of Kent's secret, Regan's and Goneril's death, the alarm to save Lear and Cordelia – Shakespeare, by the Folio text, gets all this into less than two hundred lines, with a fair amount of rhetoric and incidental narrative besides. He needs no more, though bareness does nearly turn

1 GARRICK AS KING LEAR, WITH KENT (*r.*) AND EDGAR (*l.*)
Painted by B. Wilson, engraved McArdell, 1761

THE STORM

2 T. GRIEVE'S DESIGN FOR CHARLES KEAN AT THE PRINCESS'S, 1858

3   The opening scene, Macready's Covent Garden production, 1838
"Druid circles rise in spectral loneliness out of the heath" (*John Bull*)

THE TRADITION OF "MEGALITHIC GRANDEUR", EARLY AND MID-NINETEENTH CENTURY

4   "A part of the heath with a hovel." Grey, purple-shadowed monoliths and
trilithons. Charles Kean's production, Princess's Theatre, 1858

5 MUNICH ROYAL COURT THEATRE: DESIGN BY SAVITS AND VON PERFALL, 1889
Architectural reconstruction: forestage, raised inner stage; false proscenium, with entrances, and windows above; steps to orchestra pit; combined with scenic painted cloths and curtains

6 HENRY IRVING AND ELLEN TERRY IN THE OPENING SCENE: LYCEUM, 1892
Setting by Joseph Harker: drawing by Bernard Partridge

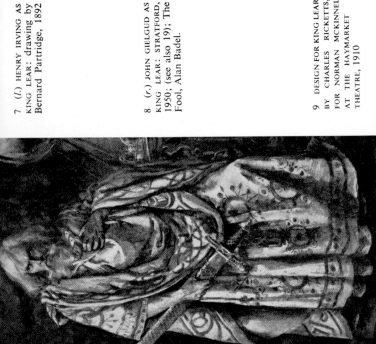

7 (l.) HENRY IRVING AS
KING LEAR: drawing by
Bernard Partridge, 1892

8 (r.) JOHN GIELGUD AS
KING LEAR: STRATFORD,
1950; (see also 19); The
Fool, Alan Badel.

9 DESIGN FOR KING LEAR
BY CHARLES   RICKETTS,
FOR NORMAN MCKINNEL
AT THE HAYMARKET
THEATRE, 1910

10 KING LEAR, WITH RANDLE AYRTON, PRODUCED BY KOMISARJEVSKY: STRATFORD, 1937
Settings and costumes by Komisarjevsky

11 DESIGN FOR KING LEAR BY NORMAN BEL GEDDES (WATER-COLOUR) 1926
Dark pillars, smoky-brown monoliths, the light ranging from pale yellow to fiery orange

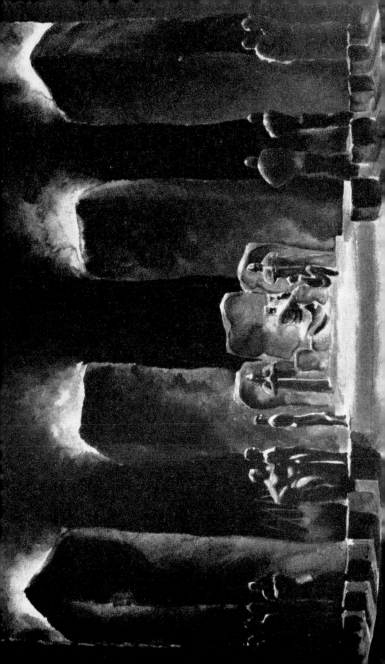

12   DONALD WOLFIT AS KING LEAR

" His King is a magnificent creation, as deeply felt as thought,
and acted with the most detailed skill." (T. C. Worsley, 1949)

Wolfit has played Lear a number of times in his
own production, which he first presented in 1943

to banality sometimes. But unless we can be held in an un-relaxed grip we may not submit to the spell.

He has kept a technical master-stroke for his ending:

> *Enter Lear with Cordelia in his arms.*

There should be a long, still pause, while Lear passes slowly in with his burden, while they all stand respectful as of old to his majesty. We may have wondered a little that Shakespeare should be content to let Cordelia pass from the play as casually as she seems to in the earlier scene. But this is the last of her, not that. Dumb and dead, she that was never apt of speech – what fitter finish for her could there be? What fitter ending to the history of the two of them, which began for us with Lear on his throne, conscious of all eyes on him, while she shamed and angered him by her silence? The same company are here, or all but the same, and they await his pleasure.[9] Even Regan and Goneril are here to pay him a ghastly homage. But he knows none of them – save for a blurred moment Kent whom he banished – none but Cordelia. And again he reproached her silence; for

> Her voice was ever soft,
> Gentle and low, an excellent thing in woman.

Then his heart breaks.

The Method of the Dialogue

The dialogue of *King Lear* is remarkable for its combination of freedom and power. Of the plays that neighbour it, the sustained melodies of *Othello* may give greater dignity. In *Macbeth* there are passages that seem to wield a sort of secret sway. *Antony and Cleopatra* has ease and breadth for its normal virtues as *Coriolanus* has strength; and, thereafter, Shakespeare passes to his last period of varied and delightful ease. But the exact combination of qualities that distinguishes

---

9 And this must not be counted as chance, for the bodies of Goneril and Regan have been brought on – why else?

the writing of *King Lear* we do not find again; nor indeed should we look to, since it is the product of the matter and the nature of the play. Shakespeare was in nothing a truer artist than in this, that, having mastered his means of expression, journeyed from the rhymed couplets and fantastic prose of *Love's Labour's Lost* to the perfected verse and balanced prose of *Henry V* and the mature Comedies, he yet fettered himself in no fixed style. He may write carelessly; here and there amid the poetic splendours we find what seem to be claptrap couplets and lines flatter than a pancake. But, his imagination once fired, the idea seldom fails of the living vesture it needs. This, it may be said, it is any writer's business to discover. But Shakespeare's art lies in the resource, which can give individual expression to a thought or emotion within the bounds, for instance, of a stretch of formal verse if his first need is for the solid strength of this; or more often, in the moulding of verse and prose into such variety of expressive form that it is a wonder any unity of effect is kept at all – yet it is. It lies in the daring by which, for a scene or two, he may dispense with all unity of form whatever, if his dramatic purpose will so profit. Witness such a seemingly haphazard mixture of verse, prose and snatches of song as we find in the scenes between Lear, Kent, Gloucester, the Fool and Poor Tom. Yet the dramatic vitality of these scenes lies largely in this variety and balance of orchestration; their emotional strain might be intolerable without it. But the root of the matter, of course, is in the imaginative vitality which he dowers the characters themselves. It is always instructive to watch Shakespeare getting his play with its crew under way, to see him stating his subjects, setting his characters in opposition. Some lead off, fully themselves from the start, some seem to hang on his hands, saying what they have to say in sound conventional phrase, some he may leave all but mute, uncertain yet, it would seem, of his own use for them. Not till the whole organism has gathered strength and abounds in a life of its own is the true mastery to be seen. Even so, in *King Lear* there is more to be accounted for. In no other of the plays, I think, unless it be *Macbeth,* are we so conscious of the force of an emotion overriding, often, a character's self-expression, and of a vision of things to which the action itself is but a foreground. And how this and the rest of the play's individuality is made manifest by the form as well as the substance of the dialogue, by the shaping and colour of its verse and prose, it is, of course, of primary importance for producer and actors to observe. There is no one correct way of speaking Shakespeare's verse and prose, for he had no one way of writing it. One way grew out of another with him. Little of the method of *Romeo and Juliet* will be left in *King Lear,* much of the method of *Hamlet* still may be. But the fresh matter of a play will provoke a fresh manner, and its interpretation must be as freshly approached.

For more reasons and in more directions than one, Shakespeare seeks strength in simplicity in the writing of *King Lear.* The noble conventional speech of its beginning will not serve him long, for this is the language of such an authority as Lear discards. There is needed an expression of those fiercer, cruder strengths which come into play when a reign of order ends and a moral code is broken. Edmund begins glibly, but is indulged neither with subtle thought nor fine phrases. Goneril becomes like a woman with a fever in her: "I'll not endure it . . . I will not speak with him . . . the fault of it I'll answer . . . I'd have it come to question . . . I would breed from hence occasions, and I shall . . . ." Mark how broken is the eloquence of Lear's appeal to Regan; mark the distraction of his

> No, you unnatural hags,
> I will have such revenges on you both
> That all the world shall – I will do such things,
> What they are yet I know not, but they shall be
> The terrors of the earth. You think I'll weep;
> No, I'll not weep:
> I have full cause of weeping, but this heart
> Shall break into a hundred thousand flaws
> Or ere I'll weep.

Here, one would say, is verse reduced to its very elements.

Shakespeare has, besides, to carry us into strange regions of thought and passion, so he must, at the same time, hold us by familiar things. Lear, betrayed and helpless, at an end of his command of self or circumstance, is dramatically set above the tyranny and logic of both by being made one with the storm, and by his harmonizing with the homely fantasies of the Fool and the mad talk of Poor Tom, till his own "noble anger" breaks the bounds of reason too. Without some anchorage in simplicity, this action and these characters would range so wide that human interpretation could hardly compass them. Kent does something to keep the play's feet firm on the ground; Gloucester a little; the Fool was to Shakespeare's audience a familiar and sympathetic figure. But himself might escape our closer sympathy were it not for his recurrent coming down from the heights to such moments as

> No, I will be the pattern of all patience;
> I will say nothing

as

> My wits begin to turn.
> Come on, my boy. How dost, my boy? Art cold?
> I am cold myself. Where is this straw, my fellow?

as

> No, I will no more. In such a night
> To shut me out! Pour on, I will endure.
> In such a night as this!

or as

Make no noise, make no noise; draw the curtains; so, so, so. We'll go to supper i' the morning; so, so, so.

This final stroke, moreover, brings us to the simplest physical actualities; Lear's defiance of the elements has flickered down to a mock pulling of the curtains round his bed. Later, when he wanders witless and alone, his speech is broken into oracular fragments of rhapsody; but the play of thought is upon actuality and his hands are at play all the time with actual things; with the flower (is it?) he takes for a coin, with whatever serves for a bit of cheese, for his gauntlet, his hat, for the challenge thrust under Gloucester's blind eyes. Let us note, too, how one of the finest passages of poetry in the play, Edgar's imaginary tale of Dover cliff, consists of the clearest-cut actualities of description. And when Lear wakes to his right senses again, simplicity is added to his garments. The tragic beauty of his end is made more beautiful by his call for a looking-glass, his catching at the feather to put on Cordelia's lips, the undoing of the button. These things are the necessary balance to the magniloquence of the play's beginning and to the tragic splendour of the storm.

Amid the sustained magnificence of the first scene we find the first use of an even more simple device, recurrent throughout the play:

> what can you say to draw
> A third more opulent than your sisters? Speak.
> Nothing, my lord.
> Nothing?
> Nothing.
> Nothing will come of nothing; speak again.

Again and again with varying purpose and effect Shakespeare uses this device of reiteration. Note Edmund's

> Why brand they us
> With base? with baseness? bastardy? base, base?
> ... Well, then,
> Legitimate Edgar, I must have your land.
> Our father's love is to the bastard, Edmund,
> As to the legitimate: Fine word, – legitimate!
> Well, my legitimate, if this letter speed,
> And my invention thrive, Edmund the base
> Shall top the legitimate.

The repetition itself does much to drive in on us the insistent malice of the man.

Lear summons Oswald with

23

> O! you sir, you sir, come you hither, sir.
> Who am I, sir?

and the tragic counterpart of this is

> Hear, Nature, hear! dear goddess, hear.

Gloucester's grieved refrain falls casually enough:

> O, madam, my old heart is crack'd, is crack'd. . .
> O, lady, lady, shame would have it hid. . .
> I know not, madam; 't is too bad, too bad.

And for a rounded elaboration of the effect, we have Lear's

> O! reason not the need; our basest beggars
> Are in the poorest thing superfluous:
> Allow not nature more than nature needs,
> Man's life is cheap as beast's. Thou art a lady;
> If only to go warm were gorgeous,
> Why, nature needs not what thou gorgeous wear'st,
> Which scarcely keeps thee warm. But, for true need—
> You heavens, give me that patience, patience I need!

Half a dozen other such instances, more or less elaborate, of major and minor importance, can be found; till we come to the effect at its crudest in

> Howl, howl, howl, howl! O, you are men of stones . . .

and to the daring and magic of

> Thou'lt come no more.
> Never, never, never, never, never!

It is a simple device indeed, but all mature artists tend to seek strength in simplicity of expression. It is, at its simplest, a very old device, and older than drama. Iteration casts, of itself, a spell upon the listener, and the very sound of that echoing "Never" can make us sharers in Lear's helplessness and despair.[10] Bradley says of this last speech that it leaves us "on the topmost peaks of poetry"; and so, surely, it does. Rend it from its context, the claim sound absurd; but dramatic poetry is never to be judged apart from the action it implies.

King Lear – are we still to think? – cannot be acted. The whole scheme and methods of its writing is a contrivance for its effective acting. This contrast and reconciliation of grandeur and simplicity, this setting of vision in terms of actuality, this inarticulate passion which breaks now and again into memorable phrases – does not even the seeming failure of expression give us a sense of the helplessness of humanity pitted against higher powers? All the magnificent art of this is directed to one end; the play's acting in a theatre.

The Characters and Their Interplay

LEAR

Lear himself is so dominant a figure that the exhaustion of his impetus to action with the play's end barely in sight leaves Shakespeare a heavy task in the rallying of its forces for what is still to do. The argument has been raised by then, moreover, to such imaginative heights that any descent from them – even Lear's own – must be precarious. They are heights that Shakespeare himself, perhaps, did not clearly envisage till the

[10] It is, moreover, an old device with Shakespeare. Set beside Lear's

> O! reason not the need . . .

Juliet's

> Hath Romeo slain himself? Say thou but 'I'
> And that bare vowel 'I' shall poison more
> Than the death-dealing eye of cockatrice.
> I am not I, if there be such an 'I',
> Or those eyes shut that make thee answer 'I'.
> If he be slain say 'I', or if not, no;
> Brief sounds determine of my weal or woe.

The puns may destroy its emotional value for us, though they did not for the Elizabethans. But the effect aimed at is about the same. The difference in the means to it may be made one measure of Shakespeare's development of his art. Not but that he could pun dramatically to the end. He came, however, to prefer single shots to fusillades.

soaring had begun. Not that there is anything tentative in the presentation of Lear. Never was character in play, one exclaims, so fully and immediately, so imminently and overwhelmingly set forth! But in this lies the actor's first difficulty.

With the dividing of the kingdom and Cordelia's rejection the trend of the action is clearly foreshadowed:

> So be my grave my peace, as here I give
> Her father's heart from her!

By all the rules of drama we know within a little what the retribution for that must amount to; and Shakespeare will not disappoint us. But equally it would seem that for this massive fortress of pride which calls itself Lear, for any old man indeed of eighty and upwards, there could be no dramatic course but declension. Who would ever think of developing, of expanding, a character from such overwhelming beginnings? Yet this is what Shakespeare does, and finds a transcendent way to do it. So the actor's difficulty is that he must start upon a top note, at what must be pretty well the full physical stretch of his powers, yet have in reserve the means of a greater climax of another sort altogether. It is here, however, that the almost ritual formality of the first scene will help him. The occasion itself, the general subservience to Lear's tyranny (Kent's protest and Cordelia's resolution only emphasize this), Lear's own assertion of kingship as something not far from godhead, all combine to set him so above and apart from the rest that the very isolation will seem strength if the actor takes care to sustain it. There need be, there must be, no descent to petulance. Lear marking the map with his finger might be marking the land itself, so Olympian should he appear. The oath by the sacred radiance of the sun is one that only he may swear. That Kent should call him an "old man" is in itself a blasphemous outrage.

> Come not between the dragon and his wrath . . . .
>
> The bow is bent and drawn, make from the shaft . . . .
>
> Nothing: I have sworn; I am firm.

Lines like these mark the level of Lear, though their fatality may be a trifle mitigated by the human surliness of

> Better thou
> Had'st not been born than not to have pleased me better

by the grim humour which lies in

> Nothing will come of nothing: speak again

in the ironic last fling at Kent of

> Away! By Jupiter,
> *This* shall not be revolked

and in the bitter gibe to Burgundy:

> When she was dear to us we did hold her so,
> But now her price is fall'n . . .

even, one would like to suspect, in the reason given for his fast intent to shake all cares of state from him, that he may

> Unburden'd crawl toward death

– for our next sight of his Majesty will show him back from hunting with a most impatient appetite for dinner! Note, too, the hint of another Lear, given us in the music of three short words – the first touch in the play of that preculiar verbal magic Shakespeare could command – when, sated with Goneril's and Regan's flattery, he turns to his Cordelia with

> Now, our joy . . .

But Lear must leave this first scene as he entered it, more a magnificent portent than a man.

He has doffed his kingship; free from its trappings, how the native genius of the man begins to show! It flashes on us as might the last outbursts of some near-extinct volcano. He is old and uncertain; but a mighty man, never a mere tyrant divested of power. He has genius, warped and random genius though it may be, and to madness, as will appear, very near allied. And Shakespeare's art lies in showing us this in nothing he does – for what he does now is foolish – but in every trivial thing that he is. All the action of the scene of the return from hunting, all his surroundings are staged to this end. The swift exchanges with the disguised Kent and their culmination:

> Dost thou know me, fellow?
> No, sir, but you have that in your countenance which I would fain call master.
> What's that?
> Authority

– his encounter with the pernickity jack-in-office Oswald, and with the frail, whimsical Fool who mockingly echoes his own passionate whimsies; all this helps set in motion and sets off a new and livelier, a heartier Lear. Not that Shakespeare bates us one jot of the old man's stiff-necked perversities. He no more asks our sympathy on easy terms for him than will Lear yield an inch to Goneril's reasonable requests. A hundred useless knights about the house – even though, from their master's point of view, they were men of choice and rarest parts – must have been a burden. Lear's striking Oswald really was an outrage; after due complaint Goneril would doubtless have reproved his impertinence – for all that she had prompted it! Even with the petted Fool, and in the very midst of the petting, out there snaps

> Take heed, sirrah, the whip!

We need look for no tractable virtues in him.

The play's adopted story has its appointed way to go, but here begins the way of Lear's soul's agony and salvation as Shakespeare is to blaze it. The change in him shows first in the dialogue with the attendant knight and the delicate strokes which inform it. The knight, dispatched to bid that mongrel Oswald come back, returns only to report the fellow's round answer that he would not. "He would not!" flashes Lear at the unbelievable phrase. But when, picking his words – as, if you were not a Kent (and there had been room at best for but one Kent at Court), no doubt you learned to do with Lear – the knight hints hesitatingly at trouble, the quiet response comes:

> Thou but remember'st me of mine own conception: I have perceived a most faint neglect of late; which I have rather blamed as mine own jealous curiosity, than as a very pretence and purpose of unkindness: I will look further into't. But where's my fool? I have not seen him this two days.
>
> Since my young lady's going into France, sir, the fool hath much pined away.
>
> No more of that; I have noted it well. Go you, and tell my daughter I would speak with her. Go you, call hither my fool. O! you sir, you sir, come you hither, sir!

– this last to the mongrel Oswald who appeared again. But Lear – can this be the Lear of the play's first scene? – to be turning his knight's "great abatement of kindness" to "a most faint neglect", and blaming, even so, his own jealous curiosity for noting it! But the Fool's grief for Cordelia he has noted well. Lest it echo too loudly in his proud unhappy heart, with a quick turn he brings the old Lear to his rescue, rasps an order here, an order there, and – takes it out of Oswald.

From now on the picturing of him is lifelike, in that it has all the varied, unexpected, indirect and latent eloquence of life. Shakespeare is at his deftest, his medium at its freest and most supple. Let the interpreter be alert too. This Lear is as quick on the uptake as it is his Fool's business to be. An unnatural quickness in an old man, is it, and some sign of a toppling brain? His silences are as pregnant. He listens and finds cheer in the Fool's chatter and song, throws him an answer or so to keep it alive, snarls now and then like an old lion if a sting goes too deep. Yet his thoughts, we can tell, are away. We must visualize this scene fully and accurately; the Fool carolling, his poor heart being heavy with Cordelia's loss he carols the more; the old king brooding; and Kent ever watchful, with a dog's eyes. Mark the effect of Goneril's appearance before her father, in purposed, sullen muteness; the Fool's speech points it for us, should we be unobservant; then her break into the prepared formality of verse, as this verse will seem, capping the loose prose of the scene and the Fool's rhyming. Mark, too, the cold kingliness of Lear's four words, all his response to her careful address:

Are you our daughter?

He resorts to irony, the fine mind's weapon, which blunts itself upon the stupid – for Goneril is stupid, and she has stupidity's stubborn strength. But when the storm of Lear's wrath does break, I think she inwardly shakes a little.

You strike my people, and your disordered rabble
Make servants of their better

sounds like scared bravado. She can wait, though, for the storm to pass; and, for the moment, it does pass in senile self-reproaches. A few more such futile outbursts, she is confident, and the extravagant old tyrant will be spent and tame enough. But, suddenly, the servants are dismissed and she is alone with husband and father. And her father, rigid, transformed, and with slow, calm, dreadful strength, is calling down the gods' worst curse upon her.

Hear, Nature, hear! dear goddess, hear!
Suspend thy purpose if thou didst intend
To make this creature fruitful! . . .

The actor who will rail and rant this famous passage may know his own barnstorming business but he is no interpreter of Shakespeare. The merely superficial effect of its deadlier quiet, lodged between two whirlwinds of Lear's fury, should be obvious. But its dramatic purpose far outpasses that. Not indifferently did Shakespeare make this a pagan play, and deprive its argument of comfortable faith in virtue rewarded, here or hereafter. And it is upon this deliberate invocation of ill that we pass into spiritual darkness. The terror of it moves Albany rather than Goneril, whom, indeed, nothing is ever to move. But as he rouses himself to plead against it Lear is gone.[11]

Now havoc begins in him. We have his raging, distracted return, tears of helpless despair punctuating hysterical threats; later the stamping, muttering impatience of his wait for his horses. We know that he sets out on a long hard ride, dinnerless after his hunting. Later we learn that the journey was wasted; he had to post on to Gloucester's. Did he ride through the night without rest or pause? Shakespeare is hunting both Lear and the play's action hard and using every device to do it.

Yet the next day when he reaches Gloucester's house – this old man past eighty, and physically we should suppose near exhaustion – he is master of himself, is his most regal self again.[12] We are given the scene with Kent awaked in the stocks to show it.

> Ha!
> Makest thou this shame thy pastime?

All the old dignity in this; there follows the brusque familiar give-and-take which true authority never fears to practice with its dependents; then again the majestic

> Resolve me, with all modest haste, which way

[11] The "Away, away" is thus spoken to the propitiatory Albany, and has no reference to the servants, who have already been sent off, nor, I think, to Lear's own departure. The point is disputable, no doubt, and I would not go to the stake for my reading of it. The Quartos have "Go, go, my people" repeated, as if his first order had not been obeyed. I must leave it to better judges of their origin and value to say whether this is mere muddlement of text. But, even if it is not, the Folio's change of phrase might cover a change of meaning too.

[12] But the outward signs of exhaustion must begin to be upon him.

> Thou might'st deserve, or they impose, this usage
> Coming from us

and the iron self-control in which the shameful tale is heard. When the tale is ended he still stands silent, while the Fool pipes for us an artless mockery (the art of this!) of his bitter and ominous thoughts. Regan too, Regan too! The grief of disillusion has now become physical pain to him,

> O, how this mother swells up toward my heart;
> *Hysterica passio*! down, thou climbing sorrow!

But he masters it.

> Where is this daughter? . . .
> Follow me not; stay here.

And, solitary in his pride, he goes to face and prove the worst.

If the play, with the invocation of the curse upon Goneril, entered an arena of anarchy and darkness, Lear himself is to pass now from personal grievance to the taking upon him, as great natures may, the imagined burden of the whole world's sorrow – and if his nature breaks under it, what wonder! And Shakespeare brings about this transition from malediction to martyrdom with great art, by contrivance direct and indirect, by strokes broad and subtle; nor ever – his art in this at its greatest – does he turn his Lear from a man into an ethical proposition. The thing is achieved – as the whole play is achieved – in terms of humanity, and according to the rubric of drama.

Lear comes back with Gloucester; the well-meaning Gloucester, whose timid tact is the one thing least likely to placate him. He is struggling with himself, with the old tyrannic temper, with his newfound knowledge of himself, with his body's growing weakness. He is like a great oak tree, torn at the roots, blown this way and that. When the half-veiled insolence of Regan's and Cornwall's greeting must, one would think, affront him, a pathetic craving for affection peeps through.

When he once more finds refuge in irony, it is to turn the edge of it against himself. But with four quick shocks – his sudden recall of the outrage upon his servant, the sound of a trumpet, the sight of Oswald, the sight of Goneril – he is brought to a stand and to face the realities arrayed against him. This must be made very plain to us. On the one side stand Goneril and Regan and Cornwall in all authority. The perplexed Gloucester hovers a little apart. On the other side is Lear, the Fool at his feet, and his one servant, disarmed, freed but a minute since behind him. Things are at their issue. His worst errors, after all, have partaken of nobility; he has scorned policy. He has given himself, helpless, into these carnal hands. He will abide, then, as nobly the fate he has courted. Note the single touch of utter scorn for the cur Cornwall, who, the moment looking likely, takes credit for those stocks.

> I set him there, sir; but his own disorders
> Deserved much less advancement.
>   You! Did you!

But all consequences he'll abide, even welcome, he'll abjure his curses, run from one ingrate daughter to the other, implore and bargain, till the depth is sounded and he stands at last surrendered, and level in his helplessness and deprivation with the least of his fellow-men.

GONERIL   Hear me, my lord,
  What need you five-and-twenty, ten, or five,
  To follow in a house where twice so many
  Have a command to tend you?
REGAN   What need one?
LEAR. O! reason not the need; our basest beggars
  Are in the poorest thing superfluous:
  Allow not nature more than nature needs,
  Man's life is cheap as beast's. . . .
                  But, for true need –
  You heavens, give me that patience, patience I need!

33

> You see me here, you gods, a poor old man
> As full of grief as age, wretched in both!

"O! reason not the need ..."! This abandoning of the struggle and embracing of misfortune is a turning point of the play, a salient moment in the development of Lear's character, and its significance must be marked. He is now at the nadir of his fortunes; the tragic heights are at hand.

It may be thought that by emphasizing so many minor points of stagecraft the great outlines of play and character will be obscured. But while Shakespeare projects greatly, asking from his interpreters a simplicity of response, lending them greatness by virtue of this convention that passes the play's material through the sole crucible of their speech and action, he yet saves them alive, so to speak – not stultified in an attempt to overpass their own powers nor turned to mere mouthpieces of mighty lines – by constant references to the commonplace (we noted more of them in discussing the methods of the dialogue). He invigorates his play's action by keeping its realities upon a battleground where any and every sort of stroke may tell.

Thus there now follows the tense passage in which Goneril, Regan and Cornwall snuff the impending storm and find good reason for ill-doing. What moralists! Regan with her

> O! sir, to wilful men,
> The injuries that they themselves procure
> Must be their schoolmasters.

Cornwall, with his

> Shut up your doors, my lord; 'tis a wild night:
> My Regan counsels well; come out of the storm.

This is surely the very voice – though the tones may be harsh – of respectability and common sense? And what a prelude to the "high engender'd battles" now imminent! Before battle is joined, however, the note of Kent is interposed to keep the play's story going its more pedestrian way and to steady us against the imaginative turmoil pending. This use of Kent is masterly; and, in the storm-scenes themselves, the contrasting use of the Fool, feeble, fantastic, pathetic, a foil to Lear, a foil to the storm – what more incongruous sight conceivable than such a piece of Court tinsel so drenched and buffeted! – is more than masterly.

But it is upon Lear's own progress that all now centres, upon his passing from that royal defiance of the storm to the welcomed shelter of the hovel. He passes by the road of patience:

> No, I will be the pattern of all patience;
> I will say nothing

of – be it noted – a thankfulness that he is at last simply

>   a man
>   More sinn'd against than sinning . . .

to the humility of

>   My wits begin to turn
> Come on, my boy. How dost, my boy? Art cold?
> I am cold myself. Where is this straw, my fellow?
> The art of our necessities is strange
> That can make vile things precious. Come, your hovel . . .

and, a little later yet, mind and body still further strained towards breaking point, to the gentle dignity, when Kent would make way for him – to the more than kingly dignity of

> Prithee, go in thyself: seek thine own ease.
> This tempest will not give me leave to ponder
> On things would hurt me more. But I'll go in:
> In, boy; go first.[13]

[13] There are practical reasons for postponing the entering of the hovel by a scene. For Kent to lead Lear elsewhere fits both with the agitated movement of the action and the freedom of Elizabethan stage method. It enables Shakespeare both to relieve the high tension of the storm-

Now comes the crowning touch of all:

> I'll pray, and then I'll sleep.

In the night's bleak exposure he kneels down, like a child at bedtime, to pray.

> Poor nakes wretches, wheresoe'er you are,
> That bide the pelting of this pitiless storm,
> How shall your houseless heads and unfed sides,
> Your loop'd and window'd raggedness, defend you
> From seasons such as these? O, I have ta'en
> Too little care of this! Take physic, pomp;
> Expose thyself to feel what wretches feel,
> That thou mayst shake the superflux to them,
> And show the heavens more just.

To this haven of the spirit has he come, the Lear of unbridled power and pride. And how many dramatists, could they have achieved so much, would have been content to leave him here! Those who like their drama rounded and trim might approve of such a finish, which would leave us a play more compassable in performance no doubt. But the wind of a harsher doctrine is blowing through Shakespeare. Criticism, as we have seen, is apt to fix upon the episode of the storm as the height of his attempt and the point of his dramatic defeat; but it is this storm of the mind here beginning upon which he expends skill and imagination most recklessly till inspiration has had its will of him; and the drama of desperate vision ensuing it is hard indeed for actors to reduce to the positive medium of their art – without reducing it to ridicule. The three coming scenes of Lear's madness show us Shakespeare's art at its boldest. They pass beyond

scenes and to provide for the continuity of the Gloucester-Edmund story. And he takes advantage of all this to show us some further battering at Lear's sanity. Note in particular the ominously broken thoughts and sentences of the end of the speech to Kent just before the hovel is reached; and these, as ominously, are set between connected, reasoned passages.

the needs of the plot, they belong to a larger synthesis.[14] Yet the means they employ are simple enough; of a kind of absolute simplicity, indeed.

The boldest and simplest is the provision of Poor Tom, that living instance of all rejection. Here, under our eyes, is Lear's new vision of himself.

> What! have his daughters brought him to this pass?
> Could'st thou save nothing? Did'st thou give them all?

Side by side stand the noble old man, and the naked, scarce human wretch.

> Is man no more than this? Consider him well. Thou owest the worm no silk, the beast no hide, the sheep no wool, the cat no perfume. Ha! here's three on's are sophisticated; thou art the thing itself; unaccommodated man is no more but such a poor, bare, forked animal as thou art. Off, off, you lendings! Come; unbutton here.

Here is a volume of argument epitomized as only drama can epitomize it, flashed on us by word and action combined. And into this, one might add, has Shakespeare metamorphosed the didactics of those old Moralities which were the infancy of his art.

> What! hath your grace no better company?

gasps poor Gloucester, bewailing at once the King's wrongs and his own, as he offers shelter from the storm. But Lear, calmness itself now, will only pace up and down, arm in arm with this refuse of humanity:

> Noble philosopher, your company

[14] It is worth noting that the Folio cuts out the lunatic trial of Regan and Goneril. This episode proves so admirable on the stage that it is hard to suppose Shakespeare's actor failed to make it effective. But if it was a question of time and a choice between two scenes, doubtless his audience would be supposed to prefer the rhetoric of the storm.

– nor will he seek shelter without him. So they reach the out-house, all of his own castle that Gloucester dare offer. What a group! Kent, sturdy and thrifty of words; Gloucester, tremulous; the bedraggled and exhausted Fool; and Lear, magnificently courteous and deliberate, keeping close company with his gibbering fellow-man.[15]

They are in shelter. Lear is silent; till the Fool – himself never overfitted, we may suppose, in body or mind for the rough and tumble of the world – rallies, as if to celebrate their safety, to a semblance of his old task. Edgar, for his own safety's sake, must play Poor Tom to the life now. Kent has his eyes on his master, watching him – at what new fantastic trick? The old king is setting two joint-stools side by side; they are Regan and Goneril, and the Fool and the beggar are to pass judgment upon them.

The lunatic mummery of the trial comes near to something we might call pure drama – as one speaks of pure mathematics or pure music – since it cannot be rendered into other terms than its own. Its effect depends upon the combination of the sound and meaning of the words and the sight of it being brought to bear as a whole directly upon our sensibility. The sound of the dialogue matters almost more than its meaning. Poor Tom and the Fool chant antiphonally; Kent's deep and kindly tones tell against the higher, agonized, weakened voice of Lear. But the chief significance is in the show. Where Lear, such a short while since, sat in his majesty, there sit the Fool and the outcast, with Kent whom he banished beside them; and he, witless, musters his failing strength to beg justice upon a joint-stool. Was better justice done, the picture ironically asks, when he presided in majesty and sanity and power?

But what, as far as Lear is concerned, is to follow? You cannot continue the development of a character in terms of lunacy – in darkness, illuminated by whatever brilliant flashes of lightning. Nor can a madman well dominate a play's action. From this moment Lear no longer is a motive force; and the needs of the story – the absolute needs of the char-

15 And Kent is unknown to Lear and Edgar to his father, as we shall sufficiently remember.

acter – would be fulfilled if, from this exhausted sleep upon the poor bed in the outhouse, he only woke to find Cordelia at his side. But Shakespeare contrives another scene of madness for him, and one which lifts the play's argument to a yet rarer height. It is delayed; and the sense of redundancy is avoided partly by keeping Lear from the stage altogether for a while, a short scene interposed sufficiently reminding us of him.[16]

His reappearance is preluded – with what consonance! – by the fantastically imaginative episode of Gloucester's fall from the cliff. There also is Edgar, the aura of Poor Tom about him still. Suddenly Lear breaks in upon them.[17] The larger dramatic value of the ensuing scene can hardly be over-rated. For in it, in this encounter between mad Lear and blind Gloucester, the sensual man robbed of his eyes, and the despot, the light of his mind put out, Shakespeare's sublimation of the two old stories is consummated. No moral is preached to us. It is presented as it was when king and beggar fraternized in the storm and beggar and Fool were set on the bench of justice, and we are primarily to *feel* the significance. Yet this does not lack interpretation; less explicit than when Lear, still sane, could read the lesson of the storm, clearer than was the commentary on the mock trial. It is Edgar here that sets us an example of sympathetic listening. His asides enforce it, and the last one:

[16] In the Quarto another preceding scene is also concerned with him.

[17] *Mad,* says the stage direction, and no more; the usual *fantastically dressed with wild flowers* is Capel's addition. But something of the sort is justified by Cordelia's speech in the earlier scene. And the dramatic purpose of them is plain: to emphasize the contrast between this and our last sight of him amid the barren wildness of the heath and the storm.

There are signs, it may be noted, that this Gloucester-Lear encounter is a second thought on Shakespeare's part. Apart from its redundance to the action, the Gloucester-Edgar scene is complete without it; and originally, one would guess, Gloucester's

> Henceforth I'll bear
> Affliction till it do cry out itself
> 'Enough, enough!' and die

was followed directly by Edgar's

> Well pray you, father!

39

> O! matter and impertinency mixed,
> Reason in madness!

will reproach us if we have not understood. The train of
fancies fired by the first sight of Gloucester, with its tragically
comic

> Ha! Goneril with a white beard!

(Goneril, disguised, pursuing him still!) asks little gloss.

> They flattered me like a dog. . . . To say 'Ay' and 'No'
> to everything I said! . . . When the rain came to wet me
> once and the wind to make me chatter, when the thunder
> would not peace at my bidding, there I found 'em,
> there I smelt 'em out. Go to, they are not men o' their
> words; they told me I was everything; 'tis a lie, I am
> not ague-proof.

Gloucester's dutiful

> Is't not the king?

begins to transform him in those mad eyes. And madness
sees a Gloucester there that sanity had known and ignored.

> I pardon that man's life: What was thy cause?
> Adultery?
> Thou shalt not die: die for adultery! No:
> The wren goes to't, and the small gilded fly
> Does lecher in my sight.
> Let copulation thrive; for Gloucester's bastard son
> Was kinder to his father than my daughters
> Got 'tween the lawful sheets.

Gloucester knows better; but how protest so to the mere er-
ratic voice? Besides which there is only the kindly stranger-
peasant near. A slight unconscious turn of the sightless eyes
toward him, a simple gesture – unseen – in response from Ed-

gar, patiently biding his time, will illuminate the irony and the pathos.

Does the mad mind pass logically from this to some uncanny prevision of the ripening of new evil in Regan and Goneril? Had it in its sanity secretly surmised what lay beneath the moral surface of their lives, so ready to emerge?

> Behold yon simpering dame
> Whose face between her forks presageth snow;
> That minces virtue and does shake the head
> To hear of pleasure's name;
> The fitchew, nor the soiled horse, goes to't
> With a more riotous appetite.[18]

But a man – so lunatic logic runs – must free himself from the tyrannies of the flesh if he is to see the world clearly:

> Give me an ounce of civet, good apothecary, to sweeten my imagination.

And then a blind man may see the truth of it, so he tells the ruined Gloucester:

> Look with thine ears: see how yond justice rails upon yond simple thief. Hark in thine ear: change places, and, handy-dandy, which is the justice, which is the thief? Thou hast seen a farmer's dog bark at a beggar? . . . . And the creature run from the cur? There thou might'st behold the great image of authority; a dog's obeyed in office.

It is the picture of the mock trial given words. But with a

[18] The (superficial) inappositeness of this passage is quoted nowadays as evidence of Shakespeare's morbid occupation, about now, with the uncleaner aspects of sex. But it is by no means inapposite to the larger moral scheme of the play. Goneril's lust has become an important factor in the action. Shakespeare cannot give much space to its developments, nor does he care to set the boys acting women to deal directly and elaborately with such matters. So he uses, I think, this queer intuition of the mad mind as a mirror in which the vileness is reflected and dilated.

difference! There is no cry now for vengeance on the wicked. For what are we that we should smite them?

> Thou rascal beadle, hold thy bloody hand!
> Why dost thou lash that whore? Strip thine own back;
> That hotly lust'st to use her in that kind
> For which thou whip'st her. The usurer hangs the cozener.
> Through tattered clothes small vices do appear;
> Robes and furr'd gowns hide all. Plate sin with gold,
> And the strong lance of justice hurtless breaks;
> Arm it in rags, a pigmy's straw doth pierce it.

Shakespeare has led Lear to compassion for sin as well as suffering, has led him mad to where he could not hope to lead him sane – to where sound common sense will hardly let us follow him:

> None does offend, none, I say, none.

To a deep compassion for mankind itself.

> I know thee well enough; thy name is Gloucester;
> Thou must be patient; we came crying hither:
> Thou know'st the first time that we smell the air
> We wawl and cry. I will preach to thee: mark . . . .
> When we are born, we cry that we are come
> To this great stage of fools.

This afterpart of Lear's madness may be redundant, then, to the strict action of the play, but to its larger issues it is most germane. It is perhaps no part of the play that Shakespeare set out to write. The play that he found himself writing would be how much the poorer without it!

The simple perfection of the scene that restores Lear to Cordelia one can leave unsullied by comment. What need of any? Let the producer only note that there is reason in the Folio's stage direction:

Enter Lear in a chair carried by servants.

For when he comes to himself it is to find that he is royally attired and as if seated on his throne again. It is from this throne that he totters to kneel at Cordelia's feet.[19] Note, too, the pain of his response to Kent's

> In your own kingdom, sir.
> Do not abuse me.

Finally, Lear must pass from the scene with all the ceremony due to royalty: not mothered –please! – by Cordelia.

Cordelia found again and again lost, what is left for Lear but to die? But for her loss, however, his own death might seem to us an arbitrary stroke; since the old Lear, we may say, is already dead. Shakespeare, moreover, has transported him beyond all worldly issues. This is, perhaps, why the action of the battle which will seemingly defeat his fortunes is min-imized. What does defeat matter to him – or even victory? It is certainly the key to the meaning of the scene which fol-lows. Cordelia, who would "out-frown false fortune's frown", is ready to face her sisters and to shame them – were there a chance of it! – with the sight of her father's wrongs. But Lear himself has no interest in anything of the sort.

> No, no, no, no! Come, let's away to prison.
> We two alone will sing like birds i' the cage:
> When thou dost ask me blessing, I'll kneel down,
> And ask of thee forgiveness[20]: so we'll live,
> And pray, and sing, and tell old tales, and laugh
> At gilded butterflies, and hear poor rogues
> Talk of court news. . . .

He has passed beyond care for revenge or success, beyond

---

[19] Shakespeare kept – and transformed – this piece of business from the old play; for Cordelia kneels, too, of course. It should be given its full value.

[20] That scene in the old play haunted Shakespeare.

even the questioning of rights and wrongs. Better indeed to be oppressed, if so you can be safe from contention. Prison will bring him freedom.

> Upon such sacrifices, my Cordelia,
> The gods themselves throw incense. Have I caught thee?
> He that parts us shall bring a brand from heaven
> And fire us hence like foxes. Wipe thine eyes;
> The good years shall devour them, flesh and fell,
> Ere they shall make us weep: we'll see 'em starve first.

Lear's death, upon one ground or another, is artistically inevitable. Try to imagine his survival; no further argument will be needed. The death of Cordelia has been condemned as a wanton outrage upon our feelings and so as an aesthetic blot upon the play. But the dramatic mind that was working to the tune of

> As flies to wanton boys are we to the gods;
> They kill us for their sport

was not likely to be swayed by sentiment. The tragic truth about life, to the Shakespeare that wrote *King Lear*, included its capricious cruelty. And what meeter sacrifice to this than Cordelia? Besides, as we have seen, he must provide this new Lear with a tragic determinant, since "the great rage ... is kill'd in him", which precipitated catastrophe for the old Lear. And what but Cordelia's loss would suffice?

We have already set Lear's last scene in comparison with his first; it will be worth while to note a little more particularly the likeness and the difference. The same commanding figure; he bears the body of Cordelia as lightly as ever he carried robe, crown and sceptre before. All he has undergone has not so bated his colossal strength but that he could kill her murderer with his bare hands.

> I kill'd the slave that was a-hanging thee.
> Tis true, my lords, he did

says the officer in answer to their amazed looks. Albany, Edgar, Kent and the rest stand silent and intent around him; Regan and Goneril are there, silent too. He stands, with the limp body close clasped, glaring blankly at them for a moment. When speech is torn from him, in place of the old kingly rhetoric we have only the horrible, half human

> Howl, howl, howl, howl!

Who these are, for all their dignity and martial splendour, for all the respect they show him, he neither knows nor cares. They are men of stone and murderous traitors; though, after a little, through the mist of his suffering, comes a word for Kent. All his world, of power and passion and will, and the wider world of thought over which his mind in its ecstasy had ranged, is narrowed now to Cordelia; and she is dead in his arms.

Here is the clue to the scene; this terrible concentration upon the dead, and upon the unconquerable fact of death. This thing was Cordelia; she was alive, she is dead. Here is human tragedy brought to its simplest terms, fit ending to a tragic play that has seemed to outleap human experience. From power of intellect and will, from the imaginative sweep of madness, Shakespeare brings Lear to this; to no moralizing nor high thoughts, but just to

> She's gone for ever.
> I know when one is dead and when one lives;
> She's dead as earth. Lend me a looking-glass;
> If that her breath will mist or stain the stone,
> Why, then she lives.

Lacking a glass, he catches at a floating feather. That stirs on her lips; a last mockery. Kent kneels by him to share his grief. Then to the bystanders comes the news of Edmund's death; the business of life goes forward, as it will, and draws attention from him for a moment. But what does he heed? When they turn back to him he has her broken body in his arms again.

And my poor fool is hang'd. No, no, no life!
Why should a dog, a horse, a rat, have life,
And thou no breath at all? Thou'lt come no more,
Never, never, never, never, never!
Pray you, undo this button; thank you, sir.
Do you see this? Look on her, look, her lips,
Look there, look there![21]

GONERIL, REGAN AND CORDELIA

Shakespeare's point of departure for all three is that of
the crude old story. Moreover, with regard to Goneril and
Regan he is quite content to assume – we shrink from the
assumption nowadays – that there are really wicked people
in the world. That admitted, these two exemplars of the fact
are lifelike enough. Their aspect may be determined by the
story's needs, but their significance does not end here; and,
within the limit afforded them, they develop freely and naturally, each in her own way.

Likeness and difference are marked from the beginning.
They are both realists. Their father wants smooth speech of
them and they give it, echoing his very phrases and tones.
They ignore Cordelia's reproaches; she is exiled and in disgrace, so they safely may. Left alone together (and the drop
here from verse to prose seems to bring us with something
of a bump to the plain truth about them), they are under no
illusions at all, we find, about their own good fortune:

> he always loved our sister most; and with what poor
> judgment he hath now cast her off appears too grossly.

There are few things more unlovely than the passionless ap-
praisement of evil and our profit in it. They are as wide-
awake to the chances of trouble ahead; but while Regan would
wait and see, Goneril means to go to meet it.

If the quarrel between King Lear and his two daughters

---

[21] Bradley has an admirable note upon this passage, just such a fine
piece of perception as we expect from him. Lear, he says, at the very
last, thinks that Cordelia lives, and dies of the joy of it.

had been brought into the law courts, counsels' speeches for Regan and Goneril would have been interesting. But what a good case Goneril makes for herself unaided! The setting-on of Oswald to provoke Lear might, one supposes, have been kept out of the evidence. True, the reservation of a hundred knights was a definite condition of his abdication. But their behaviour was impeachable; it may well have been if Lear's own treatment of Oswald set them an example. He was almost in his dotage; unbalanced certainly. His outbursts of ironic rage, the cursing of Goneril, his subsequent ravings – his whole conduct shows him unfit to look after himself. For his own sake, then, how much better for his daughters' servants to wait on him! And Regan, though she needs Goneril's prompting, makes an even better case of it; the weaker nature is the more plausible. A jury of men and women of common sense might well give their verdict against Lear; and we can hear the judge ruling upon the one point of law in his favour with grave misgiving that he is doing him no good. How then can we call Regan and Goneril double-dyed fiends? They played the hypocrite for a kingdom; but which of us might not? Having got what they wanted and more than they expected they found good excuse for not paying the price for it. Like failings have been known in the most reputable people. Their conduct so far, it could be argued, has been eminently respectable, level-headed and worldly-wise. They do seem somewhat hard-hearted, but that is all. Says the broken, mad old king:

> let them anatomize Regan, see what breeds about her heart. Is there any cause in nature that makes these hard hearts?

But from now on the truth about them grows patent. Does prosperity turn their heads? It releases hidden devils. When Gloucester's defection is discovered they waste no words.

> Hang him instantly.
> Pluck out his eyes.

And the weaker Regan grows the more violent of the two; she turns crueler even than that bloody wolf, Cornwall, her husband. For amid the scuffling a little later she can think to tell Gloucester that his own son has betrayed him; and even as he faces her, blinded and bleeding, she can jeer at him.

The devil of lust comes now to match with the devil of cruelty. Goneril has hardly seen Edmund but she marks him down with those

> strange œilliads and most speaking looks

— which rouse Regan to jealousy as quickly. In their plot upon their father they were clever enough, self-controlled, subtle. But, the beast let loose in them, they turn reckless, shameless, foolish. Regan, with a little law on her side, presumes on it; so Goneril poisons her as she might a rat. And the last note of Goneril is one of devilish pride.

> Say, if I do, the laws are mine, not thine:
> Who can arraign me for it?

Flinging this at her husband when he confronts her with the proof that she meant to have his life, she departs to take her own.

We may see, then, in Goneril and Regan, evil triumphant, self-degrading and self-destructive. It may also be that, from beginning to end, Shakespeare, for his part, sees little to choose between hot lust and murdering hand and the hard heart, in which all is rooted.

It will be a fatal error to present Cordelia as a meek saint. She has more than a touch of her father in her. She is as proud as he is, and as obstinate, for all her sweetness and her youth. And, being young, she answers uncalculatingly with pride to his pride even as later she answers with pity to his misery. To miss this likeness between the two is to miss Shakespeare's first important dramatic effect; the mighty old man and the frail child, confronted, and each unyielding.

48

> So young and so untender?
> So young, my lord, and true.

And they both have the right of it, after all. If age owes some tolerance to youth, it may be thought too that youth owes to age and fatherhood something more – and less – than the truth. But she has courage, has Cordelia, amazing courage. Princess though she be, it is no small matter to stand her ground before Lear, throned in the plenitude of his power, to stand up to him without effort, explanation or excuse. Nor does she wince at the penalty, nor to the end utter one pleading word. Nor, be it noted, does Kent, who is of her temper, ask pity for her. His chief concern is to warn Lear against his own folly and its consequences.[22] It is her strength of mind he emphasizes and praises.

> The gods to their dear shelter take thee, maid,
> That justly think'st and hast most rightly said!

Nor would she, apparently, open her mouth again to her father but that she means her character shall be cleared. And even this approach to him is formal and uncompromising:

> I yet beseech your majesty . . . .

She does (Shakespeare keeps her human) slip in, as if it hardly mattered, a dozen words of vindication:

> since what I well intend,
> I'll do't before I speak.

Yet, lest even that should seem weakness, she nullifies its effect for a finish. Nor does Lear respond, nor exonerate her except by a noncommittal growl. Still, she is not hard.

> The jewels of our father, with wash'd eyes
> Cordelia leaves you . . . .

[22] And certain small alterations from Quarto to Folio emphasize this.

49

Shakespeare has provided in this encounter between Cordelia and Lear that prime necessity of drama, clash of character; that sharpest clash, moreover, of like in opposition to like. He has added wonder and beauty by setting these twin spirits in noble and contrasted habitations. Pride unchecked in Lear has grown monstrous and diseased with his years. In her youth it shows unspoiled, it is in flower. But it is the same pride.

The technical achievement in Shakespeare's staging of Cordelia is his gain of a maximum effect by a minimum of means. It is a triumph of what may be called "placing". The character itself has, to begin with, that vitality which positive virtues give. Cordelia is never in doubt about herself; she has no vagaries, she is what she is all circumstances apart, what she says seems to come new-minted from her mind, and our impression of her is as clean cut. Add to this her calm and steadfast isolation among the contending or subservient figures of that first scene – and the fact, of course, that from this very thrift of herself the broadcast violence of the play's whole action springs – then we see how, with but a reminder of her here and there, Shakespeare could trust to her reappearance after long delay, no jot of her importance nor of our interest in her bated. Indeed, if the Folio text gives us in the main his own reconsiderations, he found his first care to reinstate her in our sympathy a scene before she reappears to be needless.[23] But at this point the play itself is beginning to have need of her return. Somehow its intolerable agonies must be eased; and amid the dreadful flux our memory of her certainty abides.

There is not, at any time, much to explain in Cordelia. Nor does she now herself protest her love and expand her forgiveness. She has not changed; elaboration would only falsify her. Not that she is by nature taciturn; she can resolve the harmonies of her mind, and Shakespeare gives a flowing music to them.

> Was this a face
> To be opposed against the warring winds?

[23] Act IV. Scene iii.

50

To stand against the deep dread-bolted thunder?
In the most terrible and nimble stroke
Of quick cross lightning? to watch – poor perdu!
With this thin helm? Mine enemy's dog,
Though he had bit me, should have stood that night
Against my fire.

But even this is not spoken to Lear. To him she still says little. It is as if speech itself were not a simple or genuine enough thing for the expressing of her deep heart. And her

No cause, no cause!

when he would welcome her reproaches, is not at all the kindly, conventional, superior "Let's forget it" of the morally offended. It is but the complement of that "Nothing" which cost her a kingdom, and as true of her in its tenderness as the other was true. For the simple secret of Cordelia's nature is that she does not see things from the standpoint of her own gain or loss. She did not beg, she does not bargain. She can give as she could lose, keeping a quiet mind. It is no effort to her to love her father better than herself. Yet this supremest virtue, as we count it, is no gain to him; we must note this too. Her wisdom of heart showed her Regan and Goneril as they were; yet it was an inarticulate wisdom and provoked evil in Lear, and could but hold her bound in patience till the evil was purged. Is there, then, an impotence in such goodness, lovely as we find it? And is this why Shakespeare lets her slip out of the play a few scenes later to her death, as if, for all her beauty of spirit, she were not of so much account? Neither good fortune nor ill can touch Cordelia herself; this is her strength and her weakness both.

For thee, oppressed king, am I cast down;
Myself could else outfrown false fortune's frown

she says; and so she could, we are sure. Then she falls into

dumbness – into such a dumbness as was her first undoing –
and passes, silent, from our sight.

Here is another positive, absolute being; he, Lear and Cordelia make a trinity of them. He has not Lear's perilous intellect nor Cordelia's peace of soul. His dominant quality is his
unquestioning courage; akin to this the selflessness which
makes it as easy for him to be silent as to speak. And he springs
from Shakespeare's imagination all complete; full-flavoured
and consistent from the first. Surer sign yet of his author's
certainty about him is the natural inconsistency of the man
as we see him. Through the first three acts there is never a
stroke in the drawing of Kent which is merely conventional,
nor yet an uncertain one. But neither is there one which,
however unexpected, need perplex us. And for a small sign
of Shakespeare's confidence in the sufficiency of his creature,
see the shrewd critical thrust which he lets Cornwall have
at him:

> This is some fellow,
> Who, having been praised for bluntness, doth affect
> A saucy roughness . . . .

Even though it be a Cornwall disparaging a Kent, the thrust
is shrewd enough for Shakespeare not to risk it unless he is
confident that Kent's credit with the audience is firm.

This variety and apparent inconsistency give great vitality.
From the Kent of the first scene, quick of eye, frank at a
question:

> Is not this your son, my lord?

impatient at half answers:

> I cannot conceive you

yet tolerant, discreetly courteous, dry, self-contained:

52

> I cannot wish the fault undone, the issue of it being so
> proper

but gentle and kindly too:

> I must love you and sue to know you better

– from this we pass without warning to the impetuous outburst against Lear; and unmannerly though this may be, it is
still dignified, collected and cool. From this to the Kent of
the borrowed accents – but never more himself than in his
disguise, to the man of

> What would'st thou?
> Service.
> Who would'st thou serve?
> You.
> Dost thou know me, fellow?
> No, sir; but you have that in you countenance which I
> would fain call master.
> What's that?
> Authority

to the Kent of the tripping of Oswald; and, at their next
meeting, with Oswald so unwary as to ask him

> What dost thou know me for?

to the Kent of

> A knave, a rascal, an eater of broken meats; a base,
> proud, shallow, beggarly, three-suited, hundred-pound,
> filthy, worsted-stocking knave; a lily-livered, action-tak-
> ing knave; a whoreson, glass-gazing, super-serviceable,
> finical rogue; a one-trunk inheriting slave; one that wouldst
> be a bawd in way of good service, and art nothing but
> the composition of a knave, beggar, coward, pandar,
> and the son and heir of a mongrel bitch; one whom I

> will beat into clamorous whining if thou deniest the least
> syllable of thy addition

to the resourceful, humorous disputant of the scene with Cornwall and Regan, and to the philosopher in the stocks, with his

> Fortune, good-night; smile once more; turn thy wheel!

Having so opulently endowed him with life, Shakespeare, we may say, can now afford to be thriftier of attention to him for a while; he had better be, we might add, or the balance of the play's interest will go awry. But it is of a piece with the character that, when misfortune overwhelms Lear, Kent should sink himself in it, that his colourfulness should fade, his humour wane, and the rest of the play find him tuned to this one key of vigilant unquestioning service; till he comes to the final simplicity of

> I have a journey, sir, shortly to go.
> My master calls me, I must not say no.

Nevertheless Shakespeare does seem in Act IV to lose interest in him, thus straitened, and he keeps him a place in the action carelessly enough. Throughout the storm-scenes, of course, his sober, single-minded concern for the King does but reinforce his dramatic credit; it is, besides, a necessary check to their delirium. He could have even less to say here, and his very presence would be a strength. It is like Kent not to fuss as poor Gloucester fusses, not to talk when he need not, to think of the morrow and do the best he can meanwhile. Shakespeare allows him – a just economy – two flashes of emotion; the first when Lear turns to him with

> Wilt break my heart?
> I'd rather break my own

he says. And once –

54

O pity!

No more than that.

It is after he has taken Lear to Dover that, as a character, he begins to live upon the credit of his past. Shakespeare seems not quite sure what more he may want of him; he only does not want him to complicate with his vigorous personality the crowded later action of the play. What his purpose may be in sustaining his disguise –

> Pardon, dear madam;
> Yet to be known shortens my made intent:
> My boon I make it that you know me not
> Till time and I think meet

– is never very clear. But Shakespeare's own purpose here is clear enough; not to spoil Lear's reconciliation with Cordelia, by adding to it a recognition of Kent. The couplet with which Kent ends the scene:

> My point and period will be throughly wrought,
> Or well or ill, as this day's battle's fought

has in the event neither much significance nor consequence. It is a safe remark and sounds well. We might suppose (we may do so, if we like; but in fact an audience will not stop to consider a commentator's point) that Kent is counting, if Lear is defeated, on serving him still in disguise, when known he could not. But he does not appear in the battle or the defeat; and this we might think (if, again, we stopped to think; but while the play is acting we shall not) as strange as his neglect which had let Lear escape to wander

> As mad as the vex'd sea; singing aloud . . . .

But the simple explanation probably is that Shakespeare finds he has no more dramatic use for Kent till he can bring him on, the play all but done, with

55

> I am come
> To bid my king and master aye good-night.

So he must just keep him in being meanwhile.

That Kent should survive so effectively to the play's end is at once a tribute to the vitality of his first projection and to the tact with which Shakespeare can navigate the shallows of his art. And the actor who can express himself and impress himself upon us as well by silence as by speech will find no difficulties in the part.[24]

THE FOOL

The Fool can never, of course, be to us what he was to the play's first audience. For them, Shakespeare's achievement lay in the double conversion of a stock stage character and a traditional Court figure to transcendent dramatic use. There are few greater pleasures in art than to find the familiar made new; but to us stage Fool and Court Fool alike are strange to start with. Court Fool has, to be sure, a likely claim to a place in the play, and can claim a place too in our historical consciousness. Grant the old King such a favourite: it is good character scheming to contrast his royal caprices with such spaniel affection; dramatic craft at its best to leave Lear in adversity this one fantastic remnant of royalty. This, and much more of intrinsic value, we cannot lose. But what, from the transcended stage Fool, did Shakespeare gain besides?

Elizabethan acting did not inhabit the removed footlight-defended stage of the theatre of today, and all its technique and conventions and the illusion it created differ appropriately in consequence; this is the constant theme of these Prefaces,

[24] If it be said that there is nothing in the Kent of Act IV which, upon analysis, belies his character, yet this Preface is concerned also with his presentment, and that is ineffective and even halting. But what of his sudden outburst in Act IV, Sc. iii:

> It is the stars;
> The stars above us, govern our conditions . . .

– is this the authentic Kent? And even if Shakespeare were here starting to develop a new phase of the man, he never goes on.

For a masterly analysis of the whole character we should turn to A. C. Bradley's lecture on *King Lear*.

and must be of any study of the staging of Shakespeare plays. But certain effects, however gained, are common to all drama, certain problems recur. A problem in the writing and acting of tragedy is the alternate creating and relaxing of emotional strain; the tenser the strain, the less long can an audience appreciatively endure it. "Comic relief" has a crude sound; but, to some degree and in some form or other, the thing it suggests is a necessity. Greek tragedy had "choric relief"; emotion in the Greek theatre was magnified and rarefied at once, and sharp transitions were neither wanted nor workable. Shakespeare had the constant shift of scene and subject, usual in his theatre, to help him; and his most strenuous scenes, we may remark, tend to be short ones.[25] We may suppose him ever mindful of the difficulty of keeping the attention of a motley audience fixed, but still alert; and in the body of a scene, if it needs must be a long one, we shall always find what may be called "points of rest and recovery".

But the problem can be stated in other terms. Tragedy, it may be said, takes us out of ourselves; how else can it be enjoyed? A dash of comedy will, by contrast, restore us to ourselves; yet, for the tragedy's sake, the less conscious of the process we are the better. Here lay for Shakespeare, in this play, the histrionic value of the Fool. He wanted no comic relief in the crude sense; but this familiar stage figure, even though turned to tragic purpose, kept for that audience, if insensibly, its traditional hail-fellow quality. Only the dramatic and human value of the character is preserved us for today to the full. Of the effect of the snatches of song and rhyme, the lyric lightening of the epic strength of these scenes, we keep only the most manifest part. The things themselves are queer to us, and this is just what they should not be. And of the friendly feeling, the sense of being at ease with ourselves,

---

25 This play apart, they are noticeably so in *Macbeth* and in *Antony and Cleopatra*. In *Hamlet* and in *Othello* it may be said they are not. But in *Hamlet* the action is – and characteristically – not consistently strenuous; and the sustaining of the anguish in *Othello* is typical of the tragedy, helps give us the heroic measure of Othello himself.

which the stage Fool, a-straddle between play and audience, could create for the Elizabethans, we save nothing at all. We have felt something of the sort as children perhaps, when, at the Pantomime, after the removed mysteries of the transformation scene, came the harlequinade and the clown, cuddling us up to him with his "Here we are again". It may seem a far cry from red-hot poker and sausages to *King Lear*. But these indigenous attributes of the Fool are the underlying strength of the part once its acting is in question; and it is Shakespeare's use and restraint and disguise of them at once that is so masterly. Out went the character, as we know, from the eighteenth-century versions of the play; nor actors nor audience, it was thought, could countenance such an aberration. Macready restored it with many misgivings and gave it to a girl to act. The producer today faces another difficulty. He finds a Fool all etherealized by the higher criticism. His first care, in the part's embodying, must be to see restored as much as may be of its lost aboriginal strength. Its actor must sing like a lark, juggle his words so that the mere skill delights us, and tumble around with all the grace in the world. Satisfy these simpler demands, and the subtleties will have their effect; neglect them, and you might as well try to play tunes on a punctured organ stop.

About the Fool's character in the personal sense there is really not much to be said, though it is a subject upon which the romantic commentator has rejoiced to embroider his own fancies. He is, not a half-wit, but – the old word fits – a "natural"; he does not, that is to say, draw all our practical distinction between sense and nonsense, the wise thing to do, and the unwise. But he lives in a logical world of his own. Lear has petted him as one pets a dog; he shows a dog's fidelity. It is foolish of him, no doubt, to follow his master into such a storm – but, then, he *is* a fool. Shakespeare, having had his dramatic use of him, drops him incontinently; this alone should label the part of merely incidental importance to the scheme of the play. But even this he makes a measure of the human pathos of the creature. We are told by the attendant knight before ever we see him:

Since my young lady's going into France, sir, the fool
hath much pined away.
No more of that; I have noted it well . . . .

Lear answers (lest we should not note it well enough). But
not a word more; above all never a hint from this professional
jester himself that he has, or has a right to, any feelings of his
own. His jests have grown bitterer lately perhaps, to suit with
Lear's changing fortunes; yet, for compensation, he is more
full of song than ever. And come weal, come woe, he sticks
to his job, sticks to it and to his master till the storm batters
him into silence. With a ha'porth of warmth and comfort in
him, he flickers bravely into jest again. But his task is done
now, and he himself pretty well done for. He tells us so in a
very short and bitter jest indeed:

And I'll go to bed at noon.

And this is the last we hear or see of him; and what happens
to him thereafter, who knows or cares? Which is quite according to the jesters' – and players' – code of professional honour, and to the common reward of its observance, as Shakespeare, of all men, would know well. To pursue the Fool
beyond the play's bounds, to steep him in extraneous sentiment,
is to miss the most characteristically dramatic thing about
him.

One minor point about the part is yet an important one.
The soliloquy which Act III, Scene ii, is made to end is
certainly spurious.[26] Its own incongruity can be left out of
the question; its offence against the dramatic situation dis-
allows it. The very heart of this is Lear's new-found care for
the shivering drenched creature at his side.

Come on, my boy. How dost, my boy? Art cold? . . .
Poor fool and knave, I have one part in my heart
That's sorry yet for thee.

[26] And surely it is time that all editions of Shakespeare put certain
passages, whose fraud can be agreed upon, in expurgatorial brackets. We
are ready for another – and another sort of – Bowdler.

Shakespeare is incapable – so would any other dramatist in his senses be – of stultifying himself by dispatching Lear from the scene immediately after, and letting him leave the Fool behind him.

GLOUCESTER, EDGAR AND EDMUND

Gloucester and his sons are opposite numbers, as the phrase now goes, to Lear and his daughters. Gloucester himself is the play's nearest approach to the average sensual man. The civilized world is full of Gloucesters. In half a dozen short speeches Shakespeare sets him fully before us: turning elderly but probably still handsome; nice of speech if a little pompous; the accomplished courtier (he seems to be Lear's master of ceremonies); vain, as his mock modesty shows, but the joking shamelessness that succeeds it is mainly swagger; an egotist, and blind, knowing least of what he should know most, of his own two sons.

> He hath been out nine years, and away he shall again.

That carelessly jovial sentence of banishment for Edmund proves his own death-sentence. Still, who could suspect the modest young newcomer, making his bow with

> Sir, I shall study deserving

of having such unpleasant thoughts in mind?

Gloucester like so many sensual men, is good nature itself, as long as things go their easy, natural way; but when they fail to he is upset, rattled. Kent's banishment, the quarrel with Cordelia and France, and the King's utter recklessness set his mind off at one tangent and another and make him an easier victim to very simple deceit. We must not, however, appraise either his simplicity or Edgar's, at this moment, with detachment – for by that light, no human being, it would seem, between infancy and dotage, could be so gullible. Shakespeare asks us to allow him the fact of the deception, even as we have allowed him Lear's partition of the kingdom. It is his starting point, the dramatist's "net's pretend", which is as essential to the beginning of a play as a "let it be granted" to a proposition of Euclid. And, within bounds, the degree of pretence makes surprisingly little difference. It is what the assumption will commit him to that counts; once a play's action is under way it must develop as logically as Euclid, and far more logically than life. The art of the thing is to reward the spectator for his concession by never presuming on it; one should rather dress up the unlikely in the likelier. Thus Shakespeare makes Gloucester, with his pother about "these late eclipses of the sun and moon", the sort of man who might at any moment be taken in by any sort of tale; the more improbable, indeed, the better. He makes Edmund plausible even if the incriminating letter is not. And what better way to confirm a nervous, puzzled, opinionated man in an error than to reason calmly with him against it? Your victim will instinctively take the opposite point of view and forget that this was yours to begin with.[27] Does not the credulous nature crave to be deceived? Moreover, Shakespeare's first concern is to develop character, to put us on terms with these people; not till that is done, he knows, will their doings and sufferings really affect us. So it suits him, in any case, to subordinate, for a little, what they do to what they are. And we part from Gloucester in this scene knowing him for a start pretty well.

The sensual man does not stand up very resolutely against blows dealt to his complacent affections. Disillusion leaves Gloucester not only wax in Edmund's hands but more help-

[27] But it follows that upon these lines we cannot be brought to a very close knowledge of Edgar too. Give him the same scope, and he must either get on the track of the truth or prove himself as great a fool as his father. So Shakespeare, now and at his next appearance, does as little with him as possible. This delays – and dangerously – our gaining interest in him. But a play survives sins of omission when the smallest sin of commission may damn it. Besides, time is valuable; and a subplot cannot, for the moment, be spared much more. The likelihood of the detail of his traffic between father and sons, the sending of letters, the "retire with me to my lodging . . . there's my key" and the rest, depends somewhat upon the large, loose organization of a great nobleman's household of that day, of which Shakespeare's audience would know well enough.

less than it belongs to him to be – fair-weather sailor though he has ever been! –in the alien troubles that now centre round him. Shakespeare's manœuvering of him through these scenes – from the welcome to the "noble arch and patron" to the moment when his guest's honoured fingers are plucking at his eyes – is a good example of the fruitful economy with which, once a character has "come alive", its simplest gesture, its very muteness is made significant. And Gloucester has been alive from the beginning; no illustration for a thesis, but un-self-consciously himself. This very unself-consciousness is turned later to tragic account. Fate's worst revenge on him is that, blinded, he comes to see himself so clearly as he is, and to find the world, which once went so comfortably with him, a moral chaos. We might wonder at the amount of agonized reflection in this kind allotted to him. But mark its culmination:

> The king is mad: how stiff is my vile sense
> That I stand up, and have ingenious feeling
> Of my huge sorrows! Better I were distract:
> So should my thoughts be sever'd from my griefs,
> And woes by wrong imaginations lose
> The knowledge of themselves.

The one thing, it seems, that the average sensual man cannot endure is knowledge of the truth. Better death or madness than that!

Yet which of us must not feelingly protest that the Gloucester, who threads and fumbles his way so well-meaningly about the family battlefield his house is turned into (much against his will), is very harshly used indeed? Is this poetic justice? He does all that one who respects his superiors may do to save Kent from the ignominy of the stocks. He does his best to pacify Lear.

> I would have all well betwixt you.

How familiar is that heartfelt cry of the man who sees no

sense in a quarrel! When he does take sides his reasons and his method are not heroic, it is true.

> These injuries the king now bears will be revenged home; there is part of a power already footed; we must incline to the king. I will look to him and privily relieve him, go you and maintain talk with the duke, that my charity be not of him perceived. If he asks for me, I am ill and gone to bed.

No, truly, it is not heroic, when battle is joined, to be ill and go to bed. But caution is a sort of a virtue; and the keeping of a family foot in each camp has good sanction. Yet who can be altogether wise? In his next breath comes

> If I die for it, as no less is threatened me, the king, my old master, must be relieved.

And this his best impulse is his undoing. Unwittingly he is telling Edmund how best to betray him. He points the way; Edmund has but to follow it – just a little further. Irony deepens when later he calls upon Cornwall to spare him in the sacred name of that hospitality which, towards his king, he himself has so spinelessly betrayed. Yet, "tied to the stake", he can "stand the course" courageously enough; and he recovers self-respect in hopeless defiance of his tyrants. With just a little luck he need never have lost it. Now he is blinded and turned helpless from his own doors. Is this poetic justice upon a gentleman, whose worst fault has been to play for safety, his worst blunder to think ill of a man without question and to believe a liar? Disquieting to think that it may be!.[28]

---

[28] For an earlier stroke of irony – only to be fully appreciated perhaps by the shade of Lady Gloucester – consider the exclamation wrung from the distracted old man at the climax of his wrath against Edgar:

> O strong and fasten'd villain!
> Would he deny his letter? *I never got him.*

And this to Edmund his bastard!

Edmund is, in wickedness, half-brother to Iago. Having no such great nature as Othello's to work on, Shakespeare has no need of such transcendent villainy; and he lessens and vulgarizes his man by giving him one of those excuses for foul play against the world which a knave likes to find as a point of departure. His first soliloquy is a complete enough disclosure. The fine flourish of

> Thou, Nature, art my goddess . . . .

(finer by its surprise for us in the mouth of the modest young man of the earlier scene), and the magnificent rejection of conventional morality narrow to their objective in

> Well, then,
> Legitimate Edgar, I must have your land.

And from this firm businesslike basis Edmund, except for pure pose, never soars again. The later

> This is the excellent foppery of the world . . . .

is enjoyable argument doubtless, and doubtless he chuckles over it. There is a sporting and imaginative touch, perhaps, in the trick that finally gets rid of Edgar; the stabbing his own arm, we feel, is to his credit. But for the rest, a strict attention to business, and a quick eye to one main chance after the other, suffice him. And this, really, is almost the loathliest thing about the man. He not only betrays his father to Cornwall, but he cants about loyalty the while. He accepts the attentions of Regan and Goneril without surprise or embarassment (he is a handsome young fellow and he knows it), calculates which will be the more desirable connection, but will leave Goneril to get rid of her husband alone if that risky task has to be undertaken. It even passes through his mind that she herself – if not Regan – may in her turn have to be "put away". His tardy repentance does not touch us; and he puts it into practice too tardily.[29] The queer snobbery which prompts him to say to the still visored Edgar

> If thou'rt noble,
>   I do forgive thee

and the still queerer vanity (at such a moment!) of

> Yet Edmund was beloved.
> The one the other poison'd for my sake,
> And after slew herself

may strike upon some ears as all but ridiculous. He is an ignoble scoundrel and he makes an ignoble end.

Still, his methods have been interesting. The first attack upon his father's credulity was, as we saw, both bold and apt; and what could be safer support to the fiction of Edgar's plot than the counterfeit truth of

> When I dissuaded him from his intent . . .
> he replied,
> Thou unpossessing bastard! dost thou think,
> If I would stand against thee, would the reposal
> Of any trust, virtue, or worth in thee
> Make thy words faith'd? No: what I should deny, –
> As this I would; ay, though thou didst produce
> My very character, I'd turn it all
> To thy suggestion, plot, and damned practice.

For masterly confounding of counsel this should rouse the admiration of the most practiced liar. Whether, later, there is need for him to be so snivellingly hypocritical with Cornwall we may question. But he is still on promotion; and that

---

[29] His "Ask me not what I know", in which he takes example from Goneril – and Iago! – is given by one Quarto and some editors to Goneril herself, with (I fancy) good enough reason.

shrewd, forthright brute, if not deceived, will be the more flattered by this tribute of vice to his virtue.

But once he is in the saddle, and when not one royal lady, but two, have lost their heads over him, what a change!

> Know of the duke if his last purpose hold,
> Or whether since he is advised by aught
> To change his course; he's full of alteration
> And self-reproving; bring his constant pleasure.

This he says publicly of no less a man than Albany, whom later he salutes with an ironically patronizing

> Sir, you speak nobly.

He is losing his head, one fears, in the flush of his fire-new fortune. Albany, however, waits his time and prepares for it; this mild gentleman should have been better reckoned with. For, of a sudden, Edmund finds that he has climbed, even as his blinded father set out in misery to climb, to the edge of a steep. And it is an apposite phrase indeed which flashes the depths on him:

> Half-blooded fellow, yes!

– from an Albany not so mild. The wheel is coming circle.

This individual catastrophe and its contriving are a good example of Shakespeare's adapting of end to means (that constant obligation of the dramatist), and of his turning disability to advantage. His very need to compress close these latter incidents of Edmund's rise to fortune helps him make it the more egregious. The fact that but a dozen speeches seem to lift the fellow towards the grasping of the very power of which Lear divested himself at the play's beginning should make our recollection of that modest young man in the background of its first scene the more amazing to us. It is, at this juncture, a breathless business for all concerned. Then at the climax comes the sudden isolation of the upstart, brave in his armour, flushed with his triumph. And Shakespeare releases the tension — and rewards himself for his economy — in the sounding of trumpets, the fine flow and colour of some heroic verse quite in his old style, and all the exciting ceremony of the duel.[30] Late in the play as this comes, and of secondary concern to the greater tragedy as it may be, not a point of its thriftily developed drama must be missed.

Edgar is a "slow starter" and shows no promise at all as a hero. Not here, however, but in Shakespeare's use of him as Poor Tom will be the actor's greater handicap. For by the time he is free from this arbitrary bondage the play has put our attention and emotions to some strain and we are no longer so well disposed to the development of a fresh serious interest. Otherwise there is every dramatic fitness in his tardy coming to his own. Edmund flashes upon us in pinchbeck brilliance; the worth of Edgar waits discovery, and trial and misfortune must help discover it — to himself above all.

> a brother noble,
> Whose nature is so far from doing harms
> That he suspects none; on whose foolish honesty
> My practices ride easy!

says Edmund of him in proper contempt. "What are you?" asks his unknowing father, when his fortunes are still at their worst. And he answers:

> A most poor man, made tame to fortune's blows;
> Who, by the art of known and feeling sorrows,
> Am pregnant to good pity.

But, by the play's end, it is to him as well as to Kent that Albany turns with

> Friends of my soul, you twain

---

[30] Compare the "defiances" of this scene with the passage between Mowbray and Norfolk in the beginning of *Richard II*.

> Rule in this realm, and the gor'd state sustain.

What are the steps by which he passes from nobody to some-body?

His very reserve at the beginning can give him a stamp of distinction, and should be made to do so. And the notion of that strange disguise would not come, we may say, to a commonplace man. Through the ravings of Poor Tom we can detect something of the mind of Edgar with its misprision of the sensual life – of his father's life, is it? We can certainly see his pitiful heart; this Shakespeare stresses. But only in the soliloquies that end Act III, Scene vi, and begin Act IV do we discover the full mind of the man[31]:

> When we our betters see bearing our woes,
> We scarcely think our miseries our foes.
> Who alone suffers, suffers most i' the mind,
> Leaving free things and happy shows behind;
> But then the mind much sufferance doth o'erskip,
> When grief hath mates, and bearing fellowship . . .

and

> Yet better thus, and known to be contemn'd,
> Than still contemn'd and flatter'd. To be worst,
> The lowest and most dejected thing of fortune,
> Stands still in esperance, lives not in fear;
> The lamentable change is from the best;
> The worst returns to laughter. . . .

We seem to have found the play's philosopher. And the sententiousness of the earlier soliloquy, differing both in form and tone from anything that has preceded it in the play, is surely a deliberate contrivance to lower the tension of the action and to prepare us for the calmer atmosphere – by comparison – of the play's ending. Shakespeare may afterwards have repented of it as sounding too sententious and as coming uselessly for its wider purpose immediately before the blind-

[31] The Folio rejects the first of those two and (see p. 16, note) the producer may be wise to.

ing of Gloucester. But Edgar's philosophy of indifference to fortune, of patience with life itself, of the good comfort of fellowship, is now, certainly, to dominate the play. It is summed up for us more than once.

> Bear free and patient thoughts

he tells his father, when, by his queer stratagem – again, it was not the notion of a commonplace mind – he has saved him from despair. His playing the peasant with the insufferable Oswald is, yet again, not commonplace; and, having killed him:

> He is dead. I am only sorry
> He had no other deathsman.[32]

To him is given the answer to Gloucester's deadly

> As flies to wanton boys, are we to the gods;
> They kill us for their sport

in

> therefore, thou happy father,
> Think that the clearest gods, who make them honours
> Of men's impossibilities, have preserved thee.

To him is given

> The gods are just, and of our pleasant vices
> Make instruments to plague us.

But before this, his good name and his father's death justly avenged, what is the first thing he says as he discloses himself to the doubly damned scoundrel lying at his feet?

> Let's exchange charity.

[32] "Chill pick your teeth, sir", suggests that he stabs him, either with a knife he wears, or, possibly, with Oswald's own dagger, wrested after a tussle.

Edgar, in fact, has become a man of character indeed, modest, of a discerning mind, and, in this pagan play, a very Christian gentleman.[33]

BURGUNDY, FRANCE, ALBANY, CORNWALL

Burgundy and France hardly outpass convention, though the one gains enough character from his laconic indifference, while the spirit and quality of France's speeches should keep him a pleasant memory to the play's end.[34]

Cornwall has "character" in abundance. He and Albany stand all but mute at their first appearance.[35] But from our next sight of him to our last he justifies in action and speech Gloucester's description:

> My dear lord,
> You know the fiery quality of the duke;
> How unremoveable and fix'd he is
> To his own course.

He is a man, we may suppose, in the prime of life; old enough, at least, to say to Edmund

> thou shalt find a dearer father in my love.

[33] He is, I think, as true a gentleman as the plays give us. And he is kept himself and no mere moralizer to the last. When Lear sinks dying, it is Edgar who starts forward to recover him, till Kent checks him with the immortal

> Vex not his ghost: O! let him pass; he hates him
> That would upon the rack of this tough world
> Stretch him out longer.

For Edgar is still very young.

[34] Here is one of the difficulties incidental to the production of such a play as *King Lear* with a company gathered in for the occasion. The quality of the actors available tends to diminish with the importance of the parts. Pay apart, an actor of authority and distinction will not attach himself to a theatre for the sole purpose of playing France. Hence the need of an established company with all its compensating opportunities. France is a powerful king and Cordelia's husband; and if he does not impress us as he should, and lodge himself in our memories, not only is the play immediately the poorer, but Cordelia, returning, is robbed of a background of great importance to her.

[35] By the text of the Quarto absolutely mute.

He is by no means a stupid man: the cynical humour with which he appraises Kent shows that. He asserts himself against his wife as Albany does not. He can speak up to Lear when need be, but he is not too swift to do it. In his vindictiveness he still keeps his head.

> Go seek the traitor Gloucester,
> Pinion him like a thief, bring him before us.
> Though well we may not pass upon his life
> Without the form of justice; yet our power
> Shall do a courtesy to our wrath, which men
> May blame but not control.

But this hardly makes him the more likeable. And though we might allow him some credit for at least doing his own dirty work, it is evident that he enjoys Gloucester's blinding, for he sets about it with a savage jest. The taste of blood seems to let loose all the wild beast in him; and, like a wild beast, Shakespeare has him dispatched. Yet Cornwall is a forceful character; and there are those who – having no more concern with them than to profit by their forcefulness – can find, strangely enough, something to admire in such men. So he may be allowed a certain dog-toothed attractiveness in performance.

Albany is at the opposite pole. He prefers a quiet life with Goneril while he can contrive to lead it, even at the cost of some self-respect.

> Striving to better, oft we mar what's well

seems to stand as his motto; and it sounds the more sententious by its setting in a rhymed couplet. His "milky gentleness", his "harmful mildness" ring true enough as accusations: does he think to tame a tigress with a platitude? His wife, quite naturally, departs to seek Regan's help without him.

Much has happened, though, by the time we see him again, when Goneril is on the full tide of reckless triumphant wicked-

71

ness. She takes no heed of Oswald's

> never man so changed

still presumes on

> the cowish terror of his spirit

and even, when she meets him changed indeed, is blind and deaf to the change. That Albany had loved his wife is made plain. We hear him speak in his quiet way of "the great love" he bore her. He has been slow to think ill of her. But he is of those who let their wrath gather beneath a placid surface till, on a sudden, it boils over, and if the cause of it lies deep they are never the same again. Shakespeare, who cannot spare much space for his development, gives us this impression of the man by allowing us chiefly these contrasted sights of him, the long interval between. And the first stern clash with Goneril has a double purpose and nets a double dramatic gain. It wins Albany the authoritative standing that he now needs in the play, and it shows us a Goneril so possessed by self-will that our own surprise at the change in him turns to surprise that she can be so oblivious of it. We may count her a doomed creature from this moment.

Henceforth he is pitted against Edmund; the aristocrat against the upstart; the man with nothing to gain for himself against the man who must win and still win or perish; the man who, to the taunt of "moral fool" can answer

> Where I could not be honest,
> I never yet was valiant

against the man who can tell his follower as he sends him to commit an atrocious murder:

> know thou this, that men
> Are as the time is; to be tender-minded
> Does not become a sword; thy great employment

> Will not bear question; either say thou'lt do't,
> Or thrive by other means.

The world's allegiance is ever swaying between such leaderships.

Albany, once in action, is as distinguished a figure as any in the play. Shakespeare endows him with a fine sense of irony. The slight sting in the tail of his compliment to Edmund after the battle:

> Sir, you have showed today your valiant strain,
> And fortune led you well

the cutting courtesy of

> Sir, by your patience,
> I hold you but a subject of this war,
> Not as a brother

his cool preparation of his stroke; the stroke itself:

> Stay yet, hear reason. Edmund, I arrest thee
> On capital treason; and, in thy arrest,
> This gilded serpent. For your claim, fair sister,
> I bar it in the interest of my wife;
> 'Tis she is sub-contracted to this lord,
> And I, her husband, contradict your banns.
> If you will marry, make your loves to me,
> My lady is bespoke

- are not bad for a moral fool.

Nor does he trust to the appearance of the unknown champion for Edmund's undoing. He throws his own gauntlet down. A touch of gallantry, though Shakespeare does not – does not need to – compromise his dignity by setting him to fight. And he is left from now to the play's end in command of its action.[36]

---

[36] Though the last speech should possibly, in accordance with the Folio, be Edgar's.

A modern audience must lose almost as much of the flavour of Oswald as of the Fool; and more still must be lost if he is stripped of his doublet and hose, forbidden his swagger and his curtseys and thrust back into the dark ages. We cannot be expected to cheer – as I doubt not Shakespeare's audience did – when Kent breaks out with

> That such a slave as this should wear a sword,
> Who wears no honesty!

nor to take the precise point of Lear's

> How now, where's that mongrel?

that newfangled fellow, neither gentleman nor plain servant, mimicking the manners of the one, doing dirtier work than the other. Kent sizes him up when he dresses him down, with enjoyable completeness; so does Lear, later, in a dozen words:

> This is a slave, whose easy-borrowed pride
> Dwells in the fickle grace of her he follows.

So does Edgar, having rid the world of him, as

> a serviceable villain;
> As duteous to the vices of thy mistress
> As badness would desire.

Oswalds have existed in every age and been good game for abuse, but the London of Shakespeare's day had evidently produced an unusually fine crop of them. His own sayings are colourless compared with what is said of him. It follows, then, that his "Ay, madams" and "No, madams", his "I'll not be strucken, my lord", his "Prithee, if thou lovest me, tell me", and his "Out, dunghill", when the peasant's cudgel threatens to knock his dishonourable sword out of his hand, must answer exactly in accent and attitude, as he himself in look and manner, to the very sort of being Shakespeare had in mind. In himself he is nothing; a "whoreson zed", an "unnecessary letter", and he should seem no more. But, as a tailor made him, he must be tailored right.

It remains to notice one or two of Shakespeare's minuter touches. When Gloucester has been blinded, branded a traitor and turned from his own house to smell his way to Dover, he finds one fearless friend; the old peasant who has been his tenant and his father's tenant "these fourscore years". The savagery of the blinding itself had stirred one common fellow to risk and lose his life stopping the worst of it. Two other common fellows have the charity to bind up the wounds; but they'll risk no more than that. The old peasant, too old himself to go far with his lord, shakes a sad head at leaving him in such company as Poor Tom, and will risk his fortunes to do Gloucester, in his ruin and disgrace, a last simple service. Close following the transcendent scenes of Lear's madness and the extreme brutality of the blinding comes this interlude of servant and peasant, of common humanity in its bravery and charity with its simple stumbling talk. The whole effect is made in a dozen lines or so, but gains importance by its homespun contrast and by its placing across the main dividing line of the play's action.

And for a happy instance of Shakespeare's power to suggest a man in a dozen words, take the reply of the Captain to whom Edmund confides the murder of Lear and Cordelia:

> I cannot draw a cart nor eat dried oats;
> If it be man's work, I'll do it.

Staging and Costume

No more need be urged, I hope, against a realistic staging of the play or anything approaching one. But whether the single alternative to this is the actuality of Shakespeare's own theatre is another question, which the producer must answer for himself. If he protests that his audience will never sit so unconsciously before a reproduction of the Globe stage as did Shakespeare's before the thing itself one cannot contradict him. But he cuts from the anchorage at his peril. And the doubt is as to whether when he has found some, presumably, atmospheric sort of background, which does not positively conflict with the play's stagecraft, the result – for all its visual beauty – will be worth the risk and the trouble.

Abide by Shakespeare's own stage, and no questions of importance arise upon the use of it. But for Edgar's moment "above", some need for the masking of Lear's "state", and again for the discovery of the joint-stools and bench in the scene of the mock trial, the play could indeed be acted upon a barer stage than was the Globe's.[37] The great chair with the unconscious Lear in it may be more conveniently carried from an inner stage, and Poor Tom will emerge more effectively from one than from a sidedoor. But this is all; and it may even be that Shakespeare minimized such localization as his theatre did afford him to give the play spaciousness of action, and to magnify his characters the more in isolating them from needless detail of circumstance. Let the producer, at any rate – and at all costs – provide for the action's swift unencumbered movement and for our concentration upon the characters themselves, in whom everything is concentrated.

As for costume, this is one of the few plays in which Shakespeare took some trouble to do more than its subject itself would do to dissociate it from his own time; though even so he will not have relied overmuch upon costume to help him. But only here and there is his own seventeenth-century patent, and that in character or incident of minor importance. The prevailing atmosphere and accent is barbaric and remote. Edmund's relationship to Iago may seem to us to give him a certain Italianate flavour, and Edgar's beginning suggests bookishness and the Renaissance. But clothe these two as we please, their substance will defy disguise. Oswald, as we have argued, is a topical picture; in the Ancient Briton he will be all but obliterated. That must be faced. Of the Fool, by shift-

[37] There are one or two signs that the stage to which the Folio version was fitted differed a little from that of the Quarto.

76

ing him back a dozen centuries, we lose little, because, as we have argued, we are bound already to lose so much. And if a Fool in a barbarous king's retinue seems to us an anachronism (though it may be doubted if – for all the preciseness that would take offence at a Henry V in doublet and hose – it will), the fantasy of the part marks it out as the fittest note of relief from consistency. To consistency in such matters no dated play of Shakespeare can be submitted. Here our main losses by desertion of seventeenth-century habit and manners will end. And such anachronism as may lie in Cordelia's chance of being Duchess of Burgundy, in "base football player" and "unfee'd lawyer", in the stocks, in some of Poor Tom's talk and Lear's ravings, and in the procedure of the challenge and the duel, will be inconsiderable however the characters are clothed.

So a producer is free to balance these items against an imagined Britain, whose king swears

> by the mysteries of Hecate and the night

(not to mention Apollo), and where a Duke of Cornwall turns public executioner. There is no doubt, I think, in which scale advantage lies. The play should be costumed according to the temper that Shakespeare has given it, a splendid barbaric temper. It is equally clear that archaeological accuracy profits nothing. Nor should the producer lose more than he need of such sophistication as Shakespeare himself retained.

The Music

About the music there is little to be said. I do not imagine much improvement possible upon "the consort of viols", to the quiet harmonies of which Lear was meant, one presumes, to be waked. The sennet that announces his first regal appearance should be noted, as well as the flourish to herald France and Burgundy, and the ceremonial difference between the two. The *Horns within*, which prelude Lear's return from hunting, ask no comment. A trumpet is used with dramatic effect before Cornwall's entrance in Act II, Scene i; it reinforces Gloucester's excitement. The same sound stirs Lear a little later and strings him up for the encounter with Goneril. And, towards the play's end, the triple sounding by the herald, to be answered, when our suspense is keenest, by Edgar's trumpet without, is a most carefully calculated dramatic effect.[38] We have noticed earlier how the battle in which Cordelia's forces are defeated is dramatically minimized; its musical symbolism consist only of an alarum and an alarum and retreat. But the *Drum afar off,* to the ominous sound of which the longest and most varied scene of the fourth act closes, has very definite value. So has the dead march with which the play itself ends.

The Fool is allotted no formal and completed song, but, needless to say, his snatches of melody should be melodious indeed. This musical and lyrical relief to the strain of Lear's passion is, as we have argued elsewhere, an essential part of the play's stagecraft. The technique of the singing should not be artificial; rather that of an accomplished folk-song singer. And where no authentically traditional tunes exist, folk music will prove a sufficient quarry.

The Text

The complications of the text are troublesome. Corruptions, obvious and suspected, apart, the producer is confronted by the problem of the three hundred lines, or nearly, that the Quartos give and the Folio omits, and of the hundred given by the Folio and omitted from the Quartos. Editors, considering only, it would seem, that the more Shakespeare we get the better, bring practically the whole lot into the play we read. But a producer must ask himself whether these two versions do not come from different prompt books, and whether the Folio does not, both in cuts and additions, sometimes represent Shakespeare's own second thoughts. In general, surely, the Folio is of better authority; it is at least more carefully transcribed. Some of its cuts are of passages which seem to have been found constructionally unnecessary. Some only "ease" the dialogue; they are of varying importance

[38] Beethoven found a similar one useful in *Fidelio.*

and aptness. Where Quarto and Folio offer alternatives, to adopt both versions may make for redundancy or confusion.[39]

To deal with the major differences. In the scene of the dividing of the kingdom the Folio's stressed identification of Albany and Cornwall, France and Burgundy, seems deliberate and is certainly valuable. Of the additions to the Gloucester-Edmund-Edgar scene the same may be said. Gloucester can hardly be shown too distracted, and the hiding-away of Edgar from his father is a good point made. But, in compensation, the Folio cuts the mockery of Gloucester's foibles with which Edmund preludes his attempt on Edgar's confidence – and one sees why.

In Goneril's first scene with Oswald the Folio's omissions save some repetition and show her to us terser and less familiar with her servant. A Folio cut in the Fool's part a little later – his rhyming upon the "sweet and bitter fool", and the joke about monopolizing – may seem at a first glance a little clumsy. But we shall hardly appreciate the gibe at monopolies unless we rewrite it "trusts"; probably the Quarto's audiences had appreciated it too well. The whole cut is a useful tightening of the dialogue. Yet a little later the Folio gives us (as the Quarto does not) a passage in which Goneril justifies herself to Albany; undoubtedly useful.

When Lear finds Kent in the stocks and has listened in silence to the story of his being set there, by the Quarto

> O, how this mother swells up toward my heart . . .

follows immediately upon Kent's story. The Folio gives the Fool a little piping song, while Lear still stands speechless, his agony upon him. The dramatic effect will be appreciably different.

Later the Folio alone gives us a passage in which Regan justifies Goneril.

In Act III, Scene i, the Folio cuts some important lines out of the Gentleman's second speech. In particular

[39] I speak from now on of "the Quarto" because for the purposes of this argument the "Pied Bull" and "Butter" Quartos might be one.

79

> Strives in his little world of man to outscorn
> The to-and-fro-conflicting wind and rain

has vanished. An inefficient actor might have been the cause
of this. A few lines later Folio and Quarto offer us alternative
cuts. That of the Folio is perhaps the clumsier of the two.
It stresses the call for Cordelia's help but barely hints at her
army's landing, which the Quarto emphasizes. We may or may
not have here the cutting of a common original (of which
still more may have existed; for of the

> servants, who seem no less,
> Which are to France the spies and speculations
> Intelligent of our state . . .

we do not hear again). The object of the cut in both cases —
and possibly the cutting of the Gentleman's speech also — is
evidently to shorten this prelude to Lear's great entrance.
What should a producer do here? Shakespeare leaves us to
the end a little unconvinced by the machinery of Cordelia's
return. There is no dramatic profit in the confusion. Neither
text may be as Shakespeare left it. But in this instance I prefer
the Quarto's to an amalgam of the two.

Of Merlin's prophecy I have spoken elsewhere.[40]

Let us in passing note the Folio's most important addition
of two lines' preparation for the critical

> Poor naked wretches, wheresoe'er you are . . . .

In them the kindness to the half-drowned Fool is emphasized;
and he is (I think) sent off the stage so that there may be no
danger whatever of discord or incongruity. The actor of the
Fool, possibly, was never quite to be relied on; and even if he
could be, there was always the chance that some buffoon in
the audience would vent an incongruous guffaw at the mere
sight of him sitting there. But, above all, by these two lines
the meaning and intention of what is to come are emphasized:

[40] P. 59.

In, boy; go first. You houseless poverty –
Nay, get thee in. *I'll pray, and then I'll sleep.*

I italicize the vitally important phrase. It is dangerous to dogmatize; but this addition has to me all the air of being a second thought of Shakespeare's own.

We come to the Folio's omission of the mock trial. Time may, as we said, have demanded some omissions, and this scene may have been chosen rather than something better liked by the actors or (seemingly) audience. It can hardly have proved ineffective, technically "daring" though it is. It certainly does not to-day; and very certainly one cannot imagine Shakespeare regretting he had written it.

The cut at the end of this scene, however, asks more consideration; for a purely dramatic reason can be found for the omission of Edgar's soliloquy. It must lower the tension of the action. This may damage the scene of Gloucester's blinding, which follows immediately; and if an act-pause if to follow, the tension will, of course, be lowered then. The chief purpose of the soliloquy, moreover, is to give Edgar a fresh start in his dramatic career. It is a quiet start, the effect of which the violent scene that follows must do much to obliterate. When the Folio, then, postpones it to the beginning of Act IV, it does Edgar a double service, as the Quarto doubles the disservice by making the second soliloquy, when it comes, seem dramatically redundant. Without hesitation, I should here follow the Folio text. The further cutting of Kent's lines, however,

Oppressed nature sleeps . . .

is probably due to a quick closing of the inner stage, which may have obviated the lifting of the sleeping Lear, and it has not the same validity.

The Folio also cuts the significant piece of dialogue between the two servants with which the third act ends. I cannot pretend to say why, if it was not that when this text was settled, the actors to speak the lines were lacking. No one need abide by this cut.

The disappearance of Edgar's "Obidicut, Hobbididance" and the rest from the first scene with his father is, I think, to the good. A few lines before he says:

> I cannot daub it further.

And in any case the effect of the mad lingo will have been exhausted in the scenes with Lear.

We next come to some ruthless cutting of Albany by the Folio. Shakespeare may have yielded here to the exigencies of bad acting or to wish to knit the action more closely. But he is taking some pains at this juncture to develop Albany, and we shall be on the safe side in keeping to the fuller text.

Now, however, the Folio omits one entire scene. It is a carpentered scene if ever there was one. It begins with a lame explanation of the nonappearance of the King of France; it goes on to a preparation for the reappearance of Cordelia and it ends with some unconvincing talk about Lear's "burning shame" and Kent's disguise. I could better believe that Shakespeare cut it than wrote it. There is, certainly, a little life in the description of Cordelia, and a case can be made for so heralding her return to the play. The rest is explanation of what is better left unexplained; and whoever, between the making of the Quarto and the Folio, discovered this —Shakespeare or another—did the play a good service, which we shall wisely profit by.

The remaining differences between the two versions show, in the Folio, a further cutting of explanatory stuff, by which we may well abide; a certain slicing into Albany and Edmund that neither hurts them much now, nor, it is true, does much to spur the action; the loss of one or two lines (Cordelia's in particular) that we shall not want to lose, and the gain of a few that seem good second thoughts. There are, besides, one or two changes that seem merely to reflect change in stage practice as between Quarto and Folio.

On the whole, then —and if he show a courageous discretion— I recommend a producer to found himself on the Folio. For that it does show some at least of Shakespeare's own reshapings I feel sure.

13 JOHN GIELGUD AS KING LEAR

PRODUCED BY GRANVILLE-BARKER AND LEWIS CASSON, OLD VIC, 15 APRIL 1940

"In 1940 I rehearsed the part with Granville-Barker for an hour and a half, day after day. Everything he said seared into my brain and I follow that interpretation still." (John Gielgud, in an interview with *The Times*, 1959)

THE BARKER-CASSON OLD VIC PRODUCTION, 1940

15 Edgar, Robert Harris; Edmund, Jack Hawkins;
Goneril, Cathleen Nesbitt; Albany, Harcourt Williams

16 CHARLES LAUGHTON AS KING LEAR, PRODUCED BY GLEN BYAM SHAW; SETTINGS AND COSTUMES, MOTLEY: STRATFORD, 1959

"Dear daughter, I confess that I am old;
Age is unnecessary."

14 Lear, John Gielgud; Kent (in stocks), Lewis Casson;
the Fool, Stephen Haggard

17 "What they are, yet I know not; but they shall be
The terrors of the earth." (II iv 284–5)

18 "When we are born, we cry that we are come
To this great stage of fools." (IV vi 187–8)

19   "With acknowledgments to the late Harley Granville-Barker."

KING LEAR, PRODUCED BY JOHN GIELGUD AND ANTHONY QUAYLE; STRATFORD, 1950

Scenery and costumes, Leslie Hurry

Goneril, Maxine Audley; Lear, John Gielgud; Regan, Gwen Ffrangcon Davies

(*left*) 17, 18   LAURENCE OLIVIER IN HIS OWN PRODUCTION OF KING LEAR,
OLD VIC, NEW THEATRE, 1946

Scenery and costumes by Roger Furse

20 MICHAEL REDGRAVE AS KING LEAR

Produced by George Devine, settings and costumes, Robert Colquhoun:
Stratford, 1953

"Give him a scene, like this at Dover, which is the
higher mathematics of acting, and he solves it in a
flash: here, and throughout the last act, was the cube
root of King Lear, 'the thing itself'." (Kenneth Tynan)

21 CHARLES LAUGHTON AS KING LEAR; STRATFORD, 1959

Produced by Glen Byam Shaw

"Now, our joy,
. . . . What can you say, to draw
A third more opulent than your sisters? Speak."

FRONTISPIECES TO KING LEAR AND CYMBELINE, ROWE'S SHAKESPEARE, 1709

22 THE STORM SCENE   23 IMOGEN'S BEDCHAMBER

Note contemporary gentlemen's costume for Lear, Kent and Gloster, and compare Edgar's theatrical costume
with No. 1. Iachimo in *costume à la romaine* lends support to Barker's view that *Cymbeline* was originally
costumed in the masque tradition, (pp. 106–7)

Among other slightly vexed questions, the following are particularly worth attention (the lineal references are to the [English] Arden Shakespeare).

Act I, Scene i, 35. There is no authority for Edmund's exit, and the producer is quite at liberty to let him stay and listen to the momentous proceedings.

Scene v, 1. I give a guess that "Gloucester" in this line is a slip for "Cornwall". There is no other evidence that Lear writes to the Earl of Gloucester, nor any reason he should, nor any evidence at all that Cornwall lived near the town.

52-3. This couplet has the sanction (as Merlin's prophecy has not) of both Quarto and Folio. But I find its authenticity hard to credit. Shakespeare could write bawdry, and sometimes at what seem to us the unlikeliest moments. This does not smack of the Fool, though, or of what Shakespeare wants of him.

Act II, Scene i, 20. *Enter Edgar*. This stage direction is wrongly placed – and typically – in modern editions. The Quarto places it four lines, the Folio a line, earlier. Even the Folio, then, shows that he enters on the upper stage and is visible to the audience before Edmund sees him. It may seem a small matter, but the difference between an independent entrance and being called on like a dog is appreciable, and can affect a character's importance. Edgar does descend, of course.

Scene ii, 168–73. "Nothing almost sees miracles, But misery . . . and shall find time From this enormous state, seeking to give Losses their remedies." Cut this much, and an actor can make sense of a passage otherwise as obscure as it is evidently corrupt.

Scene iii. I think, on the whole, that there is no scene-division here; there is not, that is to say, a cleared stage. Curtains might be drawn before Kent in the stocks, but he may as well sit there asleep while Edgar soliloquizes. On an *unlocalized* stage I doubt its puzzling even a modern audience if he does; it certainly would not have troubled Shakespeare's.

Act III, Scene iii. The Quarto stage-direction *Enter ... with lights* shows, I think, if nothing else does, the use of the inner stage for this scene.

Scene vii, 23. Neither Quarto nor Folio specifies Oswald's exit, and they get Edmund's and Goneril's wrong. But it is plain that Oswald should be gone immediately on the command to get horses for his mistress. Edmund's and Goneril's leave-taking then stands out the plainer, and the "strange œilliads and most speaking looks" that pass between them as they go may be made noticeable to Regan – and to us.

Act IV, Scene iv, 6. "Centurie" says the Quarto and "centery" the Folio; and this surely will be understood even now (and whatever the anachronism) to mean a hundred men. Why send one sentry to look for Lear? And why a sentry, any how?

Act V, Scene iii, 161. "Ask me not what I know." The Quarto gives this to Goneril and marks her exit accordingly. It is at least a question whether the Folio's change is not erroneous. For Edmund's so sudden change of front is not easily explicable.

284. This is the first and only indication that Kent's name in disguise has been "Caius". I cannot discover that any editor has commented upon the strangeness of Kent – Kent of all people, and at this moment of all others – asking Lear, apparently, a kind of conundrum. The Pied Bull Quarto at least gives no note of interrogation. If the line can be spoken as if it meant

Your servant Kent, who was your servant Caius ...

it will at least not be confusing. Can it not, perhaps, be so read? Kent in his next line plainly appropriates the question to himself.

324. The Quarto gives the last speech to Albany, the Folio to Edgar. Convention would allot it to Albany as the man of rank. "We that are young" sounds more like Edgar. But remembering how much Albany's part is cut in the Folio, it is likely, I think, that this change to Edgar was deliberately made, and therefore it should stand.

Cymbeline

Cymbeline is said to have been a product, probably the first, of Shakespeare's leisured retirement to Stratford. Professor Ashley Thorndike thinks it was written in emulation of Beaumont and Fletcher's successful *Philaster*. There are signs that it was intended for the "private" theatre of the Blackfriars. More than one editor has scented a collaborator; the late Dr Furness, in particular, put many of the play's weaknesses to this account.

The Folio labels it tragedy, but it is not; it is tragi-comedy rather, or romance. Through treachery and mischance we move to a providentially happy ending. Repentance for wrong done, and then

> Pardon's the word to all

is the moral outcome, two of the least pardonable characters having conveniently been dispatched beyond human pardon's reach. In which digest of charitable wisdom – and the easing of the occasion for it – we may see if we will a certain leisured weariness of mind. The signs of association with the Blackfriars must be looked into carefully when we come to consider the play's staging, if for no other reason than that here was a theatre far liker to our own than the open-air Globe. As for collaboration; we shall not deny Imogen to Shakespeare, nor Iachimo, the one done with such delight, the other, while he sways the plot, with exceeding skill. Here is not the master merely, but the past-master working at his ease. Much besides seems to bear his stamp, from Cloten to that admirable Gaoler. Was he as content, in his leisure, to set his stamp on such a counterfeit as the dissembling tyrant Queen? There is a slick professional competence about the writing of her, one may own. And how far is he guilty of the inepter lapses, with which the play is undeniably stained?

It is pretty poor criticism (Dr Furness owns it) to fasten all the faults upon some unknown collaborator and allow one's adored Shakespeare all the praise. Lackeying of that sort leads us first to the minor, then, if we are not careful, into the larger lunacies. Better take shelter behind Johnson, who, like a schoolmaster with cane in hand, sums up his indignation in one tremendous sentence and lets his author – this author, when need be, as well as another – know that he, at any rate, will not "waste criticism upon unresisting imbecility, upon faults too evident for detection, and too gross for aggravation". Johnson was spared the dilemmas of modern research. He would not have taken kindly to our armament of the hair sieve. Nor would he ever have subscribed, one feels sure, to the convenience of a whipping-boy, whatever other tribute he might pay to Shakespeare's majesty. Still, even he approves Pope's opinion – for he quotes it – that the apparitions of the Leonatus family and the jingle they speak were "plainly foisted in afterwards for meer show, and apparently [are] not of Shakespear".

How much further must we go? The apparitions and their rubbish –

> When once he was mature for man,
> In Britain where was he
> That could stand up his parallel,
> Or fruitful object be
> In eye of Imogen, that best
> Could deem his dignity?

– are not only, one swears, not Shakespeare's, but could hardly have been perpetrated even by the perpetrator of the worst of the rest of the play. One searches for a whipping-boy to the whipping-boy; the prompter, possibly, kept in between rehearsal and performance, thumping the stuff out and thumbing it down between bites and sips of his bread and cheese and ale.

But Furness quotes a round dozen of passages besides, which he declares Shakespeare never, never could have written; and they all, or nearly all, have certainly a very tinny ring. Did the author of *King Lear* and *Antony and Cleopatra* descend to

87

> Triumphs for nothing and lamenting toys
> Is jollity for apes and grief for boys

or to

> Th' imperious seas breed monsters; for the dish,
> Poor tributary rivers as sweet fish?

But he also, we notice, will have nothing to do – on Shakespeare's behalf – with

> Golden lads and girls all must,
> As chimney-sweepers, come to dust

and he rejects Belarius altogether on the ground, mainly, that the old gentleman's demand to be paid twenty years' board and lodging for the children he had abducted touches turpitude's lowest depths. But this surely is to deny even the whipping-boy a sense of pleasantly whimsical humour. It is hard to follow Furness all the way. There are, however, other directions in which we can look for this collaborator or interpolator; and we may possibly find, besides, a Shakespeare, who, for the moment, is somewhat at odds with himself.

The Nature of the Play

If the play's construction is his unfettered work he is at odds with himself indeed. From the beginning he has been a good craftsman, and particularly skilful in the manœuvring of any two stories into a symmetrical whole. But here the attempt results in a very lopsided affair. The first scene sees both themes stated: Imogen's marriage to Posthumus, and the strange loss, years before, of her brothers. Then Iachimo's intrigue against her is pursued and completed, most expeditiously; the entire business is done in less than twelve hundred lines, with Cloten and his wooing thrown in. But meanwhile we see nothing, and hear only once, of the young princes. Certainly Imogen cannot set out on her wanderings and encounter them any sooner than she does; and, once she does, this part of the story – it is the phase of the blending of the two stories, and customarily would be the penultimate phase of the plot as a whole—makes due progress. But what of Posthumus? He is now banished from the scene for the space of another fourteen hundred lines or so. That is bad enough. But when he does return to it, the only contrivances for his development are a soliloquy, a mute duel with Iachimo, a quite undramatic encounter with an anonymous "Lord" a talk with a gaoler, and a pointless pageant that he sleeps through. This is far worse. He was never much of a hero, but here he becomes a bore. The difficulties are plain. Once his faith in Imogen is destroyed and he has commanded her murder (and we do not need both to see him sending the command and Pisanio receiving it), there is nothing left for him to do till he returns repentant; and once he returns he cannot openly encounter any of the more important characters, or the dramatic effect of his sudden appearance in the last scene (and to that, in its elaboration, every thread, obviously, is to be drawn) will be discounted. But it is just such difficulties as these that the playwright learns to surmount. Can we see Shakespeare, past-master in his craft, making such a mess of a job? If nothing else showed a strange finger in the pie, this letting Posthumus slip from the current of the story, and the clumsiness of the attempt to restore him to prominence in it, should suffice to. Nevertheless, Shakespeare's stamp, or an excellent imitation of it, is on much of the actual writing hereabouts. One would not even swear him entire exemption from the apparitions.

> Poor shadows of elysium, hence, and rest
> Upon your never-withering banks of flowers;
> Be not with mortal accidents opprest;
> No care of yours it is; you know 'tis ours.
> Whom best I love I cross; to make my gift
> The more delay'd, delighted. . . .

That, though pedestrian, is, for the occasion, good enough.

These structural clumsinesses concern the last two-thirds of the play. The passages that Furness gibbets—the most and the worst of them—fall there too; and there we may find, besides, minor banalities of stagecraft, set as a rule in a poverty of writing, the stagecraft and writing both showing a startling change from the opulently thrifty methods that went to the making of *Coriolanus, Antony and Cleopatra, King Lear, Othello*, this play's predecessors.

Are we to debit the mature Shakespeare with the dramatic impotence of Pisanio's soliloquy:

> I heard no letter from my master since
> I wrote him Imogen was slain: 'tis strange:
> Nor hear I from my mistress, who did promise
> To yield me often tidings; neither know I
> What is betid to Cloten, but remain
> Perplex'd in all. The heavens still must work.
> Wherein I am false I am honest; not true, to be true.
> These present wars shall find I love my country,
> Even to the note o' the king, or I'll fall in them.
> All other doubts, by time let them be clear'd:
> Fortune brings in some boats that are not steer'd.

It is poor stuff; the information in it is hardly needed; it does not seem even meant to provide time for a change of scene or costume. Nor does Shakespeare now use to let his minor characters soliloquize to help his plots along.[1] There are two other such soliloquies: the Queen's rejoicing over Imogen's disappearance, rising to its forcible-feeble climax with

> gone she is
> To death or to dishonour; and my end
> Can make good use of either: she being down,

---

[1] The writing of the rest of this scene is poverty itself (in fact, from Lucius' rescue of Imogen, just before, to the beginning of the long last scene of revelation, there is – except for the character of the Gaoler – marked deterioration of writing). The First Lord's

> So please your majesty
> The Roman legions, all from Gallia drawn,
> Are landed on your coast, with a supply
> Of Roman gentlemen by the senate sent

about touches bottom. Sheridan's burlesquing in *The Critic* has more life in it.

I have the placing of the British crown.

This is nearly as redundant in matter; but villainy has its
rights, and premature exultation over the misfortunes of the
virtuous is one of them. Though it be Shakespeare at his
worst, it may still be Shakespeare. So, more certainly, is the
Second Lord's soliloquy, with which Cloten's second scene
ends. This probably owes its existence to Imogen's need of
a little extra time for getting into bed. But it adds information, and, more importantly, reiterates the sympathy of the
Court for her in her trouble. It falls earlier in the play, in
the stretch of the action that few will deny to be wholly
Shakespeare's.

But, quality of writing and the unimportance of the speakers apart, is there not a curious artlessness about nearly all
the soliloquies in the play? They are so frankly informative.
Shakespeare's use of the soliloquy is no more subject to rule
than are any other of his methods; but his tendency, as his
art matures, is both to make it mainly a vehicle for the
intimate thought and emotion of his chief characters only,
and to let its plot-forwarding seem quite incidental to this.
Antony and Cleopatra, a play of action, contains few soliloquies, and they are not of dominant importance; Coriolanus,
the man of action, is given hardly one; Hamlet, the reflective hero, abounds in them, but they are germane to idea
rather than story. Iago's soliloquies, it may be said, frankly
develop the plot. It will be truer to say they forecast it; the
dramatic justification for this being that it is a plot, in both
senses, hatched in his own brain.[2] And we notice that once
it is well under way he soliloquizes little more.

But in *Cymbeline,* what a disintegrating change! Posthumus' soliloquies are reflectively emotional enough. The first
is an outburst of rage; it would not, one supposes, have been
any differently framed for Othello or Antony. The others
contain such simply informative passages as

2 Edmunds' soliloquies in *King Lear* come into the same category.

> I am brought hither
> Among the Italian gentry, and to fight
> Against my lady's kingdom. . . .
> I'll disrobe me
> Of these Italian weeds, and suit myself
> As does a Briton peasant . . .

as the seemingly needless

> I have resumed again
> The part I came in. . . .

And one asks, without being quite sure of the answer, how far is that

> You married ones,
> If each of you should take this course, how many
> Must murder wives much better than themselves,
> For wrying but a little! . . .

meant to be addressed plump to his audience? But the flow of emotion is generally strong enough to sweep any such obstacles along.

Iachimo passes from the dramatic perfection of the soliloquy in the bedchamber to the feebleness of his repentant

> Knighthoods and honours, borne
> As I wear mine, are titles but of scorn.
> If that thy gentry, Britain, go before
> This lout as he exceeds our lords, the odds
> Is that we scarce are men and you are gods

– with which we hesitate to discredit Shakespeare in any case.

But what of that not merely ingenuously informative, but so *ex post facto* confidence from Belarius:

> O Cymbeline! heaven and my conscience knows
> Thou didst unjustly banish me: whereon,
> At three and two years old I stole these babes,

> Thinking to bar thee of succession as
> Thou reft'st me of my lands. Euriphile,
> Thou wast their nurse, they took thee for their mother,
> And every day do honour to her grave.
> Myself, Belarius, that am Morgan called,
> They take for natural father.

We shall have to search far back in Shakespeare's work for anything quite so apparently artless, and may be doubtful of finding it even there. Furness would make the collaborator responsible for Belarius. But what about the long aside – a soliloquy, in effect – by which Cornelius lets us know that the Queen is not to be trusted, and that the poison he has given her is not poison at all? This is embedded in the admittedly Shakespearean part of the play.

The soliloquies apart, when we find Imogen-Fidele, welcomed by Arviragus-Cadwal with

> I'll make 't my comfort
> He is a man: I'll love him as my brother . . .

then glancing at him and Guiderius-Polydore and exclaiming

> Would it had been so, that they
> Had been my father's sons . . .

and when the trick by which Cloten must be dressed in Posthumus' garments (so that Imogen waking by his corpse may mistake it) is not glossed over but emphasized and advertised, here, we feel, is artlessness indeed. But it is obviously a sophisticated, not a native artlessness, the art that rather displays art than conceals it.[3]

A fair amount of the play – both of its design and execution – is pretty certainly not Shakespeare's.[4] Just how much,

---

[3] For a similar artlessness of method, compare the Prospero-Miranda, Prospero-Caliban scenes in *The Tempest* by which the story is told. But *The Tempest* is a Masque rather than a play, and may properly be artificial.

[4] Both more and less, I myself feel, than Furness allows to be.

it is hard to say (though the impossible negative seems always the easier to prove in these matters), for the suspect stuff is often so closely woven into the fabric. It may have come to him planned as a whole and partly written. In which case he worked very thoroughly over what are now the Folio's first two acts. Thereafter he gave attention to what pleased him most, saw Imogen and her brothers and Cloten through to the end, took a fancy to Lucius and gave him reality, did what more he could for Posthumus under the circumstances, generously threw in the First Gaoler, and rescued Iachimo from final futility. This relieves him of responsibility for the poor planning of the whole; he had been able to refashion the first part to his liking. But why, then, should he leave so many of the last part's ineptitudes in place? Or did the unknown cling affectionately to them, or even put them back again after Shakespeare had washed his hands of the business? We are dabbling now, of course, in pure "whipping-boy" doctrine, and flaws enough can be found in it. Of the moments of "unresisting imbecility" Shakespeare must be relieved; careless or conscienceless as he might sometimes be, critcal common sense forbids us to saddle him with them. But, trying his hand at a new sort of thing (emulating Beaumont and Fletcher and their *Philaster* – why not? – he had never been above taking a hint), and if, moreover, he was trying it "by request" in hard-won leisure at Stratford, his grip might easily be looser than usual. We find him with a firmer one, that is certain, in *A Winter's Tale* and *The Tempest*. Allowing, then, for some collaboration, and some incertitude besides, at what, are we to suppose, is he aiming, what sort of play is he setting out to write? And if the sophisticated artlessness is his, what end is this meant to serve? These are the practical questions to be answered here.

He has an unlikely story to tell, and in its unlikelihood lies not only its charm, but largely its very being; reduce it to reason, you would wreck it altogether. Now in the theatre there are two ways of dealing with the inexplicable. If the audience are to take it seriously, leave it unexplained. They will be anxious – pathetically anxious – to believe you; with faith in the dose, they will swallow a lot. The other plan is to show one's hand, saying in effect: "Ladies and gentlemen, this is an exhibiton of tricks, and what I want you to enjoy among other things is the skill with which I hope to perform them." This art, which deliberately displays its art, is very suited to a tragi-comedy, to the telling of a serious story that must yet not be taken too seriously, lest its comedy be swamped by its tragedy and a happy ending become too incongruous. Illusion must by no means be given the go-by; if this does not have its due in the theatre, our emotions will not be stirred. Nor should the audience be overwhelmed by the cleverness of the display; arrogance in an artist antagonizes us. This is where the seeming artlessness comes in; it puts us at our ease, it is the equivalent of "You see there is no deception". But very nice steering will be needed between the make-believe in earnest and in jest.

Shakespeare sets his course (as his habit is, and here we may safely assume that it is he) in his very first scene. We have the immediately necessary tale of Posthumus and Imogen, and the more extraordinary one of the abducting of the princes is added. And when the First Gentleman brings the Second Gentleman's raised eyebrows down with

> Howsoe'er 'tis strange. . . .
Yet is it true, sir

we of the audience are asked to concur in the acquiescent

> I do well believe you.

For "this", Shakespeare and the First Gentleman are telling us, "is the play you are about to hear; and not only these facts, but their rather leisurely amplifying, and that supererogatory tale of Posthumus' birth, should show you the sort of play it is. There is trouble in the air, but you are not to be too strung up about it. Moreover, the way you are being told it all, the easy fall of this verse, with its light endings and spun-out sentences, should be wooing you into the right mood. And this talk about Cassibelan is to help send you back into a fabulous past in which these romantic things may legitimately happen. So now submit yourselves, please, to the illusion of them".

The beginning, then – quite properly – inclines to make-believe in earnest, rendering to the theatre its normal due. And the play's story will follow its course, nor may any doubt of its likelihood be hinted; that is a point of dramatic honour. But in half a hundred ways, without actually destroying the illusion, Shakespeare can contrive to prevent us taking it too seriously.

Cornelius lets us know at once that the poison is not poison; for, monster though the Queen is, we must not fear tragedy of that stark sort to be impending. We must be interested in watching for the working-out of the trick played upon her, and amused the while that

> She is fool'd
> With a most false effect . . . .

There is a subtler aim in the artlessness of Belarius' soliloquy. By accepting its frank familiarity we become, in a sense, Shakespeare's accomplices. In telling us the story so simply he is at the same time saying, "You see what an amusing business this playwriting is; take it, please, no more seriously than I do". The stressing of the coincidence of the meeting of the sister and her lost brothers has a like effect. We feel, and we are meant to feel, "What a pretty fairy tale!" The emphasizing of the artifice, the "folly of the fiction", by which Cloten's corpse comes to be mistaken for Posthumus' does much to mitigate the crude horror of the business, to bring it into the right tragi-comic key. Keep us intrigued by the preparations for the trick, and we shall gain from its accomplishment a half-professional pleasure; we shall be masters of the illusion, not its victims. And throughout the whole elaborate scene of revelation with which the play ends we are most artfully steered between illusion and enjoyment of the ingenuity of the thing. *We* hold all the clues; the surprises are for Cymbeline, Imogen, Posthumus and the rest, not for us. We soon foresee the end, and our wits are free to fasten on the skill of the approach to it. But there is an unexpected turn or so, to provide excitement; and the situation is kept so fully charged with emotion that our sympathy is securely held.

This art that displays art is a thing very likely to be to the taste of the mature and rather wearied artist. When you are exhausted with hammering great tragic themes into shape it is a relief to find a subject you can play with, and to be safely able to take more interest in the doing than the thing done. For once you can exercise you skill for its own sake. The pretty subject itself seems to invite a certain artlessness of treatment. But the product will have a sophisticated air about it, probably.

The Blackfriars and Its Influence

Whether the style of the play – out of whatever combination of circumstances this was compacted – owes anything (and, if so, what) to its probable connection with the Blackfriars, is not much easier to determine; for our knowledge of the stage there, and the degree of its difference from the Globe's, is still much in the realm of guesswork.

Cymbeline must be dated about 1610. It was in 1609 that the King's Men first went to act in these quieter, candle-lit surroundings. They did not desert the Globe, which remained their summer quarters; a successful play would be seen there also. The open-air theatres stayed in use for another thirty years, and the old audiences had still to be catered for. But critical opinion would now come to centre, taste to be dictated, at the Blackfriars; and the dramatists attached there would have to consider what sort of work made most effect in these changed conditions. Beaumont and Fletcher may have scored an early hit with *Philaster*[5] and so (if theatre managers of yesterday were as managers of today, and possibly they were) set a fashion which would be hastily followed. But sooner or later, a specifically indoor drama must have

[5] They had already written a play or two for the Paul's children and their indoor theatre.

developed. The change would come slowly, and not very certainly. There would be reaction against it. The elder dramatists might no more take kindly to it than would the old audience when they saw its new effects show up a little pallidly, perhaps, in the sunlight at the Globe. But the shifting from outdoors in made all the difference, finally. Our drama of today, with its scenic illusion, its quiet acting, its gains in subtlety and loss in power, was born, not upon the platforms of the innyards, but of the patronage and prosperity that produced the private theatre.

Not that indoor performances were a novelty. The children had always played indoors. Such a man as Lyly had written exclusively for them, and other dramatists gave them plays that might differ little, or not all, from those provided for their elders. But a boy Tamburlaine could "holla" his loudest and yet break no windows; though the plays did not differ, the performances would. The adult companies had played indoors too. *A Midsummer Night's Dream* has a delicacy of fibre and the early *Love's Labour's Lost* a preciosity which may show that Shakespeare devised them for select audiences. When James's Scottish extravagance replaced Elizabeth's English thrift, Court performances were frequent. But the Globe had been the breeding-ground of the greater work. *Hamlet, Othello, Lear* and *Macbeth* had come to birth there; and there force and simplicity were cardinal virtues. This was not because a slice of the audience would be uncultured (so it would be at Court), but because the theatre's every condition enhanced such virtues; the daylight, and the actors on their platform, making point-blank unvarnished appeal. Subtleties could be achieved, but they must be lodged in simple and accustomed forms; they were, as we find, thought safest and surest of effect in the comparative intimacy of the soliloquy. Scraps of scenery might come into use; but in daylight there could be nothing like scenic illusion.

What would the confined quiet of the "private" theatre bring? The style of the acting of the old plays would change; bad actors would not shout so much, and good actors could develop new delicacies of expression. The plots of new plays might well grow more elaborate and their writing more diffuse, for it would be easier to keep an audience attentive and see that no points were missed. If violence is still the thing, noise will not be. The old clattering battles may gradually go out of favour; but processions will look finer than ever, and apparitions and the like will be twice as effective. Rhetoric will lose hold a little (to regain it when the theatres grow larger and the groundlings come to their own again) and sentiment will become as telling as passion. This would bring softer and slacker versifying, and the impetus to carry through the old powerful speeches will no longer be needed. Humour may be less brisk; the pace of the acting in general will tend to slow down. Mere tendencies, all these, with little consistency to be seen in them for a long while, and recurrent reaction against them.

One speculates upon what might have happened had Shakespeare reached London as a young man, not when he did, but a generation later, to serve his apprenticeship at the Blackfriars instead of at the Theatre, the Rose and the Curtain. As it is he is an old hand when the change comes, and will live out the rest of his life retired, more or less, from the stage. But while he still wrote for it he would remain a most practical playwright. We might look to find in his latest plays signs that he was as sensitive as the youngest to this shift or direction. If *Cymbeline* was written for the Blackfriars it may well owe a few of its idiosyncrasies to that mere fact.

The Play's First Staging

Though we do not know how the stage there differed from the Globe's (and there is much about the staging at the Globe which still keeps us guessing), that the two did differ somewhat we may be sure. "The hall', Sir Edmund Chambers tells us, "was 66 ft from north to south and 46 ft from east to west ... The stage was at one end of the hall." Not much more than 20 ft of the whole length, then, would be spared to it. Of this, 8 or 10 ft would be needed for back stage and passage. That would leave a main stage 10 or 12 ft in depth, by, perhaps, the full 46 ft in width. An awkward shape; but about 10 ft each side would be taken up by the rows of stage stools. The practicable main stage would be, say, 12 ft by 26. Cramped acting-space, after the Globe, even if we deepen it by a foot or so. We do not know the height of the hall; but it could hardly match the Globe's three stories, which gave an upper stage, and room above that for the working of machines, and probably room above that again. On the other hand, if it were ceiled and not too lofty, the descent of deities enthroned would be an effective and fairly easy business, and the present apostrophe to Jupiter, with its

> This marble pavement closes, he is entered
> His radiant roof

could be exactly illustrated.

While plays had to serve for both theatres, the principles (so to call them) of the Globe staging would be likely to endure, but its practice would need to be adapted to the Blackfriars material conditions; and these – doors, openings, balconies – would have been dictated by the restricted space there and its different disposition. With more breadth than depth available, the inner stage opening might well be widened, both to improve the inner stage itself and to give better access from the main stage. The action upon the inner stage would in any case be more prominent with the main or front stage reduced in size. That was turning already into the "apron" of its final metamorphosis. But if it has now been brought to a 10 or 12 ft depth it is to suffer no further in size, nor very much in importance, for another two hundred years to come. The inner stage will be widened still more, and deepened and again deepened as opportunity serves. This, however, will be for the accommodation of the coming scenery, and to give lighting its effect; and for long the actors will confine themselves there as little as may be.

The action of *Cymbeline* evidently makes no demands that the stage at the Globe could not quite well fulfill. But one scene, at least, would be doubly effective at the Blackfriars. It would be played at either house wholly on the inner stage.

Imogen is asleep, the taper has been left burning near her. Iachimo comes softly from the trunk, steals about the room, noting all its features on his tablets, stands over her gloating. The dramatic value of all this will depend upon his expression being well seen; and the verse is written for subtle and gentle speaking. How much would not be lost on the removed inner stage of the Globe, and gained in the intimacy of the Blackfriars, where the candlelight too – the effect of it is twice emphasized – would be something more than a symbol!

One other thing about the scene should be noted. Iachimo says:

> I will write all down:
> Such and such pictures; there the window; such
> The adornment of the bed; the arras, figures,
> Why, such and such . . .

and leaves it at that. Not till two scenes later are we – and Posthumus – given the description of the room, with its tapestry of silk and silver, its chimney

> south the chamber; and the chimney-piece
> Chaste Dian bathing. . . .
>   The roof o' the chamber
> With golden cherubims is fretted: her andirons –
> I had forgot them – were two winking Cupids
> Of silver, each on one foot standing, nicely
> Depending on their brands.

The inference is plain. Whatever changes had been made at the Blackfriars, this scene was not thought to need an individual background; and Shakespeare carefully refrains from calling our attention to – something that is not there![6]

Belarius' cave, however, is a piece of scenery of some sort. The text makes this clear.

---

[6] Dramatically, as usual, he is the gainer. The Cupids and Chaste Dian and Cleopatra staring us in the face would only have distracted our attention from Iachimo. But it is excellent material for the "madding" of Posthumus, and the better for being freshly used.

A goodly day not to keep house, with such
Whose roof's as low as ours! Stoop, boys: this gate
Instructs you how to adore the heavens . . . .

A few lines later comes a casual "We house i' the rock",
but there is no definite reference to "this our pinching cave"
for thirty-eight lines. It would be a conventional, decorative
piece of scenery, probably, but very obviously a cave; the
audience could not be left, for a large part of the scene, to
wonder what it was had provoked that "Stoop, boys . . ."
and the sequent moralizing.

Of Jupiter we have spoken already; if he could descend
through an actual marble pavement of a ceiling, so much
the better. Posthumus' prison seems to call for the inner stage.
He would lie down to sleep not too far back from the line
of its opening. Sicilius and the rest, entering *as in an apparition,*
would probably come through curtains (very probably through
slits in them) behind him. *They circle Posthumus round as
he lies sleeping* means, I think, that they stand, not march,
round him.[7] When Jupiter descends, he can hardly come all
the way down. As a god he must hold the centre of the stage;
and if he did come all the way he would then obliterate the
sleeping Posthumus, who, for decorative reasons (important
when apparitions are in hand), would almost certainly be in
the centre, too. Besides, godhead is less impressive on the
ground; nor does any one want to lower those machines
further than need be – they are tricky things. He might stay
suspended in mid-air; but he would be terribly likely to swing
about. His best resting-place would be the upper stage. It is
just possible that, at the Blackfriars, this may not have been
the inconvertible, railed, low-roofed balcony which we commonly imagine for the public theatres. A deep gallery above
the inner stage, not more than 8 or 10 ft up, with its centre
open, or able to open, to the ceiling, would answer this particular purpose very well. No other use, we notice, is made of

---

7 *With music before them,* read in conjunction with *after other music,*
becomes a careless phrase for music played before they enter. It cannot
imply attendant apparitions performing upon recorders. Cf. p. 183.

the upper stage throughout the play[8]; Cloten even serenades Imogen at her door, instead of beneath her window.

The comprehensive last scene asks for the full extent of main and inner stage together, especially if Posthumus' listening *behind* is to be made effective. The First Gaoler's soliloquy – if he is to speak it on the main stage with the inner stage curtains closing behind him – may have been put in to make time for the shifting of the pallet upon which Posthumus had been lying.[9] For the rest of the action, inner stage, outer stage and the two doors we know of function normally enough.

The Style of the Play

With furnishing and costume comes the problem – if we choose to make it one – of the play's anachronisms. But why make it one? No such difficulty exists as in *Antony and Cleopatra*, over the Rome and Egypt that we learned to see, that Shakespeare had not; nor as in *King Lear*, over a Court Fool and a topical Oswald, no longer topical to us, set unconcernedly in a barbarous scene. There one can at least contend – though it is a poor plea – for tragedy and its integrity or history and its verities; but why cultivate an archaeological conscience towards *Cymbeline's* Britain and such a story as this? Shakespeare knew as well as we know that war chariots and the god Jupiter did not fit with a Posthumus made Gentleman of the King's Bedchamber, who waves his farewells with hat and glove and handkerchief, with a Cloten who fights duels and plays at bowls, a Belarius who talks of rustling at Court in unpaid-for silks, a Guiderius joking about a tailor, an Imogen disguised in doublet and hose; and – if

[8] Nor is any use made of it in *A Winter's Tale;* nor, apparently, in *The Tempest,* except upon one occasion, when the stage direction reads, instead of the usual *above: Prospero on the top (invisible).* One must not base too much upon carelessly written stage directions; one must remember, too, that stage terminology is not exact. But a systematic study of them in the plays that can be safely held to have been written for the Blackfriars will do much to tell us what the stage there was like; and the knowledge is needed.

[9] But here the question of act-division is involved. This is discussed on p. 188.

he had stopped to think about it – that in a Rome over which Augustus Cæsar ruled, Frenchmen, Dutchmen and Spaniards would not be found discussing their country mistresses, or an Iachimo making a bet of ten thousand ducats. We commonly say he was careless about these things; it is a very fertile carelessness that shows here. For from this collection of inconsistencies emerges a quite definite picture all illuminative of the fantasy of the story. In a work of art, for what other consistency should we ask?

The style of the play; this is what, above all, its staging must elucidate, for, far more than with most plays, this is its life. Its contents may be mongrel, but it has a specific style. Set Imogen in her doublet and hose beside Rosalind or Viola and – all difference of character and circumstance allowed for – note the complete change of method; the verse with its varied pace and stress, complex, parenthetical, a vehicle for a strange mixing of artifice and simplicity, of naked feeling and sententious fancy – the old forthright brilliance has given place to this.

It is style (nor of writing only; for writing is but half, or less, of the dramatic battle) that gives their due complexion to all the actualities of the play. Critics have exclaimed against the blinding of Gloucester in *King Lear*. Upon the face of it, Imogen's discovery of Cloten's headless corpse should be as horrible a business; more so, indeed, for much more is made of it. But, thanks to the style of its contriving, this passes unremarked.[10] The artless artifice of the preparations for the episode, this we have noted already. But much more is done in mitigation. We do not see Cloten killed; no moment of poignancy is allowed him; he vanishes bombasting and making a ridiculous fight of it. The next we see of him is his ridiculous head; and the boyish unconcern of the young savage who has slaughtered him puts us in the mood to make as little of the matter.

---

[10] I have not pursued comment much beyond the pages of Furness. The outcry against the blinding of Gloucester is misguided, as I have tried to show elsewhere.

> This Cloten was a fool, an empty purse;
> There was no money in't: not Hercules
> Could have knock'd out his brains, for he had none. . . .

Then, before the body is brought on, comes the long, tender passage of the mourning over the unconscious Fidele; and our attention is so fixed upon her, Cloten already a memory, that when she wakes beside the dummy corpse it is really not much more to us than a dummy and a pretext for her aria of agony. The setting of the scene, too, must have helped to rob the business of poignancy. There is one sort of realism to be gained on a bare stage and another in scenic illusion; but before a decoratively conventional cave we shall not take things too literally. The right interpretation of all this will depend upon a style of production and acting fitted to the style of the play.

Not too much emphasis, naturally, is to be placed upon so very parliamentary a war; and we notice that the stage directions for the battle are unusual.

> *Enter Lucius, Iachimo and the Romane army at one doore: and the Britaine army at another: Leonatus Posthumus following like a poore souldier. They march over and goe out. Then enter againe in skirmish Iachimo and Posthumus: he vanquisheth and disarmeth Iachimo, and then leaves him. . . . The Battaile continues, the Britaines fly, Cymbeline is taken. Then enter to his rescue, Belarius, and Arviragus. . . . Enter Posthumus and seconds the Britaines. They rescue Cymbeline and exeunt. . . . Enter Cymbeline, Belarius, Guiderius, Arviragus, Pisanio and Romane captives. The Captaines present Posthumus to Cymbeline, who delivers him over to a Gaoler.*

Here is action enough, certainly. But why are there none of the accustomed directions for alarums, drums and trumpets? And why is there such a strangely small allowance of intermediate dialogue to so much and such elaborate business? Belarius and Guiderius colour their thrusting-in with a line or so, Iachimo soliloquizes shortly between whiles, and Post-humus, the battle being over, is given a speech which might be modelled upon a messenger's in Greek tragedy. But while fighting heroically as a peasant, and when he is brought a prisoner to Cymbeline he utters not a word; and Cymbeline himself stays mute as a fish, nor seems (incidentally) to recognize his son-in-law. Stage directions make a perilous basis for argument; and we ought, it may be, to lay these to the account of some editor preparing the text for printing – for the rest, there are few enough signs of the prompt book about it. But, as it stands, the elaborate pantomime really looks not unlike an attempt to turn old-fashioned dumb show to fresh and quaint account. It is certainly not a battle by either of the very different patterns of *Antony and Cleopatra* or *Coriolanus*, nor is it at all like the simplified affair we find in *King Lear*. It has, one would say, a style of its own.

Then there are Jupiter and the apparitions; and upon them hangs that highly fictitious soothsayer with his

> The piece of tender air, thy virtuous daughter,
> Which we call 'mollis aer'; and 'mollis aer'
> We term it 'mulier' . . . .

There are, as we noted, the (for Shakespeare) archaic soliloquies, and such strokes of still more deliberate artifice in this kind as that by which, in his scene with Imogen, Iachimo is made to speak an eight-line aside, which he intends her to overhear. There is Belarius' "ingenuous instrument" sounding "solemn music" in that salutary cave.

Make all the allowance we may for the vagaries of collaboration, the result still shows strange divergence from Shakespeare's precedent work. In our art-jargon of today (or is it yesterday already?) the thing is very "amusing". At the core of the best of it the strong dramatic pulse beats still, and the craftsman still delights in the ease of his cunning. But it is Shakespeare with a difference.

If the garment of the play's writing is artifice, the costuming of the characters must take account of it. The Masque and its fancies were in vogue at the moment. We should not ascribe too much to that; but look at those drawings by Inigo Jones, then read some of the more decorative passages – Iachimo's for instance – of this verse and prose; there is a common fancy in both. These figures, though, must stand solidly and upon firm ground in their amorphous world. Shakespeare may play tricks with historic time, but to his own chronolgy – slips apart – he will be true; to his own natural history, so to speak, as well. He knows, for instance, how to etherealize nature without fantasticating the plain facts of it. When the two brothers find Fidele dead:

> Why, he but sleeps.
> If he be gone he'll make his grave a bed;
> With female fairies will his tomb he haunted,
> And worms will not come to thee.
> With fairest flowers,
> While summer lasts, and I live here, Fidele,
> I'll sweeten thy sad grave. Thou shalt not lack
> The flower that's like thy face, pale primrose, nor
> The azured harebell, like thy veins; no, nor
> The leaf of eglantine, whom not to slander,
> Out-sweetened not thy breath. . . .

No mannerism of costume, or of speech or behaviour, must be let obscure the perfect clarity and simplicity of that.

And cheek by jowl with the jingling twaddle of the apparitions (with which no one is ready to discredit Shakespeare) we find the Gaoler and his stark prose (which no one will deny him). The contrast alone makes an effect. In the morning, we must suppose, Posthumus is roused[11]:

11 We only suppose so because the vision should naturally occupy a night, and a criminal goes to his death at dawn. But, on the face of it, Posthumus is taken to prison, has his nap, sees his vision and is roused for execution, all within the time it takes Cymbeline to tidy himself up after the battle and return to his tent (as the editors have it), or wherever else the last scene may be supposed to take place. Yet another instance of the clumsiness of the penultimate section of the play's action. As to the contrast between the Gaoler's plain prose and the decorative mystery of the apparitions, though Shakespeare did not write the jingle,

GAOLER. Come, sir, are you ready for death?

POSTHUMUS. Over-roasted rather; ready long ago.

GAOLER. Hanging is the word, sir; if you be ready for that, you are well cooked.

POSTHUMUS. So, if I prove a good repast to the spectators, the dish pays the shot.

GAOLER. A heavy reckoning for you, sir. But the comfort is, you shall be called to no more payments, fear no more tavern-bills, which are often the sadness of parting, as the procuring of mirth: you come in faint for want of meat, depart reeling with too much drink; sorry that you have paid too much, and sorry that you are paid too much: purse and brain both empty – the brain the heavier for being too light, the purse too light, being drawn of heaviness: of this contradiction you shall now be quit. O, the charity of a penny cord! It sums up thousands in a trice: you have no true debitor and creditor but it; of what's past, is, and to come, the discharge: your neck, sir, is pen, book and counters; so the acquittance follows.

The elaborate pattern of this, the play upon thought and words, the sententious irony, is as sheer artifice as is the vision itself, the "ingenuous instrument", or Iachimo's overheard asides. Compare this gaoler with his cousin-german Abhorson, in *Measure for Measure*. But he is a figure of crass reality, nevertheless. And further fantastication than Shakespeare has already allowed for the fitting of him into the general scheme will be his ruin. That flash of a phrase which gives him life,

O, the charity of a penny cord!

is actuality supercharged; there is solid man summed up in it.

The problem is, then, to devise a setting and costuming which will neither eccentrically betray the humanity which is at the heart of the play nor, on the other hand, wall it

some of the other verse may well be his; and he was, one supposes, a consenting party to the main scheme of the scene.

round with ill-fitting exactitudes. Rome, Britain, the cave near the Severn, Cornelius and his drugs, Cassibelan and his tribute, these are decorative material to be turned to account; but to the play's peculiar account. Lucius must be a figure capable of

> A Roman with a Roman's heart can suffer

neighboured though he is by Iachimo, described as an Italian always, from whom comes naturally enough such talk of Posthumus as

> I never saw him sad.
> There is a Frenchman his companion, one,
> An eminent monsieur, that, it seems, much loves
> A Gallian girl at home. . . .

Cloten and Cymbeline and the Queen must be as at home in serenading and talk of knighthood and the distilling of perfumes as in argument over Mulmutius. There is no great difficulty about it once we realize that it is a problem of fancy, not of research; and how and why it was that Shakespeare saw his Princess Imogen, first with

> All of her that is out of door most rich! . . .

then in

> A riding-suit, no costlier than would fit
> A franklin's housewife,

then dressed in

> doublet, hat, hose, all
> That answer to them . . .

(a figure quite intimately familiar to his audience, that's to say), and yet gave her for her bedtime prayer:

> To your protection I commend me, gods!
> From fairies and the tempters of the night
> Guard me, beseech ye!

– why he wished both to bring her as close to us he could, at the same time transporting her, not to a distant world of historic fact, but into a timeless picture-book. He has, when he needs it, his measure of accuracy for depicting the past, though it is not ours. The Rome of *Julius Cæsar, Antony and Cleopatra* and *Coriolanus* is integrated by a very definite purpose; and it is quite other than the one which dictates these allusions to Sinon and Æneas, Gallia and the Pannonians, scattered as if from a pepper-pot, with (three several times) fairies thrown in besides.[12]

We can divine, though dimly, one or two details of the play's first costuming. Posthumus, when he returns with the Roman army, wears distinctive "Italian weeds", over which he can slip (apparently the disguise of a "poor" British soldier. In this he fights Iachimo, who does not recognize him. He then slips it off again (he is allowed but a few seconds for either change) for the encounter with the British Lord, who for his part does not recognize him as an enemy. Were the Italian weeds, then, not so very distinctive? But neither does Cymbeline recognize him when he is "presented" as a prisoner.[13] Possibly he is meant to wear some sort of visored helmet. Everything hereabouts is pretty slipshod, be the blame Shakespeare's or another's, and the audience must borrow a blind eye from Cymbeline and Iachimo.

And if "Italian weeds", had not those mute guests of Philario's, the Dutchman and the Spaniard, also some such distinguishing marks about them? Either they had or, with the Frenchman, an explanatory line or two, now lost, must have been allotted to each. Who was to know, otherwise, what they were? It would be a slight, amusing touch or so; an unusual hat or ruff, a peculiar doublet, a strange pair of

[12] It is needless to point out, surely, that by dressing the play in present-day clothes we shall *not* be reproducing the effect of the first performances. Cloten is no more to be seen in Piccadilly today than he was in the streets of Lud's-town. We only add another anachronism, which the text does not provide for.

[13] The stage direction is precise: *The Captaines present Posthumus to Cymbeline, who delivers him over to a Gaoler.* If he were recognizable the situation is too obvious not to have been enlarged upon – even by the here suspected whipping-boy!

breeches, possibly. It is no great matter; another sign, though, of the decorative bias of the play.[14]

If the scenic embryo of the cave is to be made the excuse for a full-fledged family of pictures of Britain and Rome, the designer of them must go warily to work. Just because he will not be flying so fully in the face of this play's stage-craft, he will be insidiously led into one temptation after another. He can fairly safely make, for Cymbeline's Court and Philario's house, the battlefield, Posthumus' prison, a tent, for the royal headquarters, a similar provision to that the cave makes for Imogen's adventures; a decorative back-ground, that is to say, which will be in purpose no more than furniture for the action. If he goes further towards realism or illusion he will soon find himself at odds with his theme. We may now have no such elaborate painting by words and their music of this forest and its cave as forbids us to trans-pose the moonlit wood of *A Midsummer Night's Dream* into any other medium, nor such magic invoked as will make the best paint-and-canvas versions of *King Lear's* heath or *Macbeth's* Inverness redundant and commonplace; but realism and illusion will as surely damnify the artifice in which the idiosyncrasy of this action lies. Conventional decoration may do; yet against too much of that, even, the figures of the actors will be blurred. Actors are human; they cannot con-form to arbitrary design. Artifice of scene must be measured to the artifice of the play; it should remain, simply and modestly, in the shadow of it, moreover.

---

14 Cf. *The Parlement of Pratlers*, 1593, reissued by the Franfrolico Press, 1928.

JOHN. God speed, Taylor.
TAYLOR. Welcome, sir.
JOHN. How many elles of sattin must I buy to make me a doublet?
TAYLOR. Four elles and a quarter, sir.
JOHN. And how much velvet for my breeches?
TAYLOR. If you will have them made after the Spanish fashion you must have three elles and a halfe.
JOHN. How much broad cloath must I have to make me a cloake after the Romane fashion, or a riding cloake after the Dutch maner?
TAYLOR. You must have little lesse than five elles and a halfe, to make one large enough for you with a coxcombado of the same cloth.
Philario, perhaps, wore a "cloake after the Romane fashion".

111

Nor, as we have seen, must a designer discount the description of Imogen's bedchamber, with which Iachimo whips his victim into a frenzy, by having painted us a plain picture of it in another medium first. Nor had he better bring Jupiter into a very practicable prison. Nor should he too positively define any whereabouts which the play's text leaves vague. Nor, of course, must he, whatever else he does, let any need for the shifting of his scenery obstruct the easy march of the action.

The Music

Cloten's aubade will be sung by a man or boy, and most probably to the accompaniment of a consort of viols.[15] But before its "wonderful sweet aire" we have "First a verye excellent good conceyted thing", some piece for the consort alone. A glance at the Folio text shows us why; Imogen otherwise will have but a column and a half of it in which to change from her night attire back to her princess' robes (she had had just a column of dialogue – though possibly an act-pause besides – in which to prepare for bed; but undressing is a quicker business). The consort will be employed again for the *Solemn musick* that comes from Belarius' "ingenuous instrument", and again to accompany the apparitions.

No cornets, we notice, are sounded when Cymbeline receives the Roman ambassador in state; we have already discussed the absence of drums, trumpets or alarums from the battle. This may in each case be editorial omission – or it may not.

[15] It might well have been sung by the actor of Arviragus. He, we find later, is ready enough to sing the dirge over Fidele, while Guiderius' excuse for not joining him in singing it is so palpable and overcharged that we may well set it down to domestic difficulties supervening – and the whipping-boy.

> For notes of sorrow, out of tune, are worse
> Than priests and fanes that lie.

This (it sticks fast in Furness' throat) is indeed just such a pretentious piece of nonsense as a fourth-rate writer would proudly devise for the disguising of a little difficulty – making it, in the event, ten times more noticeable.

The scene-dividing in the Folio has not been consistently done. The editor apparently set out to mark a fresh scene at every clearance of the stage. But upon the very first page he tripped; for the two Gentlemen, seeing the Queen, Imogen and Posthumus approach, will only disappear as they appear.[16] He trips again (in the other direction) when Philario and Iachimo *Exeunt* and Posthumus returns for his soliloquy,

> Is there no way for men to be, but women
> Must be half-workers? . . .

and again when Guiderius and Cloten *Fight and exeunt*. Here, in both cases, is a cleared stage, and he gives us no scene-division. Can one follow the process of his mind? If the staging was as we have been imagining, he has the cave before him, and he comes to think of "scene" in this other sense. But he is far from fixed in the notion; for a while back, when Imogen entered the cave, leaving just such a cleared stage with just such an entrance to follow, he had marked a fresh scene. In the other case he may have had the furniture of Philario's house in his mind's eye.

There are signs in the text itself that the opening or shutting of the inner stage, the drawing of its curtains, is meant to mark change of place, and, what is more important, that it is only done to that end. The scheme – if it is a scheme – does not work out with absolute consistency, but it is worth attention.[17] From the first scene till after Pisanio's account to Imogen of Posthumus' sailing, when she is sent for by

16 But it is, of course, possible that this effect, a commonplace upon the stage at the Globe, could not be so well contrived in the smaller space at the Blackfriars, and that therefore, to give the three important characters the full sweep of their "entrance", the two Gentlemen had to disappear first.

17 The so-called "alternation theory", hard pressed by Brodmeier and Allbright as a comprehensive rule of Elizabethan stagecraft, and (as that) pretty thoroughly exploded, has been applied, much modified, by Professor Thorndike to this very play and to *Antony and Cleopatra* (*Shakespeare's Theatre*, pp. 121-25). But his arrangement, and his explanation of it, differ in some significant ways from that which follows.

the Queen, there is no change of place implied (nor lapse of time[18]). Now we have both; for we are taken to Rome with Posthumus already arrived there, and this scene can best be played (though of course it need not be) with the inner stage revealed; the Dutchman and Spaniard, at any rate, will better serve such purpose as they do serve seated and in the background. We then come back to Cymbeline's Court, and, once there, neither change of place nor lapse of time is implied (nor is any furniture required; so the action can go forward on the front stage) till after Cloten's second scene and the Lord's soliloquy. By "place", of course, we need never understand anything more definite than a particular scene's action indicates.

The bedchamber-scene now occupies the inner stage; of this there is no doubt at all. The next scene contains the aubade, and would, as certainly, be played on the outer stage. It gives ample time for the removal of the bed and Iachimo's chest, and for the resetting of Philario's furniture, if the inner stage is to be used again for his house at Rome. There is not quite the same need for this; but certainly Philario and Posthumus *sound* like men sitting waiting (from the play's point of view) for Iachimo. There is also an interval of time to account for.

If the inner stage has been used again (furniture and all) for Philario's house, there might now supposedly be some difficulty, for the next scene's first stage direction begins: *Enter in state, Cymbeline, . .* and we at once envisage the conventional throne set on the inner stage. But the direction continues:

> . . . *Cymbeline, Queene, Cloten and Lords at one doore, and at another, Caius Lucius and attendants.*

So that apparent difficulty is surmounted, whether purposely or by chance.[19]

[18] The half-hour allowed Pisanio in which to see Posthumus aboard is filled up by Cloten's first scene.

[19] It could equally have been surmounted by Posthumus re-entering for his   *(cont.)*

114

There is now no change of place nor use for anything but the front stage till the introducing of Belarius, Guiderius and Arviragus discloses the cave – and the inner stage, of course. And if this "place" that the sight of the cave suggests is a little more generalized as forest than the "place" we have called Cymbeline's Court, which, in turn, was as much more generalized than Philario's house and Imogen's bedchamber, then a hypothetical plan of shifting from outer to inner stage or back only to mark change of place (and secondarily, it may be, lapse of time) works out well enough. For, Belarius and his boys departed, Pisanio and Imogen arrive.[20] They ignore the existence of the cave, as they have no use for it, but it remains in our eye as a symbol of the forest. Incidentally, the reminder that Imogen in her trouble is near her lost brothers will both sharpen and sweeten that dramatic effect.

We then return to the Court and the front stage; then again to the forest and the cave for a long stretch of action, which is broken only by that seemingly futile fifteen-line Roman irruption of two Senators and the two Tribunes. We may observe that Imogen, after two nights' wandering, is still in front of the cave. So we should put it, sitting in an "illusionary" theatre; and then, perhaps, start to argue that she might have wandered round and round. But it was long enough before audiences granted scenery such autonomy. She was in the forest before, and here she still is; that is all the sight of the cave would testify at the Blackfriars – or the Globe.

But why are we presented (upon the front stage; and the cave will be hidden) with the paltry little episode of the Senators and Tribunes? One reason is that it will not do to

Is there no way for men to be, but women
Must be half-workers? . . .

soliloquy upon the outer stage; this, indeed, he may be meant to do in any case. Moreover, the act-division, if this implied a pause, would have surmounted it. We come to that question later.

20 Rowe, re-editing the play eighty years later, quite disregards the Folio's *Scena Quarta* and brings them on in this same scene, which he, the first, has labelled "A Forest with a Cave". He sees scenes broadly in terms of scenery; just about as broadly, rather more logically, than this editor of the Folio sees them.

let the Roman invasion lapse for too long from the story; the arrival of Lucius and his legions must be prepared for. Another is that an impression of the passing of time must be given us, between Imogen's welcome to the cave and the setting-out for the morning's hunt. There is Cloten's soliloquy to serve the purpose; but if this is to be spoken with the cave in sight – as it probably should be, to "place" him in the forest – it may not be sufficient. Here, then, would seem to be change of place employed to mark lapse of time.[21]

We probably see no more of the cave once Lucius has led the weeping Imogen away. Belarius and the young princes could play their next scene before it. The question is, have they not been too identified with it for us not to remark, then, *their* never remarking that Cloten's body and Fidele's have vanished? With scenery still embryonic, it is upon nice points of this sort that good stagecraft would depend.

The panoramic process of the battle will pass upon the main stage (would pass more slickly if the two doors faced each other or even were askew instead of being flat in the wall). This will give ample time for the making of the inner stage into Posthumus' prison; and, after, there will be just enough, as we have seen, to clear it, so that the elaborate finale, with every character involved, can have all the space and freedom which main stage and inner stage together will afford.

There is, as we said, nothing very logical in this stagecraft. Its aim would seem to be to create impressions, definitely of a change of place, more vaguely sometimes of a lapse of time, without prompting the audience to ask how they have been created; but (if we divine it rightly) it may show us roughly what the use and wont was at the Blackfriars (and possibly for the Jacobean stage generally) in these matters,

---

[21] Would not the act-division, which falls after the Senators' scene, serve? One would suppose so. Then, if this is an authentic part of the play, the little scene is upon that count redundant, and it certainly has no merits of its own. But an editor might well place an act-division here to reinforce the effect of a passage of time. For the whole question see p. 188 et seq.

and how the old Elizabethan freedom very showly, almost imperceptibly, contracted. For some time to come it shrinks no further. Rowe, editing the play little less than a century later, and interpreting it, as his wont was, in terms of his own theatre, does not find such stagecraft at all strange to him. He accepts the Folios' act-division; and his localizing of scenes involves very little change. He gives us *A Palace, Rome, A forest with a cave, A* (convenient) *field between the British and Roman camps*, deduces for the finale a *Cymbeline's tent*, has a fancy for *A magnificent bedchamber;* and all this, in effect, coincides with the main stage, inner stage alternation which we have been working out.[22] Later editors, blindly turning the Folio's "scenes" into scenery, with their *A garden of Cymbeline's Palace, A public place, A room in Cymbeline's Palace, Another room, Before Cymbeline's Palace, An ante-chamber adjoining Imogen's apartments,* and so on and so forth, make, of course, a hash of the whole matter. The producer today is naturally not to be exempt from direct study of the text, and he may well prefer a closer adherence to the ways of the stage of the play's origin, when he can divine them. But if he is for something more of scenery, Rowe marks for him the limits to which he may safely go.

THE QUESTION OF ACT-DIVISION

As to act-division; have we the Folio editor working by rule of thumb without warrant of what had been done in performance (that is one question), did he reproduce what had been done (that is another), did he work with a careful eye to the play's dramatic structure (that is a third), or was its very being incarnate from the beginning in these five acts? It is dangerous to dogmatize. Let us put down the pros and cons as they occur.

For what, dramatically, do the five acts of the Folio stand? The first is preparatory, and its end leaves us expectant of Iachimo's trick; in the second the trick is consummated, and

---

[22] I should add, perhaps, that it was worked out with no reference at all to Rowe.

for a climax and a finish we are shown its effect upon Post-humus; the third act prepares the Roman invasion, shows us Imogen falsely accused and brings her to an encounter with her unknown brothers, but it actually ends upon the anti-climax of the Senators' talk with the Tribunes; the fourth act is short and has little in it but the episode of Cloten's death and Imogen's mistaking of his body (it, also, ends expectantly with the battle beginning); in the fifth act we have the rather clumsy unfolding of the battle to its issue, the spectacle in the prison, the very lengthy (it is by eighty lines the longest scene in the play) and skilful elucidation of the end. This is a fairly well proportioned arrangement; each act has its own chief interest (the last an adventitious spectacle thrown in) and bears a just relation to the whole. There is nothing inevitable about it; one could probably contrive as significant an arrangement in three acts or in four, and quite certainly shift the lines of division a little without greatly prejudicing the general effect. But this would naturally be so in a play fitted to a stage which still encourages fluidity of action; granted division, if there is a best way, there can hardly fail to be several second-best.

As to principles involved, if there were any; it is plain that act-division is not used to mark lapse of time nor change of place (is not in this play, certainly, when it so easily might be, and when scene-division, in the sense of a shifting from inner stage to centre, quite possibly is), and that while one may prefer to begin a fresh act upon a note of revived inter-est, the effectiveness of its end matters little. An act seems to exist in virtue of its content and of its relation to the play's scheme as a whole. But, with a twofold story to be told, the content must be mixed (one part of it may be dominant, of course) and the relation to the whole can hardly be exact. The Folio's authority apart, then, it will not be very easy to know an act – so to speak – when one sees it.

As to the benefit of this act-division in performance; there is no check in the interest or march of the action between first act and second, though a pause here, as we noted, might conveniently give Imogen more time to get into bed; the third act does definitely and emphatically begin a new interest, but a pause after it robs the poor little scene between the Senators and the Tribunes of one reason for its existence. The fifth act's beginning brings Posthumus back; except for this, it could be as well begun a scene or even two scenes earlier. There is no check to the march of the story here, and its themes by now are blended.

The producer of today must marshal these considerations and any others that occur to him, and come to his own conclusions. The play is not passionate and precipitate in mood like *Romeo and Juliet,* nor such a simple and neatly woven affair as *The Merchant of Venice;* it will not suffer from interruption as these must do. There are, on the other hand, no dramatically effective pauses provided (nor, if we do provide them, can the audience employ them very profitably in thinking over the likelihood of the play's story); and as the tension of the action is on the slack side already, it certainly does not need more relaxing. Four prolonged intervals will be too many. Division by subject will provide two. Iachimo's plot is worked out by the end of the Folio's Act II; Imogen's flight and her adventures by the cave have a unity of their own[23]; the Folio's fifth act, with the repentant Posthumus to set it going, makes a substantial final section.

THE LAST SCENE

The finer phases of the play's construction are to be seen in the swift forwarding of the first part of the story, in the subtle composition of Iachimo's three scenes (best studied in relation to him) and in the elaboration of the finale.

This last has not lacked praise. Steevens summed up its merits in one of those excellently comprehensive eighteenth-century phrases, calling it "a catastrophe which is intricate without confusion, and not more rich in ornament than in nature"; and Barrett Wendell tells us that "into four hundred and eighty-five lines Shakespeare has crowded some two dozen situations, any one of which would probably have been strong

---

[23] And possibly its *Scena Tertia* and *Scena Quarta* are better tagged to this than prefixed to the last division.

enough to carry a whole act".[24] It is at any rate so important a piece of the play's economy that the producer must analyse it with care and see that its every twist and turn is given value.

A final, and often a fairly elaborate, unravelling of confusions is, of course, a commonplace of Elizabethan stagecraft. Compare this one to the endings of *Measure for Measure*, *Romeo and Juliet* and *Othello*. It is far more elaborate in workmanship, but it hardly differs in kind. *Romeo and Juliet* ends upon anticlimax, no more is to be done and we have nothing left to learn; in *Othello*, the disclosures feed Othello's agony, which dominates everything; in *Measure for Measure* we share the plot's secret with the Duke, but we are kept uncertain what the end will be. But here we surmise a happy ending. Our interest must be kept alive, therefore, by the strategy of its bringing-about, and – the dramatic decencies observed – the more frankly we are shown how the thing is done, the better. That aspect of the scene is of a piece with the general artifice of the play's method; but something much better than mechanical skill is now put to use. Not only is the tangle of the story straightened; the characters are brought into harmony, and we, too, are reconciled to faith in their happiness.

For the scene to be effective one rule must be observed in its acting; it is a fundamental rule in all acting, strangely liable to neglect. Each actor must resolutely sustain his part through his long intervals of listening. The action is kept alive by a series of surprises – there are eighteen of them; each character in turn provides one, or is made its particular victim – and it must be *kept* alive, not saved from extinction in a series of jerks. We, who are not surprised, find our interest in watching for each turn to come, and the producer must see that each figure in the group has its point of vantage. As it is the last scene of the play each character is well

[24] I quote from the footnotes of the Furness Variorum. Thorndike, on the other hand, seeing in it Shakespeare's effort to beat the young Beaumont and Fletcher at their own game, is critical and calls it "a dénouement . . . so ingeniously intricate that it is ineffective on the stage . . . .". But was it – and will it be – upon Shakespeare's stage?

known to us, and can be effective, therefore, even in silence.

The main action is preluded by the knighting of Belarius and the two boys, by the doctor bringing the news of the Queen's death, and the disclosure of her villainies. Cymbeline certainly takes this very calmly, with his "How ended she?"; "Prithee, say"; and his "Proceed".[25] But the plain fact is that this Goneril-like lady has never been in place in the play, and her dismissal from it is as awkward. He seems to relapse with thankfulness upon

> Mine eyes
> Were not in fault, for she was beautiful,
> Mine ears that heard her flattery, nor my heart
> That thought her like her seeming; it had been vicious
> To have mistrusted her.

There is the authentic note again; we are back among golden unrealities.

The scheme of the scene begins to work with the entrance of Lucius, Iachimo and the other Roman prisoners; Post-humus and Imogen are among them, disguised, unknown to each other and to the rest.[26] The first chord struck comes from a certain calm savagery in Cymbeline, an answering stoicism in Lucius; this gives a firm foundation to build on. Sentiment and emotion must not come too soon; if the pendulum is to swing to harmony and peace it must be held back for a start at the other extreme. The more effective, too, in quick contrast, will be Lucius' bringing forward of the fragile Fidele and his plea for the lad to be spared, the gentle Fidele who can in an instant "look himself" into Cymbeline's graces. The transparent

[25] Nor can we acquit him of tactlessness in his prompt remark to Cornelius that

> ... death
> Will seize the doctor too.

[26] *Leonatus behind,* says the Folio's stage direction. His chief disguise now is the "Italian weeds", and these would hardly conceal him from Imogen. He may have some helmet or headdress he can throw off. But guards keep the prisoners from mingling; and, generally speaking, there is much goodwill in these disguises.

> I have surely seen him;
> His favour is familiar to me ...

is in the true key of the play's artifice. Yet Fidele can – it is another quick contrast – the next instant coldly turn his back on his benefactor, to that noble Roman's indignation and surprise. But we know that Imogen knows she has time enough in which to save him; and Cymbeline, plainly, is looking for an excuse to spare him. These grace notes enrich the theme and soften its present asperity.

Then comes the puzzle of her picking upon Iachimo, and the little mystification of her walk aside with Cymbeline – which is indeed mere excuse for the dramatist to let Belarius and the brothers, on the one hand, recognize their Fidele, Pisanio, on the other, learn that Imogen is safe; artifice unashamed, but they are thus made livelier lookers-on. Then the truth – or enough of it – is wormed from Iachimo.[27] The spider must unweave his web; and the Italian brain, operating so tortuously, sets British Cymbeline stamping with impatience: will this damned foreigner never come to the point?

But it is not, of course, upon Cymbeline chiefly that we are meant to mark the cumulative effect of the long-drawn-out confession; upon Posthumus rather, there in the background, ready for death, roused to the hearing of these horrors, mocked by this scoundrel's iterated praise of him, only so slowly seizing on the full truth; when he does, though, breaking all bounds in his agony of remorse.[28] And Imogen? The long ordeal of the telling of the story sets her before us in sharp contrast to anxious father and agonized husband

[27] Critics dispute as to whether, and why, Iachimo is purposely embroidering his story. It is the sort of dispute that the nineteenth-century idolaters of Shakespeare particularly rejoiced in, demonstrating the master's super-subtlety by their own (doubtless today we err as far in other directions). But will any audience now remember the play's early scenes in such essential detail as to be able to check his equivocations? Surely it simply is that Iachimo is "making a story of it", the "Italian brain" operating as tortuously as ever, and to no purpose now. That, at any rate, is the obvious effect made; and it is a very good one.

[28] Iachimo does not know he is there (*Enter ... Leonatus behind*), though in reality there was no reason he should not. This, again, is artifice.

both. She stands listening stonily, almost indifferently, one would say. True, her good name will be cleared; but Posthumus is dead. When she heard that her life would be spared (Fidele's life, truly; Imogen's would be safe enough, but it is the surface effect which counts here) and that any boon should be hers for the asking, she had only dully responded with

> I humbly thank your highness.

When she sees the ring, it is, she says,

> a thing
> Bitter to me as death.

She stands gazing dumbly at this enigmatically evil Iachimo, till Cymbeline has to urge her with

> On, speak to him.

Very clearly, coldly and quietly the few words come:

> My boon is that this gentleman may render
> Of whom he had this ring.

And thereafter she stays silent. These two figures make the centre of the dramatic picture. The floridly gesticulating Italian, wounded and weak, his gesture wounded, too, pitiful, a little ridiculous. And Imogen, dead at heart, white and still, gazing wide-eyed, and wondering that such wickedness can be.

Even when Posthumus is raised from the dead before her eyes she cannot of a sudden turn joyful, the ice will not break so easily. The torrent of his ecstatic self-reproach would indeed take some stemming. He is still the manly egotist. But she, when she can swear she is in her senses, thinks only of him, of calming and comforting him, forgets her disguise, but finds so inarticulate a tongue with her

> Peace, my lord! Hear, hear –

123

that, his rage unspent, he turns and strikes little Fidele to the ground. To avoid anticlimax, Pisanio is ready (and his earlier aside has brought him under our eye) with his

> O, gentlemen, help!
> Mine and your mistress! O, my lord Posthumus!
> You ne'er killed Imogen till now. Help, help!
> Mine honoured lady!

And so, recovered after a few tense moments from her swoon, Imogen also stands revealed.

Consider the dramatic achievement. The double disclosure itself is the simplest part of it, and could well be done in half a dozen different ways. But it is given emotional value by the slow crescendo which leads up – till the strain becomes intolerable – to Posthumus' outburst. This, when it comes, violently reverses the situation's appeal; the shock is not mere shock, it contains fresh stimulus both to interest and emotion. Our eyes have been chiefly on Imogen; she thinks Posthumus is dead, and, though we suffer with her, we know better. Now, of a sudden, our eyes are on Posthumus; he thinks Imogen is dead, and we know better. What matters far more, though, is that his outburst restores him a little to our sympathy. His moralizing soliloquies will have left us cold. When a man has behaved like a wicked fool he had better not be too philosophic in repentance. Posthumus, stamping and bellowing in his despair and calling for the street dogs to be set on him, is a far more attractive figure than Posthumus reasoning out retribution with the gods.

This is the scene's dramatic pinnacle. Surmounted, and the anticlimax saved, now, by an admirable little device, the theme is resolved into its key of semicomedy again. Imogen, waking from her swoon, finds "Old-dog" Pisanio fussing over her; and in a flash we have

> O, get thee from my sight.
> Thou gavest me poison: dangerous fellow, hence!
> Breathe not where princes are.
>
> > The tune of Imogen!

cries Cymbeline. It is indeed. Doublet and hose despite, the timid Fidele has vanished in the princess, very much her royal self again.

Now twenty lines are given to quite subsidiary talk about the poison. Why? So that Posthumus may be left standing apart, silent and shamed.[29] He will not face her in his unworthiness. She is watching; she understands. And in a minute, dropping her royalty, she goes to him and puts her arms around his neck. It is a fragile embrace; but the man, it seems, would fall if she did not hold him. They stand there as it might be two wrestlers with the fortune of their love. And what she says is one of those odd humorous things which make reconciliation easy, and with which Shakespeare knew so well how to temper feelings too secret and too sacred for fine words. She is half-laughing, half-crying in her joy!

> Why did you throw your wedded lady from you?
> Think that you are upon a lock, and now
> Throw me again.

This is her forgiveness; he is man enough to take it, and his amending is pledged with

> Hang there like fruit, my soul,
> Till the tree die![30]

Now the second theme, the discovery of the two princes, must be worked out; and we are brought to it by another twenty thrifty lines, which are chiefly given to Pisanio for his account of the crapulous Cloten's vanishing into the forest,

[29] Or to speak by the card, the poison-story is needed for the symmetry of the plot; the dramatist turns this to account for the more vital business of illuminating character.

[30] Dowden is the first to give us "lock" in place of the Folio's "rock", and no one, envisaging the business of the scene, can doubt that he is right. This single minute or so, felt and acted as it should be, makes the play's production worth while. And one likes to think of the dying Tennyson, the play in his hand opened at this very passage, one among those he loved best.

and are capped by the little calmly loosed thunderclap of Guiderius'

> Let me end the story:
> I slew him there

– young prince and young savage in a sentence!

From now to the end the scene runs a stabler course. Guiderius has again tuned it to dramatic pitch and holds it there in his terse defiance of his unknown father; the due dash of humour added too:

> I have spoke it, and I did it.
>
> CYMBELINE. He was a prince.
> GUIDERIUS. A most uncivil one. The wrongs he did me
> Were nothing prince-like; for he did provoke
> me
> With language that would make me spurn
> the sea,
> If it could so roar to me. I cut off's head;
> And am right glad he is not standing here
> To tell this tale of mine.

Then Belarius brings his weight into the contest, speaking, so to say, bass to the young man's tenor; Arviragus, when the chance comes, adding his alto, now tremulously, now bravely, he the only one of the three to be abashed by these regalities. The simile is permissible, for the verse takes on a regular rhythm and full-toned harmonies. The sententious contrast between

> the art of the Court,
> As hard to leave as keep, whose top to climb
> Is certain falling, or so slippery that
> The fear's as bad as falling. . . .

and the life of honest freedom in the pinching cave is here brought to visible issue. They confront each other, the noble mountaineers and the none too noble Cymbeline. Needless to say, Belarius' simple eloquence – not untinged, however, with very courtly respect – carries all before it.

The princes restored to their true father, it only remains to have Posthumus recognized as

> The forlorn soldier, that so nobly fought. . . .

This rounds in the story; and the moral scheme is completed by his forgiveness of Iachimo, which prompts Cymbeline in turn to spare his prisoners:

> Pardon's the word to all.[31]

One may own perhaps to a little impatience with the post-scriptal soothsayer, and the re-reading (surely once is enough!) of Jupiter's missive. We can call the whipping-boy to account if we will. These fifty lines are, in a strict view, dramatically redundant, and, at such a moment, dangerously so; this cannot be denied. Even so, there is a quaintness about the business which makes it a not unfitting finish to a charmingly incongruous play. It does not help to hold us spellbound in excitement to the end. But must we always insist on excitement in the theatre? Let the producer consider whether something – not too much – cannot be done to give the rococo symbolism of

> The lofty cedar, royal Cymbeline . . .

and of

> the Roman eagle
> From south to west on wing soaring aloft . . .

a significant setting.

> Laud we the gods;
> And let our crooked smokes climb to their nostrils
> From our blest altars. Publish we this peace

31 As Ruggles notes (I quote from the Furness Variorum), if Posthumus had not spared Iachimo when he had him down, there could have been no disclosure of his villainy. But this is perhaps to consider things a little too closely.

To all our subjects. Set we forward: let
A Roman and a British ensign wave
Friendly together: so through Lud's town march,
And in the temple of great Jupiter
Our peace we'll ratify. . . .

There need be no stage directions here, at any rate, to show
us Cymbeline and Lucius, Posthumus, Imogen and her brothers,
Belarius, Iachimo and the rest setting out in elaborate procession; the play dissolving into pageantry.

The Verse and Its Speaking

The verse flows with amazing ease, and often seems the very
natural rhythm of speech; yet it is set to music, in its kind, as
certainly as if it were staved and barred – time, tone and all
are dictated to a sensitive ear. The first scene sees it in full
swing; the first lengthy speech is the story of Posthumus:

I cannot delve him to the root: his father
Was called Sicilius, who did join his honour
Against the Romans with Cassibelan,
But had his titles by Tenantius, whom
He served with glory and admired success, –
So gained the sur-addition Leonatus:
And had, beside this gentleman in question,
Two other sons, who in the wars o' the time
Died with their swords in hand; for which their father,
Then old and fond issue, took such sorrow
That he quit being; and his gentle lady,
Big of this gentleman, our theme, deceased
As he was born. . . .

Straightforward narrative; not so mellifluous that the sound
can slip in at the ear and leave the sense outside; masculine,
with a few firmly finished lines, but a proportion of feminine
endings to save the whole thing from sounding too clarion;
the carried-over sentences give it speed; one rich unusual
phrase at the beginning –

I cannot delve him to the root:

– arrests attention; while the limpidity of

>   for which their father,
>   Then old and fond of issue, took such sorrow
>   That he quit being. . . .

(with the need to linger ever so slightly over the doubled consonants and sibilants) runs a fine little thread of sentiment all
unobtrusively into the speech and out again.[32]

For a still more straightforward passage, take Belarius'
soliloquy:

> How hard it is to hide the sparks of nature!
> These boys know little they are sons to the king;
> Nor Cymbeline dreams that they are alive.
> They think they are mine: and though trained up thus
>   meanly,
> I' the cave wherein they bow, their thoughts do hit
> The roofs of palaces, and nature prompts them
> In simple and low things to prince it much
> Beyond the trick of others. . . .

The first three lines, each a completed phrase, gain our attention, the feminine ending of the first and (for variety) the
similar "little" coming before the caesura of the second make
easy speaking, while the dominating "dreams" in the third
gives force – just enough; and after this, carried-over sentences
and half-elided syllables send the speech familiarly on its way.

The verse throughout is very rich in texture; and if sometimes it seems over-rich, this suits it to the frank artifice of
the play, and the actors may allow themselves a certain slight
sophistication of style for its delivery. Shakespeare in fact –
the wheel come full circle – seems almost to be cultivating

[32] From a speaker's point of view, it makes, of course, little difference
whether a doubled consonant falls in one word or connects two. Needless
to say, the symbol "th" as in "the" and "that" is not included in the
term.

a new Euphuism. It has no close likeness to the old; by the difference, indeed, we may measure something of the distance he has travelled in twenty years of playwriting.[33] It is a Euphuism of imagination rather than expression. This will often be simple enough; it is the thought or emotion behind that may be too far-fetched for the occasion or the speaker. What she means is made plain, but would Imogen, we ask, even if it took her so long to break the seals of Posthumus' letter, excogitate meanwhile to such effect as this?

> Good wax, thy leave. Blest be
> You bees that make these locks of counsel! Lovers
> And men in dangerous bonds pray not alike:
> Though forfeitors you cast in prison, yet
> You clasp young Cupid's tables.

Would Posthumus, still full of faith in Imogen, regreeting Iachimo, cap his tribute to her as one of the fairest ladies he had looked upon with

> And therewithal the best, or let her beauty
> Look through a casement to allure false hearts,
> And be false with them.

And would Cloten at any time be found reflecting

> I know her women are about her: what
> If I do line one of their hands? 'Tis gold

---

[33] But the degree of likeness will depend upon how much of Cymbeline we allow to be Shakespeare's. Biron's

> Light seeking light doth light of light beguile
> So, ere you find where light in darkness lies,
> Your light grows dark by losing of your eyes

has, for instance, a more than distant likeness to Arviragus'

> Nobly he yokes
> A smiling with a sigh, as if the sigh
> Was that it was, for not being such a smile;
> The smile mocking the sigh . . . .

But then Furness – and others of his opinion, supposedly – will allow Shakespeare none of this.

Which buys admittance; oft it doth; yea, and makes
Diana's rangers false themselves, yield up
Their deer to the stand o' the stealer; and 'tis gold
Which makes the true man kill'd and saves the thief;
Nay, sometimes hangs both thief and true man; what
Can it not do and undo?

Cloten's sentiments, no doubt; but "Diana's rangers" are
hardly within his intellectual range.[34] Is Pisanio so confirmed
a moralizer that, even though Imogen be stupent with horror
at the accusation of adultery, he (and his author) must keep
her standing there while he informs us that

          'tis slander,
Whose edge is sharper than the sword, whose tongue
Outvenoms all the worms of Nile, whose breath
Rides on the posting winds and doth belie –
All corners of the world – kings, queens and states,
Maids, matrons; nay, the secrets of the grave
This viperous slander enters.

And if he does stop to think of the peril it will be to her com-
plexion to wander disguised through the forest, is this how
he will warn her of it?
              nay, you must
Forget that rarest treasure of your cheek,
Exposing it – but, oh, the harder heart!
Alack, no remedy! – to the greedy touch
Of common-kissing Titan. . . .

These are, indeed, sheer lapses from dramatic integrity.
They are not the worst to be found in the play; but we cannot,
as with the worst, simply deny them all to Shakespeare. They
are the failures, the spoiled specimens of a method which is

[34] Furness refuses Shakespeare's responsibility for the lines, and
argues that Cloten is too much of an ass to have such ideas. Cloten
is by no means pure ass; a diseased vanity is his trouble; with Caius
Lucius he puts up a by no means despicable show of the bluff, blunt
Englishman.

half-successful in such effects of antithesis and conceit of thought as Posthumus' later

> ... so I'll die
> For thee, O Imogen, even for whom my life
> Is, every breath, a death

as Imogen's rather schoolma'amish (but Iachimo at the moment is certainly making her feel most uncomfortable)

> pray you,
> Since doubting things go ill often hurts more
> Than to be sure they do – for certainties
> Either are past remedies, or, timely knowing,
> The remedy then born – discover to me
> What both you spur and stop.

It is, however, only the parenthesis that overloads this and robs it of spontaneity.

For complete success in making the formal antithetical phrase do dramatic service take the Queen's description of Imogen:

> she's a lady
> So tender of rebukes that words are strokes
> And strokes death to her.

For a clever woman's bitter-sweet summing-up of her foe, what could be better? Take Pisanio's reproachful

> O, my master!
> Thy mind to her is now as low as were
> Thy fortunes. . . .

Brooding indignation does gather itself into just such epitome. We shall not even find his description of the departing Posthumus, standing on deck,

> Still waving, as the fits and stirs of 's mind

> Could best express how slow his soul sail'd on,
> How swift his ship,

out of keeping. It is in the key of the scene; and Imogen, we
feel, thrilled through with love and faith, might move a stone
to eloquence.

And coming to Iachimo, how else should the subtle, tricky
Italian express himself but in paradox and overwrought
metaphor? The device of the asides, that are meant to be
overheard while Imogen re-reads the letter he has brought
her, is pure artifice. But it seems no more the dramatist's than
Iachimo's, touches, on that stage, the limits of convention, but
by no means exceeds them; and the high-coloured, harlequin
phrases are all Iachimo's own.

> What, are men mad? Hath nature given them
>   eyes
> To see this vaulted arch and the rich crop
> Of sea and land, which can distinguish 'twixt
> The fiery orbs above and the twinned stones
> Upon the numbered beach, and can we not
> Partition make with spectacles so precious
> 'Twixt fair and foul?
> IMOGEN.   What makes your admiration?
> IACHIMO. It cannot be i' the eye; for apes and monkeys,
> 'Twixt two such shes, would chatter this way and
> Contemn with mows the other: nor i' the judg-
>   ment;
> For idiots, in this case of favour, would
> Be wisely definite; nor i' the appetite;
> Sluttery, to such neat excellence opposed,
> Should make desire vomit emptiness,
> Not so allured to feed.
> IMOGEN. What is the matter, trow?
> IACHIMO.   The cloyed will –
> That satiate yet unsatisfied desire, that tub
> Both filled and running – ravening first the lamb,
> Longs after for the garbage.

IMOGEN.   What, dear sir,
          Thus raps you? Are you well?
IACHIMO.   Thanks, madam, well.

This is the new Euphuism *in excelsis*. For yet another taste
of it, here is his outburst to her some fifty lines later.

> O dearest soul, your cause doth strike my heart
> With pity that doth make me sick! A lady
> So fair, and fastened to an empery,
> Would make the great'st king double, to be partner'd
> With tomboys hired with that self-exhibition,
> Which your own coffers yield! with diseased ventures,
> That play with all infirmities for gold,
> Which rottenness can lend nature! such boil'd stuff
> As well might poison poison!

But the mature dramatist has turned decorative flourishes to
strict dramatic account. Belarius and his cave and his bluff
talk stand for rustic honesty; here, at the other end of the
scale, is this degenerate Italian, come to Cymbeline's Court

>   ... to mart
>   As in a Romish stew, and to expound
>   His beastly mind. . . .

and he presents us, in his arrogance, with an approach to a
travesty of himself, which is also a travesty of the very medium in which he exists. A subtle and a daring piece of craftsmanship, germane to this hybrid tragi-comedy. Instead of
opposing the heroic and the comic, Shakespeare blends the
two. But the integrity of the character must be preserved; it
would not do for Iachimo to become even half-conscious of
what a figure he cuts in the eyes of the gods – and in ours.
And it is this that is achieved by the modulating of the
medium itself. Artifice is its norm throughout the play; but
the range is wide. Iachimo's mean of expression lies at the
florid end, and itself ranges from the polished prose by which

he asserts himself among his fellows in Rome (made here and there a little plainer to suit the blunt Englishman's understanding), from the argute, sensuous verse of the soliloquy over the sleeping Imogen (the man himself, this), from the elaborate, parenthetical repentance at the last, even to the high-coloured complexity of these speeches, in which, as we said, he is meant to seem to us not only pretentious and false, but – all unconsciously, and that he may not rank as too tragic a villain – just a trifle ridiculous.

For simpler and subtler examples of this moulding of verse and its conventions to the expression of character, we can turn to Imogen, and notably to the scene in which she learns from Pisanio what is Posthumus' doom for her. The verse is full of metaphor; but it is all (or nearly all; we have noted a peccant passage or so) directly dramatic, prompted by the occasion, by the very properties of the scene.

> Come, here's my heart,
> (Something's afore't – soft, soft! we'll no defence)
> Obedient as the scabbard! What is here?
> The scriptures of the loyal Leonatus,
> All turn'd to heresy? Away, away,
> Corrupters of my faith! You shall no more
> Be stomachers to my heart. Thus may poor fools
> Believe false teachers: though those that are betrayed
> Do feel the treason sharply, yet the traitor
> Stands in worse case of woe. . . .

We are conscious neither of the metaphor nor of the structure of the verse, only of its music. The fusion of substance into form is complete.

Even when the prompting is not immediate, it is but at one remove.

> False to his bed! What is it to be false?
> To lie in watch there, and to think on him?
> To weep 'twixt clock and clock? If sleep charge nature,
> To break it with a fearful dream of him,

And cry myself awake? That's false to 's bed, is it?

We have seen her lying so, glad to have tired herself by hours of reading to the point of sleep.
  She has dressed for her journey in the

> ... riding-suit, no costlier than would fit
> A franklin's housewife.

There will, then, be sufficient strangeness in the now unroyal look of her to sharpen for us, to strengthen by its touch of incongruity (though we shall not guess why) the image of

> Poor I am stale, a garment out of fashion;
> And, for I am richer than to hang by the walls,
> I must be ripp'd . . . .

That it is a princess speaking who has stooped to her subject, to a marriage at once made desolate and homeless, is vividly implicit in

> When thou sees't him,
> A little witness my obedience. Look!
> I draw the sword myself: take it, and hit
> The innocent mansion of my love, my heart;
> Fear not; 'tis empty of all things but grief;
> Thy master is not there, who was indeed
> The riches of it. . . .

These are the subtler strokes. But the simplest actualities are – given a place. They talk of the tired horses, of the doublet, hat and hose she is to wear; and the talk is matched with action. The language is ordinary, and the brief sentences would often disintegrate the verse if the rhythm were not kept regular. But this triple combination, of simple speech, short sentence and regular rhythm, gives an effect of familiar strength. Imogen is speaking:

> Thou toldst me, when we came from horse, the plac

Was near at hand: ne'er long'd my mother so
To see me first, as I have now. Pisanio! man!
Where is Posthumus? What is in thy mind
That makes thee stare thus? Wherefore breaks that sigh
From the inward of thee? One but painted thus
Would be interpreted a thing perplexed
Beyond self-explication: put thyself
Into a 'haviour of less fear, ere wildness
Vanquish my staider senses. What's the matter? . . .

Two lines that can be strictly scanned; the third has "Pisanio!
man!" for its two last beats, each word being one; five more
regular lines, only the sense and the sentences breaking their
regularity; two lines with feminine endings to ease the rhythm
and a long sentence running through them to give them, for
the finish, continuity and strength.

The technique of the scene's writing can so be analysed
through speech after speech. But the art of it is not calculated; it shows us a Shakespeare so at one with his medium
that he manipulates it as easily, as instinctively as he expects
his actors, in their turn, to move and speak. Too easily, if
anything; tension will slacken, ideas tangle, and with emotional pressure lacking, the verse will hang loose. But it is
still a very far cry from this easy freedom that has succeeded
the decorative contrivings of the earlier plays, the ordered
march of the rhetoric of the Histories, and the tragic passion in which he fired verse as in a furnace – it is still a far
cry from this to the flaccidities of a Massinger or Shirley,
or of Fletcher at his worst. Dryden, in the end, had good
reason to bring some discipline to bear. Whatever Shakespeare's metrical willfulness, his verse will be pregnant with
drama; and in this, this only, will be found the significance
of its vagaries. Verse was his supreme dramatic resource.
We may well expect to find it, in its full development of
craftsmanship, alive with purpose, a very inventory for the
acting of the play; and to find it so in this play more than
another, for romantic substance is malleable into many
delicate effects.

Its dictation can be minute. Can anyone miss the indrawn gasping sob with which

> To break it with a fearful dream of him,
> And cry myself awake? That's false to 's bed, is it?

finishes? Or not hear how the expanding vowels and doubled consonants conspire to give Pisanio's long-bottled up

> Hence, vile instrument!
> Thou shalt not damn my hand

just the explosiveness it should have? Or not find the Imogen that, once disillusioned about Posthumus, has little faith left for anyone or anything, that will suspect Pisanio of murdering him and poisoning her, in the quick exchange of

IMOGEN. But speak.
PISANIO. Then, madam,
I thought you would not back again.
IMOGEN. Most like,
Bringing me here to kill me!

and in that contemptuous, bitter, Iachimo-poisoned

> Some Roman courtezan!

The play abounds in such matter for her. In the first scene her attitude to her father (and her private opinion of his weakly tyrant's temper), the quality of her love for her husband, the dead blow that his banishment is to her, the uncompromising dignity with which she suffers it, are all summed up for us in five lines.

IMOGEN. I beseech you sir,
Harm not yourself with your vexation:
I am senseless of your wrath; a touch more
rare

> Subdues all pangs, all fears.

CYMBELINE.   Past grace? obedience?
IMOGEN.   Past hope and in despair; that way, past
                grace.

And when, twenty lines later, news comes as she stands there with the Queen, of Cloten's flourishing attack on the departing Posthumus:

> Your son's my father's friend; he takes his part.
> To draw upon an exile! O, brave sir!
> I would they were in Afric both together,
> Myself by with a needle, that I might prick
> The goer-back. Why came you from your master?

That is another view of her: the scornful girl, flashing artless indignation at her stepmother. Note the daintily vixenish "Afric . . . needle . . . prick", with slick syllables joining them; then the sudden imperious turn upon Pisanio. Tune, time, attitude, movement, what amout of stage direction could make them plainer?

Effect after effect will be found lodged in the simple cadence of the verse. Take these few more lines from Cymbeline's rating of his daughter,

>   That mightst have had the sole son of my
>   queen!
> IMOGEN.   O blessed, that I might not! I chose an eagle,
>   And did avoid a puttock.
> CYMBELINE.   Thou took'st a beggar; wouldst have made
>   my throne
>   A seat for baseness.
> IMOGEN.   No, I rather added
>   A lustre to it.
> CYMBELINE.   O, thou vile one!
> IMOGEN.   Sir. . . .

Shrill puerile scolding in the monosyllables of the first line;

the blend in Imogen of pugnacity and respect shown by one overflowing line, the next truncated; Cymbeline's anger then gathering and deepening in weightier words, the last three regular lines giving strength, the shortening sentences adding violence to the quarrel – till, after the full stop of that "Sir!", Imogen resolves it into a calmer, but still very positive

> It is your fault that I have loved Posthumus;
> You bred him as my playfellow. . . .

Half the effect of Cloten's first scene lies in the peculiar pattern given to the action of it by the Second Lord's strange succession of asides. Cloten is crossing the stage, returning to his apartments from the frustrated duel, the First Lord fawning on him. The Second Lord follows, five paces or so behind, commenting on the conversation he can just overhear. There will be a very slight midway pause; then the walk continues. Within reach of the door Cloten turns and sees the Second Lord for the first time, catches him, probably, in the midst of his final mocking aside, suspects nothing though – for who would dare to laugh at him? Then follows

CLOTEN.	You'll go with us?
FIRST LORD.	I'll attend your lordship.
CLOTEN.	Nay, come, let's go together.
SECOND LORD.	Well, my lord

and the three depart; the Second Lord constrained to congee too. A scene of no great importance; it serves to introduce Cloten, and to fill up the "half-hour" needed for Posthumus' embarking. But its odd perambulation gives it comic distinction; the passing across the stage hints at the passing of time; the slipping-in of the asides keeps it moving and denies it solid emphasis.

There is, naturally, less flexibility in the writing of the prose scenes. Iachimo's provoking of the wager is remarkable rather for the way in which the close-knit, unrelaxing sentences are made to suggest a certain intellectual power in the man. Posthumus is no fool; he can to a point play up to him. But early in the scene, and in the midst of the prose, has come his heartfelt tribute to his Imogen:

> She holds her virtue still and I my mind

– and, of itself, the sudden melody of the single line of verse proclaims the honest romantic fellow, tempting prey to a sensualist cynic. We seem to see Iachimo stalking him in the stealthy prose line that follows pat:

> You must not so far prefer her 'fore ours of Italy.

In the verse scenes, on the other hand, a sudden line of free rhythm may be used to ease the strain of a situation; as when Imogen accepts Iachimo's apology for his experimental libelling of Posthumus with a

> All's well, sir: take my power i' the court for yours.

The limpid flow of the line does, indeed, far more than this; it speaks – its sense apart – of the nobly innocent nature, ready to be twice deceived. We hear the selfsame tune when Arviragus welcomes her to the cave:

> The night to the owl and morn to the lark less welcome.

In the very tune there is generous frank affection, flowing from a nature like her own.

The free rhythm of long, simply worded lines makes its best effect in the pastoral scenes. It fits with pathos and gentle humour, not with wit; wit asks for the discipline of stricter scanning or of prose. When Imogen, disguised as Fidele, has been discovered in the cave:

> Good masters, harm me not.
> Before I entered here I called; and thought
> To have begged or bought what I have took; good troth,

> I have stolen nought; nor would not, though I had found
> Gold strewed i' the floor. Here's money for my meat:
> I would have left it on the board so soon
> As I had made my meal, and parted,
> With prayers for the provider

the form and colour of the lines redouble their meaning; the timid half-line for a beginning, the appeal of the long, evenly stressed, all but monosyllabled sentence, the apologetic hiatus that ends the last line but one – it is all a painting in sound of helpless indomitable Imogen.[35]

More regular verse, thriftily worded, simply phrased, and of a fine virile swing, is to be found when it it wanted; as it is for Imogen's flashing response to Iachimo's first crude attempt upon her.

> What ho, Pisanio!
> The king my father shall be made acquainted
> Of thy assault: if he shall think it fit
> A saucy stranger in his court to mart
> As in a Romish stew, and to expound
> His beastly mind to us, he hath a court
> He little cares for, and a daughter who
> He not respects at all.

And it is instructive to compare Imogen's outbreaking horror and grief, when she wakes to find the headless body beside her, with Juliet's when the Nurse brings her, as she thinks, the news of Romeo's death. Between that

> I am not I, if there be such an 'I',
> Or those eyes shut that make thee answer 'I' . . .

and

> Damn'd Pisanio
> Hath with his forged letters – damn'd Pisanio –
> From this most bravest vessel of the world

[35] Early editors merely surmised a word missing from the penultimate line, and filled in the gap with a "thence" or "hence". A banal solution.

> Struck the main-top! O Posthumus! alas,
> Where is thy head? where's that? Ah me, where's that?
> Pisanio might have kill'd thee at the heart,
> And left this head on. How should this be? Pisanio!
> 'Tis he and Cloten: malice and lucre in them
> Have laid this woe here. O, 'tis pregnant, pregnant!
> The drug he gave me, which he said was precious
> And cordial to me, have I not found it
> Murderous to the senses? . . .

what a gulf! From purely verbal effect, a dervish-whirling
feat of elocution, we have passed to a subtly elaborate use
of parenthesis and reiteration, which gives us, as nearly
naturally as need be, her anguish and the reeling agonies of
her mind, yet never destroys the integrity of the verse nor
breaks from the mood of the play.

There are, as always, those pregnant phrases and passages,
in which all that is most significant in a character or the turn
of an event will seem to be packed, or by which a whole
scene may suddenly be keyed to a strange nobility.

We have Iachimo's self-portrait reflected from his very
painting of Posthumus, unfaithful, slavering,

> . . . with lips as common as the stairs
> That mount the Capitol . . .
>   . . . by-peeping in an eye
> Base and illustrous as the smoky light
> That's fed with stinking tallow . . .

There is the painting of the candle-lit silence of Imogen's
bedroom, of the night and its passing. It ranks among Shakespeare's masterpieces of mere writing; from that

> The crickets sing, and man's o'er-laboured sense
> Repairs itself by rest . . .

to the

> Swift, swift, you dragons of the night, that dawning
> May bare the raven's eye! I lodge in fear;

Though this a heavenly angel, hell is here
One, two, three! Time! Time!

There is the description of the dead Fidele:

GUIDERIUS.   How found you him?
ARVIRAGUS.   Stark, as you see:
Thus smiling, as some fly had tickled slumber,
Not as death's dart, being laugh'd at; his
    right cheek
Reposing on a cushion.
GUIDERIUS.   Where?
ARVIRAGUS.   O' the floor;
His arms thus leagued: I thought he slept,
    and put
My clouted brogues from off my feet, whose
    rudeness
Answer'd my steps too loud.

There are a dozen other such luminous passages, and more.

Finally it is worth noting how full of concrete imagery the verse is. This would be so. The mood of the play is not introspective, but romantic, concerned with things as they seem, and with emotion little purged by thought. The expression of it will rightly be picturesque.[36]

The Characters

In the best of these, and in these (one must qualify it) at their best, we find the unfailing Shakespeare. Imogen is the life of the play; it would be a pedestrian affair without her. Posthumus, in execution as in quality, is only half a hero, a torso of the study of a man, but he is justly viewed. Iachimo is excellently done. If the last part of the story had more use for him, and if he did not suffer such a dull wordy declension from his brilliant beginning, he might rank as a

---

[36] The actual text of the play is unusually troublesome, but I do not propose to discuss all the minor difficulties here. They are complicated, and, in some cases, so much matter for bibliographers that it would not be for me to venture an opinion.

masterpiece in his kind. Cloten has blood and bones, is by
no means a mere stage figure of fun. He is, indeed, an un-
common if not unique item in the Shakespearean catalogue,
a comic character drawn with a savagely serious pen. Nor
are Guiderius and Arviragus mere romantic fictions, for all
their provenance from that pasteboard cave. Guiderius, in
particular, exists in his own right, stands firmly on his feet.
He is, in a double sense, set against Cloten, true heir against
usurper, noble barbarian beside degenerate debauchee. And
as the bestial truth beneath the comic mask turns convention
into character with the one, so it is with Guiderius once he
is set in motion; copybook maxims will by no means contain
him. Caius Lucius, little as we see of him, stands clear cut
as a soldier and a gentleman; and as an instance of temperance in character made interesting – nothing is harder to do.
There is vigour enough in Belarius and enough stability in
Pisanio to beget belief in them while they are on the scene.
But, apart from their use to the story, they have little life
in them, and Cymbeline and his Queen have less.

The Queen is indeed worth some study as a failure. She
is given fairly prominent place. She has to dominate husband
and son, be double-faced to Imogen, cajole Pisanio, she is
even allowed a most masculinely impressive address to the
Roman envoy. She soliloquizes; no advantage is denied her.
But never is she co-ordinate into a human being. How account
for it? For one thing, her wickedness proves of singularly
little effect. Imogen is not taken in by her, nor are Pisanio
and Cornelius. Pisanio does metaphorically swallow the
"poison-cordial" as Imogen does actually; but the episode
is so obviously – and very clumsily – contrived for the sake
of the sensational waking beside the headless corpse that it
can hardly reflect much dramatic credit upon the poor lady.
It really looks as if Shakespeare, committed to the story and
not interested enough to remodel this part of it, had said to
her, as he sat down to write scene after scene: "Well, come
alive if you can". And when with her fifth scene it becomes
clear that – very excusably under such treatment – she cannot, he finishes her off, the quality of her last couplet telling

us pretty plainly what he thinks of her and her wicked-step-mother banalities:

> ... and my end
> Can make good use of either: she being down,
> I have the placing of the British crown.[37]

Most unfair treatment; but dramatists do sometimes behave so to their unsatisfactory offspring.

IACHIMO

It is cursory criticism that will see in Iachimo a shadow of the master-villain with the "Italian brain". He is made of quite other stuff than Iago, and it is very solid stuff too. He is most objectively viewed (a corollary of the picturesque figurative method of the play's writing, a corrective, for Shakespeare, to its romantic spirit, would seem to be a colder detachment from the characters – Imogen excepted – than usual), and he and his villainy are nicely suited to the story and its ending; for from the first there is something fantastic about the fellow, and no tragically-potent scoundrel, we should be sure, will ever come out of a trunk. He is wicked for the pure pleasure of it, for the sake of the sport; there could hardly be a more hazardous speculation than the adventure in seduction into which he incontinently plunges. At the bottom of the business is his vanity. The very first note struck from him – and Shakespeare, we know, will mean it to be a leading note – is of that grudging envy which vanity can breed. He is speaking of Posthumus:

> Believe it, sir, I have seen him in Britain: He was then of a crescent note; expected to prove so worthy as since he hath been allowed the name of: but I could then have looked on him without the help of admiration, though the catalogue of his endowments had been tabled by his side and I to peruse him by items.

No woman, he is confident, can resist him (though his opinion

37 She has, to be quite accurate, still another, a broken one.

24   SAMUEL REDDISH (1737–85) AS POSTHUMUS AND
JOHN PALMER (1745–98) AS IACHIMO
Oil painting by Thomas Parkinson, 1778
Posthumus disarms Iachimo in the battle. See pp. 105–6 for the stage directions
and Barker's comments. Garrick supplied words for this episode in his 1761
version :—

    Post.   Or yield thee, *Roman*, or thou diest!
    Iach.   Peasant, behold my breast.
    Post.   No, take thy life and mend it.   (*Exit Post.*)

25 WILLIAM ('GENTLEMAN') SMITH (1730–85) AS IACHIMO
Painted and engraved by W. Lawranson, 1784

26 IMOGEN, BARBARA JEFFORD; IACHIMO, DEREK GODFREY
Produced by Michael Benthall, Old Vic, 1956

27–28 ELLEN TERRY AS IMOGEN AT THE LYCEUM, 1896

"I think as Imogen I gave the *only* inspired performance of these last sad years . . . Sir Laurence Alma-Tadema did the designs for the scenery and dresses . . . and I have to thank him for one of the loveliest dresses I ever wore." (*Memoirs*, 1933)

29 IMOGEN'S BEDCHAMBER

Barker's comments on staging, pp. 101, 112, show that he could not have
approved of this design. He praises the dramatic skill with which "Shakespeare
carefully refrains from calling our attention to—something that is not there!",
so that, two scenes later, Iachimo's description—"chaste Dian bathing", the
andirons, "two winking Cupids of silver, each on one foot standing", etc.—
makes "excellent material for the 'madding' of Posthumus"; but here, "staring
us in the face would only have distracted our attention from Iachimo."

THE PLAYERS' SHAKESPEARE, 1923

30 THE CAVE OF BELARIUS

Barker considered that, as originally staged, this "would be a conventional, decorative piece of scenery", but "very obviously a cave". By virtue of its style this background would rob Imogen's awakening beside Cloten's headless corpse of some of its poignancy. "There is one sort of realism to be gained on a bare stage and another in scenic illusion, but before a decoratively conventional cave we shall not take things too literally". (pp. 101–2, 105)

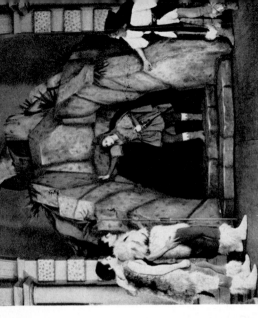

INNER STAGE OF A PERMANENT SET, WITH TEN CHANGES, BY JOHN GOWER PARKS, FOR CYMBELINE; PRODUCER, IDEN PAYNE: STRATFORD, 1937

31   Imogen's Bedchamber   32   The Cave of Belarius

Imogen, Joyce Bland; Iachimo, Donald Wolfit

33   CYMBELINE, PRODUCED BY MICHAEL BENTHALL; SCENERY AND COSTUMES, LESLIE HURRY; STRATFORD, 1949

The Queen, Wynn Clark; Imogen, Kathleen Michael; Posthumus, Clement McCallin; the Queen's Dwarf, Timothy Bateson

34 CYMBELINE, STRATFORD, 1957

Producer, Peter Hall; permanent set and costumes, Lila de Nobili

Cymbeline, Robert Harris; the Queen, Joan Miller; Imogen, Peggy Ashcroft

Barker, stressing the play's "decorative bias" and "the fantasy of the story", sees the setting and costuming as "a problem of fancy, not of research", but advises that "artifice of scene must be measured to the artifice of the play" and "should remain, simply and modestly in the shadow of it." This richly romantic, pictorial background captured the fairy-tale atmosphere, but was overcrowded with detail, took up too much stage space and called too much attention to itself. An enchanted landscape of hills, shaggy with dark woods, threaded by winding paths, revealed glimpses of mysterious archways and twisting stairs, the pillars and fan-vaulting of a ruined abbey, the square tower of a village church and a handsome renaissance interior, all framed in a proscenium of giant oaks.

of women is so low that the compliment he pays himself is a poor one), and when Imogen does, he has his trick in store; he will do anything but own himself beaten. He is a sensualist and something of an aesthete. He has a quick and sensitive mind. He can size up another man's weaknesses, and play on them with artistic skill.

Posthumus proves fairly easy quarry. For there will be, one fears – though he may mask it with good manners – just such a slight complacency about Posthumus as a life-diet of praise and nothing but praise is likely to produce; it does not, at any rate, give one overmuch interest in other people's points of view. Even this banishment, his first misfortune, is a kind of tribute to his conquering charm. His lessons are all to learn. He is a little patronizing, too; the more British, and the blinder for that.

In some such terms, while he leaves him to change greetings with the Frenchman, and the two of them fight their old battles over, Iachimo will be summing up the stranger. Then he goes delicately to work. His first approach:

Can we with manners ask what was the difference?

the Frenchman must respond to. Posthumus does not like the look of this fellow, insinuating himself into the conversation, hinting, is he? ("with manners" indeed!), that they are ill-mannered to leave him out of it. Forced to speak to him, he can give him, at any rate, a straight snub.

IACHIMO. That lady [Posthumus' so vaunted mistress] is not now living, or this gentleman's opinion by this worn out.
POSTHUMUS. She holds her virtue still and I my mind.

But it takes more than a line of blank verse, however conclusive its cadence, to defeat Iachimo. Adroitly:

You must not so far prefer her 'fore ours of Italy.

147

And as Posthumus, after all, is a guest here, the ironic appeal to his courtesy cannot be ignored. With his response to it (which is a little crude, perhaps, but he has small turn for irony),

> Being so far provoked as I was in France . . .

Iachimo has him in hand, and he begins to play him.

It is an amusing, if unequal, contest. On the one side, delicate dialectic, ironic humour, the salty cynical mind. On the other, Posthumus does his blunt, blundering best, encounters at every point; but with only his plain British common sense and simple pride in his Imogen for weapons, he has much ado even to keep his touchy British temper.

Iachimo's tactics are to lead his man on to challenge *him* to make good his boast that with "five times so much conversation" he'll "get ground" even of this paragon among ladies and "make her go back even to the yielding". Patently, that will be the better position to be in; and we mark him feeling for the steps to it, every faculty alert. In this finesse lies the interest of the scene. It is Posthumus' moral sense that he plays upon (better sometimes to attack a man at what he thinks his strongest point than at one he knows to be weak); and how artfully he moves from the disarming tribute of

> I make my wager rather against your confidence than her reputation . . .

– which is a seeming retreat from the cynical

> You may wear her in title yours; but, you know, strange fowl light upon neighbouring ponds . . .

– through the designedly preposterous

> . . . commend me to the court where your lady is, with no more advantage than the opportunity of a second con-

148

ference, and I will bring from thence that honour of hers which you imagine so reserved

to the provocative, brutal

> If you buy ladies' flesh at a million a dram, you cannot preserve it from tainting. . . .

Posthumus is duly shocked by this last:

> This is but a custom of your tongue; you bear a graver purpose, I hope,

is his comment. Yet somehow or other – he would be infinitely at a loss to say how – within a minute more, for all Philario can do, the outrageous wager is laid. What notion he has of what he is after, poor muddlehead, must lie in

> My mistress exceeds in goodness the hugeness of your unworthy thinking: I dare you to this match: here's my ring.

Imogen shall show the world, so she shall, and this contemptible foreigner in particular, what an English lady is.

It is, we may say, if we take a detached view of the business, a thing that no man in his senses could ever be brought to do. Better not be too sure of that; is there any conceivable folly that some man has not at some time committed? But Shakespeare, it must be remembered, is not approaching his dramatic problem by that way. He has chosen a story; his task is to make the events of it look likely. He need not even make them seem so in calm retrospect; the best of audiences will be content to be convinced at the time. The facts he must take for granted (if he does, so shall we); and it is in the characters themselves, in the why and wherefore of the things they do, nor in that only, but in the processes by which men's minds, shot with vanity or passion, work and can be made to work, oftenest to their own confusion, that we are to be interested. Too fine a study for the theatre, it will sometimes prove to be; and much preoccupation with it goes with dangerously dwindling regard – or capacity! – for the enlivening of plain-as-a-pikestaff issues. But Shakespeare's art has been consistently developed towards this end, the popular borrowed story and his own businesslike sense of the stage serving to keep the balance roughly true. He had always the soliloquy to turn from a confidential talk about the plot into a mirror of a mind's working; and once the whole action of a play and every means he could command were bent to show us how the acid of Iago's guile eats into Othello's heart. Iachimo's is a prettier game, and there is but a scene or so in which to play it. It can be the more subtly, and must be the more cleverly, played for that. One might even suspect that Shakespeare was attracted by its very difficulties. Put the problem thus: here were a hundred and eighty lines (he could not allow himself much more) with which to introduce Iachimo and let him persuade Posthumus to this preposterous wager, and persuade us that he *had* persuaded him. The thing asked some doing. But, absorbed by that curious combat of disparate minds, we shall admit when the scene ends that it has been done.

But what possesses Iachimo, we ask, who can turn Posthumus round his finger, to make such a crassly blundering approach to Imogen that he comes within an ace of being thrown neck and crop from the Court? The answer is an index to the man, and shows no more inconsistency in him than goes to make him a living character, not, as he might have been – as the Queen is – a mere joint in the mechanism of the plot. It is an illuminating inconsistency. He has a keen eye for a man's weaknesses; they are food for his cynicism and a sop to his vanity. But the ways of such honest innocence as Imogen's are without the range of his understanding. For, even if we must acknowledge it, we cannot understand what we do not believe in.

At a first sight of her he guesses she will be no good game for a seducer. Still, he has his trick of the trunk in reserve, so why not try? He makes the classic opening moves; marvels at her beauty, cryptically deplores the lucky husband's gross unworthiness – overdoes this somewhat, to her puzzled amusement.

We must, by the way, make liberal allowance in this scene for the exigencies of dramatic time; its effects, in fact, may be said to disregard time altogether. We shall not question Iachimo's rising to these deliberate ecstasies within a minute of his arrival (though note the touch of the comic in them that discounts any incongruity there may seem to be); nor will it trouble our sense of likelihood that within ten more he should have played out his first game and lost it. Mere haste is not meant to be his error. The scene is framed to another pattern, as a conspectus of the assault upon Imogen; the effect would be poorer strung out in terms of time. But, while the verse and its modulations provide colour and excitement, the business of the scene and the shifting of the subject of its talk give the checks and suspensions and slackenings that the use of time would give.

Iachimo's next move is to rid himself of the watchful Pisanio, who leaves them most unwillingly, not liking the look of the stranger at all. Then, alone with her, he stands deliberately mute, as oddly so as he was oddly eloquent a moment since, till she must break the silence with

> Continues well my lord? His health, beseech you?
> Well, madam!

he answers, putting a chapter of considerate mystery into two words! She tries again:

> Is he disposed to mirth? I hope he is.

He sees the opening and swiftly takes it:

> Exceeding pleasant; none a stranger there
> So merry and so gamesome; he is call'd
> The Briton reveller.

This is not quite what she expects, nor, even in her generous love, can be too glad of.

> When he was here,
> He did incline to sadness, and oft-times
> Not knowing why.
> I never saw him sad. . . .

Deftly now he gets to work, picking at the fabric of her faith with a fascinatingly evil skill. Imogen is, after all, not a woman of the world. Rome, seen from the shelter of her British Court, is Babylon. The picture of the Frenchman, mocked at for faithfulness to his "Gallian girl at home" by a Posthumus

> . . . who knows
> By history, report, or his own proof,
> What woman is, yea, what she cannot choose
> But must be . . .

— by Posthumus, who thought far otherwise of women here, and of her (here is not there, though), a little sears her mind.

Note that they are his own convictions which Iachimo lends to Posthumus; thus they sound the more credible as he vents them; this is the accepted technique of slander. But though he does excellently for a while, with his obvious wish to be quite just to Posthumus, with his flair for that unusual mingling in Imogen of humility and pride (two strengths that love and sacrifice have turned into a weakness he can play upon, with his pity of her that shames and angers her at once (he is bringing her, he must feel sure, into a very likely mood), the one warped factor in his combination — is himself. In slandering Posthumus he paints himself to her, all unaware. For who but he is now

> . . . by-peeping in an eye
> Base and illustrous as the smoky light
> That's fed with stinking tallow . . .

– at Imogen! – oblivious of him yet, her grieved mind far away. It is he, who thinks he knows

> What woman is, yea, what she cannot choose
> But must be . . .

that can mirror himself – to Imogen – in the significance of those

> diseased ventures,
> That play with all infirmities for gold,
> Which rottenness can lend nature! such boil'd stuff
> As well might poison poison!

can, when at last she does turn to him, make confident attempt – upon Imogen! – with

> Should he make me
> Live like Diana's priest, betwixt cold sheets,
> While he is vaulting variable ramps,
> In your despite, upon your purse? Revenge it.
> I dedicate myself to your sweet pleasure,
> More noble than that runagate to your bed,
> And will contrive fast to your affection
> Still close as sure. . . .
> Let me my service tender on your lips.

Where indeed is the Iachimo, subtle, dexterous, shrewd, that could turn Posthumus round his finger? Vanished in this slavering, lascivious fool!

Chastity – and married chastity, that larger virtue – is the chief theme of the play. Imogen is its exemplar. Iachimo and Cloten, the clever fellow and the blockhead, are alike blind in lust. In the story Shakespeare borrowed the villain relies only on his trick, makes no attempt at all on the wife's virtue.[38] But Iachimo's insensate blunder (Cloten's bestiality too) is most germane to the play he evolves from it.

He makes, does Iachimo, a most brilliant recovery, never-

[38] This is true also of *Westward for Smelts,* the other possible source.

theless; winning her forgiveness out of hand with his ingenious

> O happy Leonatus! I may say
> The credit that thy lady hath of thee
> Deserves thy trust, and thy most perfect goodness
> Her assured credit . . .

and the rest of the dithyramb. If we feel that she now is a
bit of a fool to be taken in by him – well, he is a foreigner,
it must be remembered, and all foreigners are eccentric; he
had shown himself so upon the moment, in those strange ex-
tollings of her beauty. Besides, to hear Posthumus praised,
when no one here dares praise him any longer! Even that

> He sits 'mongst men like a descended god:
> He hath a kind of honour sets him off,
> More than a mortal seeming . . .

will not sound over-extravagant to her. Iachimo, once he can
rein in that satyr-demon of his, knows how to win her good
opinion.

His sensuality is dominant again in the soliloquy in her
bedchamber. Here is Iachimo, his stallion vanity quiescent,
the artist in life. Yet from

> Cytherea,
> How bravely thou becom'st thy bed! fresh lily!
> And whiter than the sheets! . . .

he must still pass to

> That I might touch!
> But kiss; one kiss! . . .

and risk his whole enterprise on the chance that she will
wake as he kisses her:

> Rubies unparagon'd

How dearly they do't! . . .[39]

But, his lickerishness appeased, he can refine it again to

> 'Tis her breathing that
> Perfumes the chamber thus: the flame o' the taper
> Bows toward her, and would under-peep her lids
> To see the enclosed lights, now canopied
> Under these windows, white and azure-laced
> With blue of heaven's own tinct

– which are arguably the most purely beautiful lines in the play.

By now we have the figure fully drawn in, and coloured too. Iachimo, then, is the sensual aesthete, the amoral man. And this scene is, among other things, an exercise in the perversion of the sense of beauty. As we watch him weaving his evil web around her, making his damning inventory, even to the mole upon her breast,

> cinque-spotted, like the crimson drops
> I' the bottom of a cowslip . . .

we should be made to feel him only the wickeder for his seeing the while how beautiful in her purity she is. But Shakespeare, we may note, does not weaken the character by cant.

> Though this a heavenly angel, hell is here.

A modern villain would hardly be so simple-minded.

[39] The text, surely, leaves us in no doubt that he kisses her. Most editors will not have this at any price, their sensibilities being offended by the notion of it, and they find ingenious reasons why he should not – he would never risk waking her – and still more ingenious (mis)interpretations, since they must then have them, of the manifest "How dearly they do't". But a kiss is no more likely to wake her than is the stealing of the bracelet, even if Shakespeare were one to trouble about such trifles. And our sensibilities are meant to be offended. The sight of the fellow smacking his own lips that have just polluted hers should veritably make us squirm.

Back in Rome, with men to encounter, Iachimo is his
masterful self again. A bracelet, after all, is not irrefragable
evidence; he will need to have his wits well about him. Shakespeare sees that he has; the "madding" of the victim into
belief in his betrayal is as skilfully contrived as was his bringing to the point of the wager (and it presents the dramatist
with no easier a problem).

Posthumus, chafed by his exile, wears, while he waits, that
positively confident front which may so often mask, not a
doubt, but the fear of one. He greets Iachimo with stiffly
tolerant good nature, even rallies him, rather frostily, upon
his failure. Behind that too there may be lurking the shadow
of the shadow of a doubt. Iachimo, as before, watches his
man, keeps a cryptic countenance, lets Posthumus make what
he will of

> Your lady
> Is one of the fairest that I have looked upon

and waits to be questioned. Posthumus cannot question him;
that would be to admit a doubt. He holds to his raillery:

> Sparkles this stone as it was wont? or is't not
> Too dull for your good wearing?

Iachimo counters it by assuring him coolly and categorically
that

> the ring is won.

POSTHUMUS. The stone's too hard to come by.
IACHIMO.   Not a whit,
> Your lady being so easy.
POSTHUMUS.   Make not, sir
> Your loss your sport: I hope you know that we
> Must not continue friends.

So far, so good. Here is the quarry lured from behind his
humorous defence, pricked to the beginnings of anger. Then,
with a yet more categorical

156

                    but I now
Profess myself the winner of her honour,
Together with your ring, and not the wronger
Of her or you, having proceeded but
By both your wills

Iachimo brings him to the direct grim challenge of

              If you can mak't apparent
That you have tasted her in bed, my hand
And ring is yours: if not, the foul opinion
You had of her pure honour gains or loses
Your sword or mine, or masterless leaves both
To who shall find them

– and to make it, we note, Posthumus must needs bring from
the far back of his consciousness the brutal image of that
"tasted her in bed". It will stay staring at him now, and
Iachimo knows better than to disturb it by a word. For his
part, he will avoid all mention of Imogen for awhile. Distrust
shall be left to work. So he launches into his elaborate, choice
description of the bedchamber, which the exile knows so well,
making the lost joy of it yet more vivid to him, quickening
his senses to render them the more vulnerable, smirching
the picture with just one lewd parenthesis, one drop of ir-
ritant poison to the compound; yet for all his hardihood making so reticent a case of it that Posthumus, though puzzled,
is reassured. But to feel reassured is to feel that you have
needed assurance. And, having brought him to this state of
sensitive, unbalanced discomfort, he produced the bracelet.
   The bracelet is good evidence, and far better than Iachimo
has till this moment known, for he did not know Posthumus
had given it her. But how quick he is to seize the advantage,
and to better it!

POSTHUMUS.   . . . is it that
           Which I left with her?
IACHIMO.   Sir – I thank her – that.

> She stripped it from her arm; I see her yet;
> Her pretty action did outsell her gift
> And yet enrich'd it too. . . .

(Posthumus sees her yet; and writhes)

> . . . she gave it me
> And said she prized it once.

Even so, a bracelet – this bracelet, even! – ranged with things of its own kind, inanimate things, put plump down on a table, might be matter for reason, for argument. Iachimo makes better use of it than that.

> I beg but leave to air this jewel; see!
> And now 'tis up again . . . .

Held for a horrid moment in the husband's face, and then returned so caressingly to his bosom, it seems a living thing. Posthumus makes one clutch at reason:

> May be she plucked it off
> To send it me.

But Iachimo is ready for this, has led him, indeed, into the trap of it.

> She writes so to you, doth she?

Whereupon, without more warning, this hero and his brittle faith collapse.

He is but half a hero; and while things went so smoothly with him, while he was Cymbeline's favourite,

> . . . most praised, most loved,
> A sample to the youngest, to the more mature
> A glass that feated him

what chance had he to store up resistant virtues? And exile

has been hard on him. Still, it is a pretty ignominious collapse.
Soothed by Philario, he makes yet one more clutch at common sense. The bracelet was stolen. Iachimo has his oath in
reserve:

> By Jupiter, I had it from her arm

nor is he perjured swearing it; and with this the wretched
Posthumus is utterly undone.

> Hark you, he swears; by Jupiter, he swears.
> 'Tis true: – nay, keep the ring – 'tis true: I am sure.
> She would not lose it: her attendants are
> All sworn and honourable: – they induced to steal it!
> And by a stranger!

They, who are nothing to him, may be trusted; she, who is
all the world, no! An admirable stroke! Iachimo has won.
He contemplates in quiet detachment this moral fool demor-
alized. Such a short step is it from the boast of "her pure
honour" to

> Never talk on't;
> She hath been colted by him.

Partly to seal his victory, partly, one supposes, for the simple
pleasure of seeing the human animal suffer, he goes on:

> If you seek
> For further satisfying, under her breast –
> Worthy the pressing – lies a mole, right proud
> Of that most delicate lodging: by my life,
> I kiss'd it, and it gave me present hunger
> To feed again, though full

– to discover (interesting phenomenon!) that the victim now
asks to be tortured:

> No swearing.
> If you will swear you have not done 't you lie,

159

> And I will kill thee if thou dost deny
> Thou'st made me cuckold

– with which, and a little more raging, he breaks from them in impotent fury. The shocked Philario gazes after him:

> Quite besides
> The government of patience! you have won:
> Let's follow him and pervert the present wrath
> He hath against himself.
>   With all my heart!

The artist in Iachimo must be conscious of a fine piece of work done; and he feels, for the moment, quite good-natured.

It has been worth while, perhaps, to subject these three scenes to such close analysis, for this is how their actors must work at them, and their artistry ranks high even among Shakespeare's mature achievements of the kind.

CLOTEN

Cloten (pronounced "Clotten" to rhyme – most appropriately – with "rotten", by warrant of the pun "I have sent Cloten's clotpole down the stream", which is reinforced by several spellings in the Folio) is far from being a merely comic character. His aspect is amusing; without that much mitigation, the truth about him (and Shakespeare does not shirk it) would be intolerable in such a play – in any play! He stands in the character-scheme contrasted with Iachimo; scoundrels both, the coarse numskull beside the clever hedonist, but each, as we saw, the other's complement in lechery – with Imogen, but for providence, their victim. He is a booby; even so, less booby than brute, and debased brute at that.

The first we hear of him is as

> a thing
> Too bad for bad report . . . .

We see him with one sycophant companion, and another mocking him, all but to his face. It is harsh, unsavoured mirth, though; and we shall hardly laugh at him, unless as harshly. For to laugh at a man is to be at least in the way of forgiving him; and Cloten, gibbeted for vermin from the start, is turned round and round till all the foulness under his folly can be seen, to be slaughtered like vermin at last. Shakespeare was to evolve a little later a more picturesque and far more pardonable monster. But this civilized Caliban!

He is not pure poltroon. He challenges Posthumus (pretty confident, no doubt, that the "gentlemen at hand" will part them) and fights the hefty young Guiderius (who is only armed, it would seem, with hunting knife and club[40]). He has as much courage, that's to say, as will go to make a bully.

> Would there had been some hurt done!

– but not, of course, to him. He is lit up for us in that line; and shortly by two more. Never was there a more patient man in loss, his ironic flatterer tells him. He is

> . . . the most coldest that ever turned up ace.
> CLOTEN.   It would make any man cold to lose.
> FIRST LORD.   But not every man patient after the noble temper of your lordship. You are most hot and furious when you win.
> CLOTEN.   Winning will put any man into courage.

It will never enter his thick head that he is being laughed at. Cockered and coached by his mother, and thanks to his tailor, he makes some sort of figure at Court, woos Imogen, assails her with "musics" in the morning, being told this will "penetrate", orders the musicians about, we notice, as if they were dogs. The music not penetrating sufficiently, he must bribe her ladies, he thinks; his own idea, this. He goes about it with true delicacy:

[40] "With his own sword," says Guiderius," . . . I have ta'en his head from him."

> There's gold for you;
> Sell me your good report.

When she does at last give him a word he manages to start with

> Good morrow, fairest sister: your sweet hand.

But soon he is hectoring her too. He is not in love with her, needless to say. She is "this foolish Imogen"; when he has got her he will "have gold enough", that is all. He makes not a little noise at the reception of the Roman envoy. Critics have objected that Cymbeline would never admit such a blockhead to his counsels. Bless their innocence! At such Courts as Cymbeline's any loud-voiced bully who is in royal favour, given chance to say

> Come, there's no more tribute to be paid. . . .

and damn the consequences, will have his cheering backers. What's Rome to them? But when the fighting comes it will be one of them that Posthumus finds

> Still going? This a lord! . . .
> To-day how many would have given their honours
> To have saved their carcasses! took heel to do't,
> And yet died too. . . .

Yet Cloten rises to a sort of dignity when he bids farewell to Lucius with

> You hand, my lord.
> Receive it friendly; but from this time forth
> I wear it as your enemy.

Even Cloten, we are tempted to say, can show himself at his country's call to be a soldier and a gentleman.

One of Shakespeare's touches of grim mischief, this; for he has not done with him. Imogen fled and in disgrace, the gallant gentleman scents the opportunity for another sort of wooing of her. He will pursue her, dressed (the story demands it) in the very garments Posthumus wore at their leave-taking, those that she said she held, the meanest of them – that insult particularly rankles! – in more respect than his "noble and natural person"; and

> With that suit upon my back, will I ravish her; first kill him, and in her eyes; there shall she see my valour, which will then be a torment to her contempt. He on the ground ... and when my lust hath dined ... to the Court I'll knock her back, foot her home again ...

"When my lust hath dined ..."! Shakespeare can, on occasion, lodge a fair amount of meaning within four words, give us the marrow of a man in them too. This is Cloten with the comic mask lifted, the soldier and gentleman shed, the beast showing. A Cloten hardly in his right mind, one would suppose – even *his* right mind. He does, a little later, when he recapitulates the programme, seem to realize that her father

> ... may haply be a little angry for my so rough usage; but my mother, having power of his testiness, shall turn all into my commendations. ...

A Cloten merely weaving these Alnaschar fancies for his private delight, is he? By no means. War is beginning; his fine defiance of the Romans and the Court's applause of it have swollen his vanity yet higher; he and his kind, surely, are to have things their own way now; his appetites are whetted. The Clotens of the world, in Shakespeare's age, or Cymbeline's, or any other, ask no more than opportunity. Scarcely a comic character!

POSTHUMUS

Iachimo's victim we have already studied; is there more to be said for Imogen's husband? It will be hard for any dramatic hero to stand up, first to such praise as is lavished upon Posthumus before we see him (though when we do he is not given much time or chance to disillusion us), next against the discredit of two scenes of befoolment, then against banishment from the action for something like a dozen scenes more. Nor in his absence are we let catch any lustrous reflections of him. Were he coming back, Othello-like, to do his murdering for himself, we might thrill to him a little. He is a victim both to the story and to the plan of its telling. Even when he reappears there is no weaving him into the inner thread of the action. He cannot, as we say, openly encounter any of its prime movers without prejudicing the elaborate revelations saved up for the last scene. He can only soliloquize, have a dumb-show fight with Iachimo, a didactic talk with an anonymous "Lord" who has nothing to say in return, a bout of wit with a gaoler who has much the best of it; worst of all, he becomes the unconscious centre of that jingling pageant of his deceased relatives – a most misguided attempt to restore interest in him, for we nourish a grudge against him for it. One can detect, nevertheless, unworked veins of interest in the man. He is among those who live (the benefits of their natural happy egoism apart), rather by credulity than faith, and not at all by judgment, whose moral balance, then, is easily upset, hard to recover, no solid base being there to rest it on. No wisdom in him, nor ever likely to be much; but, in its place, some humility of heart.

> And sweetest, fairest,
> As I my poor self did exchange for you
> To your so infinite loss. . . .

That is not spoken to Imogen the princess, but to the woman; he knows himself, for all men's praise of him, coarse clay beside her. We like him too for his boyish boastfulness of her perfections – it is its very innocence that sets the cynic Iachimo compassing his downfall – and can find something pitiful in the as boyishly passionate disillusionment of

> Could I find out

> The woman's part in me! For there's no motion
> That tends to vice in man but I affirm
> It is the woman's part: be it lying, note it,
> The woman's; flattering, hers; deceiving, hers;
> Lust and rank thoughts, hers, hers; revenges, hers.
> Ambitions, covetings, change of prides, disdain,
> Nice longing, slanders, mutability,
> All faults that may be named, nay, that hell knows,
> Why, hers in part or all, but rather, all;
> For even to vice
> They are not constant, but are changing still
> One vice but of a minute old for one
> Not half so old as that. . . .

Whoever has not at some time felt the better for such an outburst (no inconvenient plot of a play pending to translate it into action), let him laugh at poor Posthumus.

But there is matter of more interest in his remorse. It overwhelms him before ever he has learned that Imogen is guiltless, and here is the drift of it:

> You married ones,
> If each of you should take this course, how many
> Must murder wives much better than themselves,
> For wrying but a little! . . .
> Gods! if you
> Should have ta'en vengeance on my faults, I never
> Had lived to put on this: so had you saved
> The noble Imogen to repent, and struck
> Me, wretch, more worth your vengeance.

Neither Othello nor Leontes, those other exemplars of the jealous husband repentant, reach this point of view. It belongs to the humility of heart which, we may like to think, was what Imogen found to love in him. And it is the same humility and generosity – for the accepting of forgiveness makes as much call on generosity as offering it, and more – that takes him back to her with no wordy repentance, no closer promise of amendment than his

> Hang there like fruit, my soul,
> Till the tree die!

He finds his new faith in her, and in himself, in her forgiveness of him. She understands; and so should we.

GUIDERIUS AND ARVIRAGUS

They are dowered with some of the best poetry in the
play; but there is more to them than this.[41] They stand, of
course, for products, the very choicest, of the simple life.
What would they have come to be at Court; with Imogen for
a sister, it is true, but with Cloten for a stepbrother besides?
As it is, they skip ruddy and skin-clad from their cave, ex-
horted by the good Belarius:

> Stoop, boys: this gate
> Instructs you how to adore the heavens, and bows you
> To a morning's holy office: the gates of monarchs
> Are arch'd so high that giants may jet through
> And keep their impious turbans on, without
> Good morrow to the sun. Hail, thou fair heaven!
> We house i' the rock, yet use thee not so hardly
> As prouder livers do.
> GUIDERIUS.   Hail, heaven!
> ARVIRAGUS.   Hail, heaven!

Nor does he let any other occasion, great or small, pass unim-
proved. Luckily for their characters (dramatically speaking,
at any rate) they are at once set in opposition to this sort of
thing; it is the simplest dramatic recipe for giving a scene
life. But it is not till Guiderius, in particular, comes into
action on his own account (this shows the authentic dramatist
too) that he effectively reveals himself. Himself, and another aspect of the simple life at once. Cloten, we shall agree,

---

[41] Burdened with some few vapidities besides – of the worst of which,
though, we have argued, Shakespeare can hardly have been guilty.

gets no more than his deserts. But when Guiderius appears, swinging his head as a gardener might a turnip:

> This Cloten was a fool, an empty purse;
> There was no money in 't: not Hercules
> Could have knock'd out his brains, for he had none:
> Yet I not doing this, the fool had borne
> My head as I do his

– departing a moment later with

> I'll throw 't into the creek
> Behind our rock, and let it to the sea,
> And tell the fishes he's the queen's son, Cloten:
> That's all I reck

– here is simplicity with a vengeance, we feel. And young Arviragus' only comment is

> Would I had done 't –
> So the revenge alone pursued me! Polydore,
> I love thee brotherly – but envy much
> Thou hast robb'd me of this deed.

The slaughterhouse side of the business is mitigated as much as may be, by more sententious talk from Belarius, by the contrasting fancy of the dirge over Fidele, by the palpable artifice of the whole affair. But Shakespeare keeps the values of his picture true. Beside the tailored brute the noble savage is as sharply drawn; and, at the salient moment, made no merely flattering figure. There is another side to the simple life.

IMOGEN

When Shakespeare imagined Imogen (for she is to be counted his, if anything in the play can be) he had but lately achieved Cleopatra. And whether meant to be or no, they make companion pictures of wantonness and chastity; and, of women, are the fullest and maturest that he drew. Chastity, faith, fidelity, strike the ideal chord in *Cymbeline*; and Imogen is their exemplar.

But a pleasantly human paragon! She has married without her father's consent (a grave matter that in Shakespeare's time), has been a clandestine wife for some while, what is more, under Cymbeline's very nose – which shows, for a start, some ability in deception.[42] Doubtless her stepmother is a tyrant and worse, and the prospect of Cloten as a husband would justify much; but her father has excuse for his anger. And she does not – before his courtiers too! – yield him very great respect, granted that he inspires very little. We find her answering him, indeed, with something uncomfortably near to condescending irony, an invidious weapon to be wielded by the young against the old.

> I beseech you, Sir,
> Harm not yourself with your vexation:
> I am senseless of your wrath. . . .

She has retorts, calm and conclusive, for his every splutter; she is not, from the parent's point of view, an easy young lady to manage.

It is, of course, her innate truthfulness and, even more, her inextinguishable sense of realities which are to blame; couple, these with as inextinguishable a courage, and we have the first flush of the effect she is meant to make upon us. Her first words are to tell us that she is not for a moment taken in by her stepmother's ready smiles. She has nothing save

[42] Furness falls into the (for him) amazing error of supposing that the marriage had not been consummated, that it is in the nature of a "troth-plight". But, apart from repeated "husbands", this is to ignore Posthumus' specific

> Me of my lawful pleasure she restrained
> And pray'd me oft forbearance; did it with
> A pudency so rosy . . . .

And as to the still threatened marriage with Cloten (another difficulty he makes) the Second Lord speaks definitely enough of

> . . . that horrid act
> Of the divorce he 'ld make.

Relationship and situation are made amply clear.

her courage with which to meet her father's powerful wrath;
but that is enough, and somehow, somewhere Posthumus will
be restored to her. And, princess to the marrow though she
be, her

> Would I were
> A neat-herd's daughter, and my Leonatus
> Our neighbour shepherd's son!

is no mere flourish of a phrase. She has not condescended to
Posthumus.

> ... he is
> A man worth any woman ....

she says. What more is there to say? She is princess most in
her utter unself-consciousness. Pisanio is her servant, and she
orders him about sharply enough.[43] But, as she trusts him,
why should she not show him how fathom-deep she is in
love? When he comes back to tell her of the ship's sailing:

> Thou should'st have made him
> As little as a crow, or less, ere left
> To after-eye him.
> Madam, so I did

(stolid, honest, categorical Pisanio!)

> I would have broke mine eye-strings, crack'd them, but
> To look upon him, till the diminution
> Of space had pointed him sharp as my needle:
> Nay, followed him, till he had melted from
> The smallness of a gnat to air; and then
> Have turned mine eye and wept. But, good Pisanio,

[43] More properly he is Posthumus' servant left with her for a faithful
watchdog. The Queen's repeated reference to him as hers – in particular
the

> Your faithful servant ...
> This hath been

has something of irony in it. For he has obviously helped the two of
them to conceal the marriage and hoodwink the Court.

When shall we hear from him?

                                    Be assured, Madam,
With his next vantage.

(Much solid heartening comfort in Pisanio! And how, by the way, Shakespeare does love that word "air"!) Imogen speaks half to herself now; her thoughts aboard the ship.

      I did not take my leave of him, but had
     Most pretty things to say: ere I could tell him
     How I would think on him, at certain hours,
     Such thoughts or such; or I could make him swear
     The shes of Italy should not betray
     Mine interest and his honour; or have charged him,
     At the sixth hour of morn, at noon, at midnight,
     To encounter me with orisons, for then
     I am in heaven for him; or ere I could
     Give him that parting kiss which I had set
     Betwixt two charming words, comes in my father,
     And like the tyrannous breathing of the north,
     Shakes all our buds from growing.

The long-drawn-out sentence, fading to an end, paints the flagging of her spirit from that intense

      I would have broke my eye-strings, crack'd them ...

to the loneliness of the prospect she faces. The fresh simplicity of it all; the little joke about the "shes of Italy" (which is to come back upon her in poisoned earnest, as such jokes will); the wifely sanctity of the

                              ... for then
            I am in heaven for him ...

— such strokes complete the statement of her; gallant, generous, royal, innocent, unguarded. To round it in:

Enter a lady.
                              The queen, Madam,
          Desires your highness' company

– and the girl-wife stiffens to princess again.

Would she for one moment tolerate Iachimo, credit his
excuse for his outrage upon her, or accept his apology? There
are the claims of the borrowed story; and once again Shakespeare – artfully, tactfully, and by what he leaves out or suggests far more than by what he puts in – brings them to tally
with the character he is creating.

This queer foreigner comes from Posthumus. That in itself will frank him past much eccentricity of behaviour. But
though she makes remorseful amends for her harsh misjudg-
ment of him her courtesy turns cool, even to wariness. And
it is her pathetically pretty fancy to have the plate and jewels
near her for a while, only because

          My lord hath interest in them . . .

– to do even so much for him! – that serves to bring the fatal
necessary trunk into her bedchamber.

Her attitude throughout the scene is quietly eloquent of
her miseries. And when Iachimo, spreading his net, baits her
with a little pity, her quick proud resentment speaks of other
pitying eyes, which follow her now about the Court, to which
she'll turn as proud a front; even as the wistful

                              My lord, I fear,
          Has forgot Britain

with its unspoken, questioning echo "is forgetting me?" tells
of happy humilities of love left starving, comfortless, to wear
down to secret self-distrust.

We see her braving the worst of her afflictions, her wooing
by the wretched Cloten; the high-mettled courage that she
showed her father is edged here with a sharper scorn – the
object of it so contemptible! But the strain of the misery is

telling on her; that final, gratuitously defiant fling at the
Queen, for answer to Cloten's

> I will inform your father.
>> Your mother too!
> She's my good lady, and will conceive, I hope,
> But the worst of me . . .

savours of desperation.

The godsend, then, of the news that Posthumus has returned, is at Milford Haven, expects her there!

> O, for a horse with wings! Hear'st thou, Pisanio?
> He is at Milford Haven: read and tell me
> How far 'tis thither. If one of mean affairs
> May plod it in a week, why may not I
> Glide thither in a day? Then, true Pisanio –
> Who long'st like me to see thy lord; who long'st –
> O, let me 'bate – but not like me – yet long'st,
> But in a fainter kind. O, not like me;
> For mine's beyond beyond: say, and speak thick, –
> Love's counsellor should fill the bores of hearing,
> To the smothering of the sense – how far it is
> To this same blessed Milford.

In a moment all the stored suffering and doubt convert into
oblivious joy, and she is at the height, again, of her old confident vitality. The lines are yet another example of the raising
of simple, seemingly natural speech to poetic power, and of
Shakespeare's maturest craft in this kind.[44] The whole scene
is finely contrived. For Imogen clouds have vanished; but
the glum, taciturn figure of Pisanio to remind us that they
are gathering more blackly than she can imagine. She appeals
to him:

[44] And some of us – nineteenth-century playgoers – can remember Ellen Terry speaking and acting them, and seeming, for those few moments,
to fill the Lyceum Theatre with dancing sunbeams. There was the fine
achievement, too, of Irving's Iachimo – with its angular grace and intellectual art.

> Prithee, speak;
> How many score of miles may we well ride
> Twixt hour and hour?

PISANIO.   One score 'twixt sun and sun,
> Madam, 's enough for you and too much too.

IMOGEN.   Why, one that rode to 's execution, man,
> Could never go so slow. . . .

As it is to hers, he knows – and we know – that she is going, the joke is a grimly good one. She enjoys it!

> But this is foolery.
> Go, bid my woman feign a sickness, say
> She'll home to her father; and provide me, presently,
> A riding-suit no costlier than would fit
> A franklin's housewife.

Reluctantly he departs to obey her; and off she flies to make herself ready. This is the last we are to see of the princess, of the imperious Imogen.

The sight of her in the drab riding-suit will speak of changing and diminishing fortune; she is adventuring into a strange unprivileged world, made the stranger, the more ominous, by Pisanio's silence as the two of them go on their way. At last she wins the truth from him; and rather, we note, by pleading than command – she is conscious already of her declension. He hands her the fatal letter.

But she is very Imogen in her meeting of the blow. She risked all when she loved Posthumus and married him. Her trust has brought her to this. It never occurs to her to try to escape the reaping of what she has sown. That she is innocent is beside the point. When she gave herself she made no reservation that it should be for as long as he loved her, or treated her well, or as it might suit with her self-respect. So, "When thou sees't him", she tells Pisanio,

> A little witness my obedience. Look!
> I draw the sword myself: take it, and hit

> The innocent mansion of my love, my heart.
> Fear not; 'tis empty of all things but grief;
> Thy master is not there, who was indeed
> The riches of it. . . .

We have had just a flash, though, of her shrewd, unilluded temper:

> Iachimo,
> Thou didst accuse him of incontinency;
> Thou then look'dst like a villain; now, methinks,
> Thy favour's good enough. Some jay of Italy,
> Whose mother was her painting, hath betray'd him.

She knows (she thinks) the fate of such a handsome hero, finding another Court to flatter him. *She* fell a victim to him. She is wrong; it is the mud of Iachimo's flinging that has stuck, as mud will; shrewdness, wounded, does thus go astray. We hear the transcendent Imogen again in

> And thou, Posthumus, thou that didst set up
> My disobedience 'gainst the king, my father,
> And make me put into contempt the suits
> Of princely fellows, shalt hereafter find
> It is no act of common passage, but
> A strain of rareness: and I grieve myself
> To think, when thou shalt be disedged by her
> That now thou tirest on, how thy memory
> Will then be pang'd by me . . .

– for in such perception and detachment lies greatness of soul. Her grief it is that is stressed; grief that such faith as hers, such love as theirs, should be thus brought to ruin.

> All good seeming,
> By thy revolt, O husband, shall be thought
> Put on for villainy. . . .

It is love and faith itself – all that she knew of good in an evil world – which stand betrayed.[45]

But while she may grieve nobly, meek mournfulness is no part of her nature, nor has she much patience with Pisanio's remorse.

> The lamb entreats the butcher; where's thy knife?
> Thou art too slow to do thy master's bidding,
> When I desire it too.

PISANIO.   O gracious lady,
> Since I received command to do this business
> I have not slept one wink.

IMOGEN.   Do 't, and to bed then.

He means to spare her and save her, has some hope of the future. She hardly believes him (what should she believe in now!) or cares to be saved. But her native pride (at least she will never return to the father she has defied), her courage and the instinctive hope that dwells in her youth (though she admits none of Posthumus, nor indeed any, yet she will act as if she did), all conspire to set her on the path he opens to her. Stoically:

>   this attempt
> I am soldier to, and will abide it with
> A prince's courage

– with the old dignity that her drab garmenting cannot disguise; with a new quietude. When they part, her answer to his

>   may the gods
> Direct you to the best!
>   Amen: I thank thee

– in the four words (if an actress can speak them) is an Imogen white from the fire.

[45] A touch of this nobility was left to Posthumus too. He speaks, his letter to Pisanio says, "not out of weak surmises, but from proof as strong as my grief". The word can, of course, be used in the mere sense of injury. But Imogen certainly does not so use it, and we may read the deeper meaning into it here as well.

We shall hardly know her as Fidele; the tiny fragile figure, once so commanding in her Court brocades and lately buckramed in her riding-gown. Nor is this all the change. Her utter helplessness, as she wanders lost in the forest, breeds a new humour in her; a sense, half comic, half pathetic, of what is ridiculous in her plight, of fellowship with the wretched, in their follies, even in their sins, a whelming sense of the pitifulness of things and of poor humanity astray.

> I see a man's life is a tedious one:
> I have tired myself, and for two nights together
> Have made the ground my bed. . . .

It needs no more than that and an empty stomach to make one very tolerant. Even Posthumus' wronging of her rouses no bitterness in her now:

> My dear lord!
> Thou art one o' the false ones . . .

– only a wistful, still loving, regret.

The conventional disguise, the sententious tone of the play (doubly sententious in these scenes around the cave), are turned to good account for this latter phase of the picturing of Imogen. They help her steer the nice course between comedy and tragedy that the story demands. As she enters the cave:

> Best draw my sword; and if mine enemy
> But fear the sword like me, he'll scarcely look on 't.
> Such a foe, good heavens!

That ever-useful joke at once blunts the tragic edge of the business. The marvel of her meeting with her brothers is dramatically subdued by the matching of such frank artifice as Arviragus'

> I'll love him as my brother,
> And such a welcome as I'ld give to him
> After long absence – such is yours; most welcome!

with her

> Would it had been so, that they
> Had been my father's sons! . . .

It must be kept subdued, not only for the sake of the elaborate
finale of revelations, but because a fresh emotional interest
here, which involved Imogen, would discount the intensity
of the climactic moment of her waking beside Posthumus'
supposed corpse. This itself we find very subtly prepared for;
producer and actors must carefully note how.

She is wooed from the worst of her sorrow by such
brotherly love. Once again – far more effectively here indeed – the sense of indeterminate time gives atmosphere to
the picture. For "two nights together" she has made the
ground her bed; that is long enough to leave her starving,
and there is no more point in the exactitude. But we are
not to calculate that she reaches the cave one afternoon and
is found seemingly dead in it the morning after. We are
simply to see her gratefully happy with these good companions, the cruelties of the Court fading to oblivion, while
she busies herself with homely duties:

BELARIUS.   Pray, be not sick,
           For you must be our housewife.
IMOGEN.   Well or ill,
           I am bound to you.
BELARIUS.   And shalt be ever.
                            (She goes into the cave.)
           This youth, howe'er distressed, appears he hath
                had
           Good ancestors.
AVIRAGUS.   How angel-like he sings!
GUIDERIUS. But his neat cookery! he cut our roots in char-
                acters,
           And sauced our broths, as Juno had been sick,
           And he her dieter.

An idyllic interlude, with its idyllic sequel in the speaking

177

of the dirge over the dead boy. For if Imogen is to survive
to happiness, Fidele is dead. The three good companions are
to meet again, but never in this wondrous world – which will
fade for them (as imaginings of it do for us) into the commonplace; even as

> Golden lads and girls all must,
> As chimney-sweepers, come to dust.

With the dirge and the departure of Belarius and the boys
their idyllic life ends too – they pass to war and its realities.
And Imogen returns to consciousness to fancy herself upon
her lonely desperate journey again –

> Yes, sir, to Milford Haven; which is the way? –
> I thank you. – By yond bush? Pray, how far thither?
> 'Ods pittikins! can it be six mile yet? –
> I have gone all night. . . .

– with the friendly comfort of the cave become a dream.
Her last waking words had been the smiling

> Well or ill,
> I am bound to you

and by the contrast the horror of the waking is redoubled.
But now that we have reached this most effective situation,
we must own it, and the whole business of it, to be, from one
point of view at least, dramatically inexcusable. It is a fraud
on Imogen; and we are accomplices in it. We have watched
the playwright's plotting, been amused by his ingenuity. We
shall even be a little conscious as we watch, in this sophisticated play, of the big bravura chance to be given to the
actress. But Imogen herself is put, quite needlessly, quite
heartlessly, on exhibition. How shall we sympathize with such
futile suffering? And surely it is a faulty art that can so make
sport of its creatures.[46]

[46] Hermione's reported death in *A Winter's Tale* is a somewhat similar

178

All this is true. But tragi-comedy – in this phase of its development, at least – is a bastard form of art; better not judge it by too strict aesthetic law. Tact can intervene; that reconciling grace which sometimes makes stern principle so pleasant to forswear. And Shakespeare palliates his trick with great dramatic tact; he veils its crudity in beauty (a resource that seldom fails him) and even manages to make it serve for some enriching of his character.

The atmosphere of artifice in which the whole play moves – in these scenes in the forest it is at its densest – helps soften, as we saw, the crudity of the butchered corpse. The long, confused waking (dream, to Imogen's drugged senses, only emerging into dream) tempers the crassness of the horror too. Such a touch of sheer beauty as

> Good faith,
> I tremble still with fear; but if there be
> Yet left in heaven as small a drop of pity
> As a wren's eye, fear'd gods, a part of it! . . .

will sweeten it. And from the positive

> A headless man! The garments of Posthumus!
> I know the shape o's leg: this is his hand;
> His foot Mercurial. . . .

we are carried very quickly to the agonized climax and as quickly on. There is no shirking. Shakespeare, once committed, will have every ounce of his effect.

fraud; but to this we are not made party. We should not sympathize overmuch with Leontes, in any case. But if we knew that he was suffering needlessly would not the retributive balance of the scene be truer, its dramatic value greater, therefore? This (if so) is sacrificed to the surprise of the living statue at the end. Would it not be better if we were in the secret and our interest set upon the effect of the revelation on Leontes? Once we know the story the practical test is hard to make. But there are more signs than one that Shakespeare never fully "found himself" in this new form of play. For how seldom, in earlier plays, have we ever had to ask, when he was in the vein and going full swing, whether there could be a more effective way of doing whats to do!

> O Posthumus! alas,
> Where is thy head? where's that? Ah me, where's that?
> Pisanio might have kill'd thee at the heart,
> And left this head on ...

is material for as blood-curdling an exhibition as any actress
need wish to give. But – here is the master-stroke – even
while she is thus racked, and beyond endurance, Imogen's
heart is purging of a deeper pain. There is no remotest reason
for her jumping to

> Pisanio,
> All curses madded Hecuba gave the Greeks,
> And mine to boot, be darted on thee! Thou,
> Conspired with that irregulous devil, Cloten,
> Hast here cut off my lord. . . .

She does not even know of Cloten's attempt to suborn him.
But her suffering – and her sex, if we like – is excuse for
anything of the sort. And to find that Posthumus, even though
she finds him dead, was not after all her reviler and would-be
murderer, cleanses and exalts her grief. Shakespeare does not
insist on this. Imogen, for one thing, is not in a very analytical
or explanatory mood. It is as clear as he needs it to be. He
leaves it to become effective in the acting:

> That confirms it home:
> This is Pisanio's deed and Cloten's: O!
> Give colour to my pale cheek with thy blood,
> That we the horrider may seem to those
> Which chance to find us: O, my lord, my lord!

She rallies from delirium; the pictorial phrase is a resolution
into the play's proper key; and in the simple "O, my lord,
my lord!" spoken as it can be spoken – we are to hear, as
she faints away, her reconciliation with her dead.

Nevertheless, contrive as he may, it is a pretty damnable
practical joke; and Shakespeare, the creator of Imogen, must

now pay the price of Shakespeare the showman's escapade.[47] He does; to whatever else he may yield we shall not find him at this time of day finally playing false to character. A happy ending may be the play's due, but Imogen can make no full recovery from what has been pure poignant tragedy for her. When the kind hands of Roman enemies recover her from her "bloody pillow" she stands tongue-tied at first. Lucius has to question and question before she answers his "What art thou?" with

> I am nothing: or if not,
> Nothing to be were better.

She is stunned and dazed; what wonder! She will follow whither she is bid:

> But first, an 't please the gods,
> I'll hide my master from the flies, as deep
> As these poor pickaxes can dig. . . .

The royal Imogen, to whom Posthumus kneeled with his

> My queen! my mistress!

who could gallantly defy her father and his Queen, and laugh at the brute Cloten and his wooing, has travelled far. "Happy ending" looks little congruous with the sight of her now.

So Shakespeare finds. He frees her from the action for four full scenes, gives her time, as it were, for recovery; but restored to it, restored to husband and father, united to her brothers, her path fair before her, she is a wounded woman still. Her ring on Iachimo's finger; that only means she may learn how all the evil came to pass, the tale cannot bring her dead back to life; she listens to its verbiage in numb silence. When it does, when by miracle Posthumus stands there before her, the very joy leaves her speechless; she can only

---

47 Or we may, of course, make the whipping-boy the original culprit, if we prefer.

cling to him and stammer helplessly. Just for one moment, when she turns upon Pisanio, she rallies to "the tune of Imogen", and they know her by it. The "happy ending" is duly brought about. But Shakespeare gives her little more to say; that little quiet and colourless, almost. He could not in conscience set her – or set any of them – merrymaking.

Lady Martin, who wrote pleasant reminiscences of Miss Helen Faucit's applauded performances of Shakespeare's heroines, ends the study of Imogen with a sentimental picture of a slow decline (the play being over), of her dying –" . . . fading out like an exhalation of the dawn" – surrounded by the rest of the cast in appropriate attitudes of grief and remorse. This is certainly not criticism; and one is apt to smile at such "Victorian" stuff, and to add "and nonsense" as one puts the book down. But there is something to be said for acting a part if you want to discover those last few secrets about it that the author knew but did not see fit to disclose. And Lady Martin is essentially right here. The figure of Imogen is lifelike, of a verity that transcends the play's need; and the blows that Shakespeare had to deal her were death-blows. It is something of a simulacrum that survives. But there is a truth to life in this too.

No one will rank *Cymbeline* with the greater plays. It is not conceived greatly, it is full of imperfections. But it has merits all its own; and one turns to it from *Othello,* or *King Lear,* or *Antony and Cleopatra,* as one turns from a masterly painting to, say, a fine piece of tapestry, from commanding beauty to more recondite charm.

Julius Caesar

Julius Cæsar is the gateway through which Shakespeare passed to the writing of his five great tragedies. He had *Henry V* close behind him, *Hamlet* was not far ahead; between times he writes the three mature comedies, *Much Ado About Nothing, As You Like It* and *Twelfth Night*. In the themes, emphasis and methods of the work of this year or two we may watch the consummating development of his art.

Henry V gives the last touch to a hero of happy destiny. We might call it the latest play in which rhetoric for rhetoric's sake prevails. Shakespeare makes it occasion for a complaint of the inadequacy of his theatre to his theme. And it is, as one says, altogether a man's play. Woman's interest rules the three comedies, further, they contain much prose and make no extraordinary demands upon staging or acting. *Julius Cæsar*, again, is the manliest of plays. For the first time, too, Shakespeare fully submits his imagination to the great idea of Rome; new horizons seem to open to him, and there is to be no return to the comparative parochialism of the Histories. Nor, with this far mightier theme to develop, do we have any hint of discontent with the means to his hand. No Chorus bows apology for the bringing of the foremost man of all the world upon such an unworthy scaffold.[1] And for Philippi, not only must a few ragged foils suffice, we are back to the simple convention by which whole armies face each other across the stage. His playwright's mind is clearly not troubled by such things now. What chiefly occupies it in the planning and writing of *Julius Cæsar*? He is searching, I think we may answer, for a hero, for a new sort of hero. The story offers him more than one, and does not force him to a choice. He chooses, in the event, but haltingly. Very significantly, however.

From the beginning Shakespeare's dramatic development has lain in the discovering and proving of the strange truth that in the theatre, where external show seems everything,

---

[1] It may well be, however, that with *Henry V* Shakespeare had surmised a patriot audience's instinct to demand for their hero trappings that a legendary foreigner like Cæsar could do well enough without.

the most effective show is the heart of a man. No need to suppose it was lack of resource in stage furnishings drove him to the drama of inward struggle, triumph and defeat. That choice was innermostly made, and no playwright worth calling one but will make it on demand, whatever the theatre he writes for. Henry V is not weakened as a character by lack of a pawing charger, but neither would he be more of a hero set astride one. In himself he is by no means all rhetoric; witness the scene with his father and the soliloquy before Agincourt. But his career has the power and the glory for an end; and the parade of this, at its best, only cumbers your hero – at its worst may make him ridiculous. Henry finishes a fine figure of a man; but long enough before Shakespeare has done all he can with him, and our retrospect is rather of the youthful junketings with Falstaff. For his next hero it is in quite another direction he turns. The next true hero is Hamlet: and Hamlet, foreshadowed in Rosaline's Romeo, in Richard II, in Jaques, is imminent in Brutus. A hero, let us be clear, is the character of which a dramatist, not morally, but artistically, most approves. Macbeth is a hero. Shakespeare's sympathy with Brutus does not imply approval of the murder of Cæsar; it only means that he ultimately finds the spiritual problem of the virtuous murderer the most interesting thing in the story. Brutus best interprets the play's theme: Do evil that good may come, and see what does come!

He is more interested, as he always has been, in character than in plot. He pays, goodness knows, small respect to the plots of the three contemporary comedies; they live by character alone. This, however, is history again, and plot must count. But it is not the homespun of Holinshed, nor the crude stuff of the *Famous Victories*. Plutarch gives him, not only the story he must abide by, but characters already charged with life. His task now is less to elaborate or invent than to capture and transmit as much of such events and such men as his little London theatre will hold. It is a feat of stagecraft to show us so many significant facets of this more than personal tragedy, a finer one to share out the best of the play's action among three chief characters and yet hardly lessen the strength of any of them.

But Shakespeare will never be too sure that he understands these Romans. He does not instinctively know their minds, as he knew Henry's or Hotspur's or Falstaff's. He is even capable of transcribing a fine-sounding passage from Plutarch and making something very like nonsense of it. He never gets to grips with Cæsar himself; whether from shrewd judgment that he could not manœuver such greatness in the space he had to spare, or, as looks more likely, from a sort of superstitious respect for it. In which case – well, idols, as we know, are apt to be wooden. Casca, raw from Plutarch, has mettle enough to ride off with a scene or two. Decius Brutus, Ligarius, Lucilius are lifted whole from his pages. And the story itself and its power, once Shakespeare is in its grip, can breed from him moment after moment of pure drama. In no earlier play do the very messengers and servants partake as they do in this. But Brutus, Cassius and Antony, though he has found them alive, he must set out to recreate in his own terms. He does it by trial and error, with a slip here and there, not disdaining a ready-made patch that comes handy; the transformation is never, perhaps, complete. But he seems to be giving them their fling, tempting them to discover themselves, passionate himself to know the truth of them, whatever it may be, and ready to face it. From no other play, probably, does he learn so much in the writing. Collaborating with Plutarch he can be interpreter and creator too. He finds what is to him a new world of men, which he tests for dramatic worth by setting it on this stage of his. *Julius Cæsar* is an occasion to which he never falls back.

The Characters

BRUTUS

That the development of Brutus should be slow is proper enough; such characters do not too readily reveal themselves. Shakespeare builds the man up for us trait by trait; economically, each stroke of value, seldom an effect made merely for its own sake. With his usual care that the first things we learn shall be essential things, that very first sentence – measured, dispassionate, tinged with disdain – by which Brutus transmits to Cæsar the cry in the crowd:

A soothsayer bids you beware the Ides of March

gives us so much of the man in perfection; and its ominous weight is doubled in his mouth, its effect trebled by the innocent irony. Brutus draws aside from the procession to the games, withdrawn into himself.

> I am not gamesome: I do lack some part
> Of that quick spirit that is in Antony.
> Let me not hinder, Cassius, your desires;
> I'll leave you.

The strain of self-consciousness, that flaw in moral strength! A suspicion of pose! But self-consciousness can be self-knowledge: Shakespeare holds the scales even.

> Into what dangers would you lead me, Cassius,
> That you would have me seek into myself
> For that which is not in me?

Wisdom itself could give no apter warning. But is this next passage, in Brutus, something of a flourish, or in Shakespeare a touch of an earlier quality?

> What is it that you would impart to me?
> If it be aught toward the general good,
> Set honour in one eye and death i' the other,
> And I will look on both indifferently;
> For let the gods so speed me as I love
> The name of honour more than I fear death.

It will be captious to call it so. The lines come hard upon the first of those shouts which are perhaps the acclaiming of Cæsar as king. Brutus is not a passionless man, though he may both despise passion and dread it. A minute later he is saying:

> I would not, so with love I might entreat you,
> Be any further mov'd.

Let the actor be wary, however, with that moment of rhetoric; and let him see that his Brutus does not compete here with Cassius. For the jealous, passionate Cassius, to whom and to whose mood eloquence and rhetoric are natural, must indisputably dominate this scene.

Brutus, if we are to learn more of him, needs a different setting. It is soon found. We see him in the calm of night. He is kindly to his sleepy page, gracious to his guests. We see him alone with his wife, left all alone in the quiet with his thoughts. Much comment has been spent upon the first soliloquy in this scene:

> It must be by his death: and, for my part,
> I know no personal cause to spurn at him. . . .

Wise editors have found this inconsistent, some with their own ideal of Brutus, some, rather more reasonably, with the fully drawn figure of Shakespeare's play. But, at this stage of its development, why should we be puzzled? If the argument is supersubtle and unconvincing, why should it not be? It may be that Shakespeare himself is still fumbling to discover how this right-minded man can commit his conscience to murder, and why should his Brutus not be fumbling too? This is how it will seem to an audience, surely.

The scene's marrow is the working of Brutus' mind, alone, in company. He is working it to some purpose now. But because it is, by disposition, a solitary mind, unused to interplay, and because the thoughts are not yet fused with emotion, that commoner currency between man and man, the scene may seem to move a little stiffly and Brutus himself to be stiff. Is not this, again, dramatically right? Would he not speak his thoughts starkly, while the rest only listen and acquiesce? – though Cassius does interpose one broken sentence of protest. They respect him, this upright, calm, self-contained man. He can command, but he cannot stir them; he is not a born

leader. If the scene lacks suppleness and ease, one thought
not prompting another revealingly, if it burns bright and hard,
with never a flash into flame, so it would have been. But see
how Shakespeare finally turns this very stiffness and suppression
to a greater emotional account, when, after the silence Brutus
keeps in the scene with Portia, the cry is wrung from him at
last:

> You are my true and honourable wife,
> As dear to me as are the ruddy drops
> That visit my sad heart.

For let no one imagine that the overwhelming effect of this
lies in the lines themselves. It has been won by his long im-
passiveness; by his listening, as we listen to Portia, till he and
we too are overwrought. It is won by the courage with which
Shakespeare holds his dramatic course.

Our sympathy with Brutus has next to weather the murder,
through the planning and doing of which he stalks so nobly
and disinterestedly and with such admirable self-control, and
our interest in him to survive the emotional storm raised and
ridden by Antony. This last might, one would think, sweep
him forever from his place in the play. The contriving of his
recovery is, indeed, a most remarkable technical achievement.
It depends upon several things. For one, upon Shakespeare's
honest but ruthless treatment of Antony and his appeal to
the mob; we too may be carried away by his eloquence, but
the worth of it and of the emotions it rouses is kept clear to
us all the time. For another: had he, as playwright, not been
faithful to Brutus and his stern consistency, Brutus would fail
him now; but now, the emotional debauch over, the stoic's
chance is due. And the fourth act opens, it will be remembered,
with a most unpleasant glimpse of Antony, the plain blunt
man, triumphant, coolly dealing out death sentences –

> These many then shall die; their names are pricked

– and, as coolly, preparing to leave his colleague Lepidus in the lurch. After that the stage is reset for Brutus and his tragedy.

In the clash with Cassius, Shakespeare, intent upon the truth about the man, shows him, we may protest, no undue favour.

CASSIUS. Most noble brother, you have done me wrong.
BRUTUS. Judge me, you gods! wrong I mine enemies?
    And, if not so, how should I wrong a brother?
CASSIUS. Brutus, this sober form of yours hides wrongs;
    And when you do them —
BRUTUS.   Cassius, be content;
    Speak your griefs softly. . . .

By the stoic's moral code it is Cassius himself, of course, who is in the wrong. But which of us might not side with him against this comrade, who, with war declared, will be just to his enemies; and, with things going desperately for his side, must needs stiffen his stiff conscience against some petty case of bribery? Is this a time for pride in one's principles? Cæsar is dead – what matter now why or how? – and the the spoils must be scrambled for, and the devil will take the hindmost. Cassius is no mere opportunist; yet so weary and distracted is he, that it almost comes to this with him. And he is answered:

                What! shall one of us
    That struck the foremost man of all this world
    But for supporting robbers, shall we now
    Contaminate our fingers with base bribes,
    And sell the mighty space of our large honours
    For so much trash as may be grasped thus?

Noble sentiments doubtless! But to depreciate and dispirit your best friends, to refuse their apologies for having lost patience with you, to refuse even to lose your own in return? Brutus tries many of us as high as he tries Cassius. And what is so quelling to the impulsive, imperfect human being as the cold realism of the idealist?

CASSIUS.   When Cæsar liv'd, he durst not thus have
          mov'd me
BRUTUS.   Peace, peace! you durst not so have tempted
          him.
CASSIUS.   I durst not?
BRUTUS.   No.
CASSIUS.   What? durst not tempt him?
BRUTUS.   For your life you durst not.

Supercilious, unforgiving – and in the right! And when anger
does rise in him, it is such a cold, deadly anger that poor passionate Cassius only breaks himself against it. Yet there is
a compelling power in the man, in his integrity of mind, his
truth to himself, in his perfect simplicity. Even the detached,
impersonal,

CASSIUS.   You love me not.
BRUTUS.   I do not like your faults.
CASSIUS.   A friendly eye could never see such faults.
BRUTUS.   A flatterer's would not. . . .

though we may palate it no better than its immediate hearer
does, is and sounds the simple truth. Cassius cannot, somehow, be simple. The dagger and the naked breast – who would
be more surprised than he, we feel, were he taken at his
word? But when Brutus relents his moral guard goes down
so utterly; there sweeps over him such a sense of the pitifulness, not of Cassius and his self-conscious passion only, but
of all these petty quarrels of human nature itself, of his own:

When I spoke that I was ill-tempered too.

It is a child making friends again with his fellow-child.
    Shakespeare has now all but prepared us for the scene's
great stroke; for the winning stroke in Brutus' own cause with
us. The quarrel is over and the "jigging fool" has been dismissed. Cassius took his turn as mentor when Brutus snapped
at the wretched poet.

Bear with him, Brutus, 'tis his fashion.[2]

They set themselves to their business and call for a bowl of wine; we are in the vein of workaday. The one confesses to his "many griefs"; the other responds with kindly platitude. And to this comes the simple answer, three naked words completing it:

BRUTUS.   No man bears sorrow better: Portia is dead.
CASSIUS.   Ha! Portia!
BRUTUS.   She is dead.
CASSIUS.   How 'scaped I killing when I crossed you so!

The seal is set upon Brutus' pre-eminence in the play, which from now to its end is to be, in its main current, the story of the doom towards which he goes unregretful and clear-eyed.

Hamlet, we have said, originating in Richard and Romeo, is imminent in Brutus; but the line of descent is broken. Shakespeare, we may add, fails in Brutus just where he will succeed in Hamlet; he is instinctively searching, perhaps, to express something which the poet in Hamlet will accommodate, which the philosopher in Brutus does not. Having lifted his heroic Roman to this height, he leaves him, we must own, to stand rather stockishly upon it. There is more than one difficulty in the matter; and they were bound to come to a head. Brutus reasons his way through life, and prides himself upon suppressing his emotions. But the Elizabethan conventions of drama – and most others – are better suited to the interpreting of emotion than thought. The soliloquy, certainly, can be made a vehicle for any sort of intimate disclosure. Shakespeare has converted it already from a direct telling of the story or a length of sheer rhetoric, but not to turn it into a length of mere reasoning. His actors could, indeed, better hope to hold their audiences by fine sounds than by mental process alone. Brutus' soliloquies in Act II are all but pure thought, and in their place in the play, and at this stage of his development, are well enough, are very well. But – does Shakespeare feel?

[2] Cf. p. 116 also.

– you cannot conduct a tragedy to its crisis so frigidly. Had Brutus been the play's true and sole hero a way might have been found (by circling him, for instance, with episodes of passion) to sustain the emotional tension in very opposition to his stoic calm. The murder of Cæsar and its sequel sweeps the play up to a passionate height. The quarrel with the passionate Cassius, and the fine device of the withheld news of Portia's death, lift Brutus to an heroic height without any betrayal of the consistent nature of the man. But now we are at a standstill. Now, when we expect nemesis approaching, some deeper revelation, some glimpse of the hero's very soul, this hero stays inarticulate, or, worse, turns oracular. The picturing of him is kept to the end at a high pitch of simple beauty; but when – so we feel – the final and intimate tragic issue should open out, somehow it will not open. When Cæsar's ghost appears:

BRUTUS. Speak to me what thou art.
GHOST. Thy evil spirit, Brutus.
BRUTUS.   Why com'st thou?
GHOST. To tell thee thou shalt see me at Philippi.
BRUTUS. Well: then I shall see thee again.
GHOST. Ay, at Philippi.
BRUTUS. Why, I will see thee at Philippi, then.

That may be true Brutus, but it comes short of what we demand from the tragic hero of this calibre. And before Philippi, a step nearer to the end of this work the Ides of March began, we have from the philosopher so confused a reflection on his fate that we may well wonder whether Shakespeare himself, transcribing it from a mistranslated Plutarch, is quite certain what it means.[3]

We are left with

[3]   Even by the rule of that philosophy
              By which I did blame Cato . . .

Furness collects four full pages of notes endeavouring to discover exactly what Brutus does mean.

                    O! that a man might know
      The end of this day's business ere it come;
      But it sufficeth that the day will end,
      And then the end is known.

That is the voice, they are all but the very words of Hamlet.
Shakespeare is to run the gamut of the mood of helpless doubt
– the mood which has kept Hamlet our close kin through three
disintegrating centuries – to more if not to better purpose.
With Brutus it but masks the avoiding of the spiritual issue.
And he is sent to his death, a figure of gracious dignity, the
noblest Roman of them all, but with eyes averted from the
issue still.

                    Countrymen,
      My heart doth joy that yet in all my life
      I found no man but he was true to me. . . .
      Night hangs upon mine eyes; my bones would rest,
      That have but labour'd to attain this hour.

   The plain fact is, one fears, that Shakespeare, even if he
can say he understands Brutus, can in this last analysis *make*
nothing of him; and no phrase better fits a playwright's particular sort of failure. He has let him go his own reasoning way,
has faithfully abetted him in it, has hoped that from beneath
this crust of thought the fires will finally blaze. He can conjure
up a flare or two, and the love and grief for Portia might
promise a fusing of the man's whole nature in a tragic passion
outpassing anything yet. But the essential tragedy centered in
Brutus' own soul, the tragedy of the man who, not from hate,
envy nor weakness, but

            only, in a general honest thought
            And common good to all . . .

made one with the conspirators and murdered his friend; this,
which Shakespeare rightly saw as the supremely interesting
issue, comes to no more revelation than is in the last weary

                            193

Cæsar, now be still:
I killed not thee with half so good a will.

Shakespeare's own artistic disposition is not sufficiently attuned to this tragedy of intellectual integrity, of principles too firmly held. He can appreciate the nature of the man, but not, in the end, assimilate it imaginatively to his own. He is searching for the hero in whom thought and emotion will combine and contend on more equal terms; and when the end of Brutus baffles him, here is Hamlet, so to speak, waiting to begin. For the rest, he at least reaps the reward, a better than Brutus did, of integrity and consistency. He never falsifies the character, and, in its limited achievement, it endures and sustains the play to the end. He had preserved, we may say, for use at need, his actor's gift of making effective things he did not fully understand; and the Brutus of the play will make call enough upon any actor, even should he know a little more about the historic Brutus – whom, after all, he is not here called on to understand – than Shakespeare did.

CASSIUS

Cassius, the man of passion, is set in strong contrast to Brutus, the philosopher; and to stress the first impression he himself will make on us, we have Cæsar's own grimly humorous assessment of him:

> Yond Cassius has a lean and hungry look;
> He thinks too much: such men are dangerous . . . .
> I fear him not;
> Yet if my name were liable to fear,
> I do not know the man I should avoid
> So soon as that spare Cassius. He reads much;
> He is a great observer, and he looks
> Quite through the deeds of men; he loves no plays,
> As thou dost, Antony; he hears no music;
> Seldom he smiles, and smiles in such a sort
> As if he mocked himself, and scorned his spirit
> That could be moved to smile at any thing.

> Such men as he be never at heart's ease
> Whiles they behold a greater than themselves,
> And therefore are they very dangerous. . . .

– a Puritan, that is to say, something of an ascetic, and with
the makings of a fanatic in him too. Already it will not be,
to Shakespeare's audience, a wholly unfamiliar figure. A
dangerous man, doubtless; and as much so sometimes to his
friends, they will feel, as to his enemies.

> Into what dangers would you lead me, Cassius,
> That you would have me seek into myself
> For that which is not in me?

the besought Brutus protests. At the best a man difficult to
deal with; jealous and thin-skinned; demanding much of his
friends, and quick to resent even a fancied slight. His very
first approach to Brutus:

> I do observe you now of late:
> I have not from your eyes that gentleness
> And show of love as I was wont to have. . . .

And in their quarrel the burden of his grievance is

> You love me not.

An egoist certainly; yet not ignobly so, seeking only his own
advantage. Convinced in a cause – as we find him convinced;
that Cæsar's rule in Rome must be free Rome's perdition – he
will fling himself into it and make no further question, argue its
incidental rights and wrongs no more, as Brutus may to weariness. For argument will have now become a kind of treason.
There lie doubt and the divided mind, which he detests in
others, and would dread in himself, since there lies weakness
too, while passion will carry him through, and give him power
to goad others on besides. Egoist he is, yet not intellectually
arrogant. He sees in Brutus the nobler nature and a finer mind,

and yields to his judgment even when he strongly feels that it is leading them astray. These principles! It would have been practical good sense to add Antony's death to Cæsar's; it was foolish to a degree – rapidly it proved so – to let him speak in the market place later; that was a petty business, after all, about Lucius Pella and his bribes; and to what does Brutus' insistence on his strategy lead them but to Philippi? It is as if he felt that in some such yielding fashion he must atone for those outbursts of rage that he will not control. And yet, despite exasperating failings, the man is lovable, as those which are spendthrift of themselves can be, and as – for all his virtues – Brutus is not.

Cassius is by no means all of a piece, and makes the more lifelike a character for that. He ruthlessly demands Antony's death (the cause demands it), but in a desperate crisis, with danger threatening, he can take sudden thought for Publius' age and weakness. He has marked respect for Brutus; but he does not scruple to play tricks on him, with the letter laid in the Prætor's chair, the placard pinned to the statue. And, despite his outbursts of passion, he can calculate at times pretty coolly. Why does he not go with the rest on that fatal morning to conduct Cæsar to the Senate House? He has said he will go –

> Nay, we will all of us be there to fetch him

– and it will not be sudden timidity, certainly, that sways him. Do second thoughts suggest that since Cæsar, as he knows, mistrusts him, his presence may rouse suspicion? Shakespeare leaves this to be implied – or not, since we may not remark his absence. Yet he has been so prominent a figure in the earlier scenes, that we can hardly help remarking it.[4]

He is cynical, and can be brutally downright. While Brutus is appealing to Antony's higher nature (Cæsar dead there between them) he comes out plump with a

---

[4] The omission of his name among the entrants may, of course, be a mere slip. In that case it is his silence throughout the scene which will be remarkable – which the actors of Cæsar and Cassius, at any rate, could hardly help making so.

> Your voice shall be as strong as any man's
> In the disposing of new dignities.

But his deep affection for Brutus rings true; even in the midst
of their quarrel, when he hears of Portia's death, as they
mutually say farewell.

> BRUTUS.   For ever, and for ever, farewell, Cassius!
>   If we do meet again, why, we shall smile;
>   If not, why then this parting was well made.
> CASSIUS. For ever, and for ever, farewell, Brutus!
>   If we do meet again, we'll smile indeed;
>   If not, 'tis true this parting was well made

– there is harmony in the echoing exchange itself; and they do
not meet again.

The cynical Cassius shows in the soliloquy:

> Well, Brutus, thou art noble; yet, I see,
> Thy honourable metal may be wrought
> From that it is disposed: therefore 'tis meet
> That noble minds keep ever with their likes;
> For who so firm that cannot be seduced? . . .

– it is at this very moment that he is scheming to seduce his
much-admired friend by the papers thrown in at his window
and other such devices. Beneath his enthusiasms and rash
humours there is a certain coldness of passion, which gives
him tenacity, lets him consider and plan, the tension of his
temper never slackening; and it is in this combination of opposites that the man is most dangerous. He will put his very
faults to use, do things for his cause that he never would for
himself, yet not, as with Brutus, studiously justifying them. His
hatred for Cæsar the tyrant may well be rooted in jealousy
of Cæsar the man; if so, he is at no pains to disguise it. But
he is incapable of protesting his love for him at one moment,
while – on principle – he will strike him down the next.

So forthcoming a man, so self-revealing as he naturally is,

what character could better animate the play's opening, and get the action under way? But there must soon come a check. No play can continue at such a strain, to the fatiguing of actors and audience both. It comes with this very soliloquy,

> Well, Brutus, thou art noble. . . .

and here, if Shakespeare meant to dig deeper into Cassius' nature, would be the chance. But he avoids it. Brutus is to be the introspective character, the play's spiritual hero, so to speak; and there will not be room for two. Nor (as we said) is Cassius the man to spend time in self-searching, though he urges Brutus to. So the soliloquy – the only one allotted him – matched against the extraordinary vitality of the earlier dialogue, falls a little flat, runs somewhat mechanically, rather too closely resembles one of those conventional plot-forwarding discourses to the audience, to which Shakespeare has long learned to give richer use; and it demands the final whip-up of that rhymed couplet. At this juncture, then, and for a while longer we learn little more about Cassius. In the scene of the storm that follows he is eloquent and passionate still. But it is the same gamut that he runs. And in the scenes which follow this he strikes the same notes, of a rather arid desperation. Not until the later quarrel with Brutus is he fully and strikingly reanimated; but then indeed the intimacy opens up, of which we shall have felt deprived before. We have no deliberate and explanatory self-confession (that, again, belongs to Brutus), simply an illustrative picture of Cassius in word and action, companion to that earlier one.

He has not changed, yet circumstances have changed him. In that paradox lies the tragedy of such natures. He was jealous of Cæsar then, and he has turned jealous of Brutus now; of his friend as he was of his enemy. So Cæsar read him aright:

> Such men as he be never at heart's ease
> Whiles they behold a greater than themselves. . . .

He slights Brutus' generalship as he once contemned Cæsar's

courage. He is as quick and as shrewd and as shrewish as ever. But then it was:

> Well, honour is the subject of my story. . . .

and now he is prudently excusing a rogue, with his own honour in question. The one-time eloquent candour has turned to blustering and scolding. Yet, even while he rages, he knows he is in the wrong. His pride is little more than a mask. And the lofty Brutus has but to soften towards him – one touch of simple humanity suffices – and he breaks down like a child. He is pleading now:

> O, Brutus!
> > What's the matter?
> Have you not love enough to bear with me,
> When that rash humour which my mother gave me
> Makes me forgetful?

And from now on, as if – so we noted – in atonement, he will follow the younger man's mistaken lead, convinced as he is that it is mistaken. He only craves affection:

> > > O, my dear brother,
> This was an ill beginning of the night:
> Never come such division 'tween our souls!
> Let it not, Brutus

abases himself – he, the elder soldier – with that

> Good night, my lord

the now indulgent Brutus quickly preventing him with a

> Good night, good brother.

But thus it is with these catastrophic natures. They spend themselves freely, but demand half the world in exchange. They behave intolerably, try their friends' patience beyond all bounds, confidently expecting, for the sake of their love for them, to be forgiven. They know and confess to their faults, but with no intention of amendment; you must take them, they say, "as they are".

Old Cassius still!

mocks Antony, when the two meet again, parleying before the battle. And certainly the sharp tongue is by then as sharp as ever. At which point we remark too that the quarrel with Brutus and the reconciliation after have proved to Cassius both relief and comfort. For despite ill-omens, and his unchanged distrust in Brutus' soldiership, he proclaims himself

> fresh of spirit and resolved
> To meet all perils very constantly.

But, the battle joined, in the fury of fancied defeat he will kill his own standard-bearer, and himself, in his impatient despair. Old Cassius still!

ANTONY

> There is a tide in the affairs of men,
> Which, taken at the flood, leads on to fortune. . . .

Mark Antony cannot always talk so wisely, but he takes the tide that Brutus loses. He is a born opportunist, and we see him best in the light of his great opportunity. He stands contrasted with both Cassius and Brutus, with the man whom his fellows respect the more for his aloofness, and with such a rasping colleague as Cassius must be. Antony is, above all things, a good sort.

Shakespeare keeps him in ambush throughout the first part of the play. Up to the time when he faces the triumphant conspirators he speaks just thirty-three words. But there have already been no less than seven separate references to him, all significant. And this careful preparation culminates as significantly in the pregnant message he sends by his servant from the house to which it seems he has fled, bewildered by the catastrophe of Cæsar's death. Yet, as we listen, it is not the message of a very bewildered man. Antony, so far, is certainly – in what we might fancy would be his own lingo – a dark horse. And, though we may father him on Plutarch, to English eyes there can be no more typcially English figure than the sportsman turned statesman, but a sportsman still. Such men range up and down our history. Antony is something besides, however, that we used to flatter ourselves was not quite so English. He can be, when occasion serves, the perfect demagogue. Nor has Shakespeare any illusions as to what the harsher needs of politics may convert your sportsman once he is out to kill. The conspirators are fair game doubtless. But Lepidus, a little later, will be the carted stag.

> A barren-spirited fellow; one that feeds
> On abject orts and imitations,
> Which, out of use and staled by other men,
> Begin his fashion: do no talk of him
> But as a property . . .

to serve the jovial Antony's turn! This is your good sort, your sportsman, your popular orator, stripped very bare.

The servant's entrance with Antony's message, checking the conspirators' triumph, significant in its insignificance, is the turning point of the play.[5] But Shakespeare plucks further advantage from it. It allows him to bring Antony out of ambush completely effective and in double guise; the message foreshadows him as politician, a minute later we see him grieving deeply for his friend's death. There is, of course, nothing incompatible in the two aspects of the man, but the double impression is all-important. He must impress us as uncalculatingly abandoned to his feelings, risking his very life to vent them. For a part of his strength lies in impulse; he can abandon himself to his feelings, as Brutus the philosopher cannot. Moreover, this bold simplicity is his safe-conduct now. Were the conspirators not impressed by it, did

[5] As Moulton demonstrates in an admirable passage.

it not seem to obliterate his politic side, they might well and
wisely take him at his word and finish with him then and
there. And at the back of his mind Antony has this registered
clearly enough. It must be with something of the sportsman's
– and the artist's – happy recklessness that he flings the temptation at them:

> Live a thousand years,
> I shall not find myself so apt to die:
> No place will please me so, no mean of death,
> As here by Cæsar, and by you cut off,
> The choice and master spirits of this age.

He means it; but he knows, as he says it, that there is no
better way of turning the sword of a so flattered choice and
master spirit aside. It is this politic, shadowed aspect of
Antony that is to be their undoing; so Shakespeare is concerned to keep it clear at the back of our minds too. Therefore he impresses it on us first by the servant's speech, and
Antony himself is free a little later to win us and the conspirators both.

Not that the politician does not begin to peep pretty soon.
He tactfully ignores the cynicism of Cassius,

> Your voice shall be as strong as any man's
> In the disposing of new dignities.

But by Brutus' reiterated protest that Cæsar was killed in
wise kindness what realist, what ironist – and Antony is both
– would not be tempted?

> I doubt not of your wisdom.
> Let each man render me his bloody hand. . . .

And, in bitter irony, he caps their ritual with his own. It is
the ritual of friendship, but of such a friendship as the blood
of Cæsar, murdered by his friends, may best cement. To
Brutus the place of honour in the compact; to each red-handed

devotee his due; and last, but by no means least, in Antony's love shall be Trebonius who drew him away while the deed was done. And so to the final, most fitting apostrophe:

Gentlemen all!

Emotion subsided, the politician plays a good game. They shall never be able to say he approved their deed; but he is waiting, please, for those convincing reasons that Cæsar was dangerous. He even lets slip a friendly warning to Cassius that the prospect is not quite clear. Then, with yet more disarming frankness, comes the challenging request to Brutus to let him speak in the market place. As he makes it, a well-calculated request! For how can Brutus refuse, how admit a doubt that the Roman people will not approve this hard service done them? Still, that there may be no doubt at all, Brutus will first explain everything to his fellow-citizens himself, lucidly and calmly. When reason has made sure of her sway, the emotional, the "gamesome", Antony may do homage to his friend.

Be it so;
I do desire no more

responds Antony, all docility and humility, all gravity – though if ever a smile could sharpen words, it could give a grim edge to these. So they leave him with dead Cæsar.

In this contest thus opened between the man of high argument and the instinctive politician, between principle (mistaken or not) and opportunism, we must remember that Antony can be by no means confident of success. He foresees chaos. He knows, if these bemused patriots do not, that it takes more than correct republican doctrines to replace a great man. But as to this Roman mob – this citizenry, save the mark! – whoever knows which way it will turn? The odds are on the whole against him. Still he'll try his luck; Octavius, though, had better keep safely out of the way meanwhile. All his senses are sharpened by emergency. Before ever Octavius' servant can speak he has recognized the fellow and

guessed the errand. Shakespeare shows us his mind at its
swift work, its purposes shaping.

> Passion, I see, is catching, for mine eyes,
> Seeing those beads of sorrow stand in thine,
> Began to water

– from which it follows that if the sight of Cæsar's body can
so move the man and the man's tears so move him, why,
his own passion may move his hearers in the market place
presently to some purpose. His imagination, once it takes fire,
flashes its way along, not by reason's slow process though in
reason's terms.[6]

To what he is to move his hearers we know: and it will be
worth while later to analyse the famous speech, that triumph
of histrionics.[7] For though the actor of Antony must move
us with it also – and he can scarcely fail to – Shakespeare has
set him the further, harder and far more important task of
showing us an Antony the mob never see, of making him
clear to us, moreover, even while we are stirred by his
eloquence, of making clear to us just by what it is we are
stirred. It would, after all, be pretty poor playwriting and
acting which could achieve no more than a plain piece of
mob oratory, however gorgeous; a pretty poor compliment
to an audience to ask of it no subtler response than the mob's.

[6] How many modern actors upon their picture stage, with its curtain
to close a scene for them pat upon some triumphant top note, have
brought this one to its end twenty lines earlier upon the familiar, tremendous, breathless apostrophe (did Shakespeare ever pen such another sentence?) that begins,

> Woe to the hand that shed this costly blood!
> Over thy wounds now do I prophesy . . .

But to how untimely an end! The mechanism of Shakespeare's theatre
forbade such effects. Cæsar's body is lying on the main stage, and
must be removed, and it will take at least two people to carry it. Here
is one reason for the arrival of Octavius' servant. But as ever with
Shakespeare, and with any artist worth his salt, limitation is turned to
advantage. If dead Cæsar is to be the mainspring of the play's further
action, what more forceful way could be found of making this plain
than, for a finish to the scene, to state the new theme of Octavius'
coming, Cæsar's kin and successor?

[7] See p. 134.

But to show us, and never for a moment to let slip from our sight, the complete and complex Antony, impulsive and calculating, warm-hearted and callous, aristocrat, sportsman and demagogue, that will be for the actor an achievement indeed; and the playwright has given him all the material for it.

Shakespeare himself knows, no one better, what mere histrionics may amount to. He has been accused of showing in a later play (but unjustly, I hold) his too great contempt for the mob; he might then have felt something deeper than contempt for the man who could move the mob by such means; he may even have thought Brutus made the better speech. Antony, to be sure, is more than an actor; for one thing he writes his own part as he goes along. But he gathers the ideas for it as he goes too, with no greater care for their worth than the actor need have so long as they are effective at the moment. He lives abundantly in the present, his response to its call is unerring. He risks the future. How does the great oration end?

> Mischief, thou are afoot;
> Take thou what course thou wilt!

A wicked child, one would say, that has whipped up his fellow-children to a riot of folly and violence. That is one side of him. But the moment after he is off, brisk, cool and businesslike, to play the next move in the game with that very cool customer, Octavius.

He has had no tiresome principles to consult or to expound.

> I only speak right on....

he boasts;

> I tell you that which you yourselves do know.

An admirable maxim for popular orators and popular writers too! There is nothing aloof, nothing superior about Antony. He may show a savage contempt for this man or that; he has a sort of liking for men in the mass. He is, in fact, the common man made perfect in his commonness; yet he is perceptive of himself as of his fellows, and, even so, content.

What follows upon his eloquent mourning for Cæsar? When the chaos in Rome has subsided he ropes his "merry fortune" into harness. It is not a very pleasant colloquy with which the fourth act opens.

ANTONY. These many then shall die; their names are pricked.

OCTAVIUS. Your brother too must die; consent you, Lepidus?

LEPIDUS. I do consent.

OCTAVIUS.   Prick him down, Antony.

LEPIDUS. Upon condition Publius shall not live, Who is your sister's son, Mark Antony.

ANTONY. He shall not live; look, with a spot I damn him.

The conspirators have, of course, little right to complain. But four lines later we learn that Lepidus himself, when his two friends have had their use of him, is to fare not much better than his brother – than the brother he has himself just given so callously to death! Can he complain either, then? This is the sort of beneficence the benevolent Brutus has let loose on the world.

But Antony finishes the play in fine form; victorious in battle, politicly magnanimous to a prisoner or two, and ready with a resounding tribute to Brutus, now that he lies dead. Not in quite such fine form, though; for the shadow of that most unsportsmanlike young man Octavius is already moving visibly to his eclipse.

These, then are the three men among whom Shakespeare divides this dramatic realm; the idealist, the egoist, the opportunist. The contrast between them must be kept clear in the acting by all that the actors do and are, for upon its tension the living structure of the play depends. And, it goes without saying, they must be shown to us as fellow-creatures, not as abstractions from a dead past. For so Shakespeare saw them; and, if he missed something of the mind of the Roman, yet these three stand with sufficient truth for the sum of the human forces, which in any age, and in ours as in his, hold the world in dispute.

OCTAVIUS CÆSAR

He tags to the three another figure; and perhaps nothing in the play is better done, within its limits, than is the outline of Octavius Cæsar, the man who in patience will reap when all this bitter seed has been sown. He appears three times, speaks some thirty lines, and not one of them is wasted. We see him first with Antony and Lepidus. He watches them trade away the lives of their friends and kinsmen. And when Antony, left alone with him, proposes to "double-cross" Lepidus, he only answers,

> You may do your will;
> But he's a tried and valiant soldier.

It is the opening of a window into this young man's well-ordered mind. Lepidus is a good soldier, he approves of Lepidus. But Antony is powerful for the moment, it won't do to oppose Antony. Lepidus must suffer then. Still, should things turn out differently, let Antony remember that this was his own proposal, and that Octavius never approved of it.[8]

By the next scene, however, this quiet youth has grown surer – not of himself, that he has no need to be, but of his place amid the shifting of events.

ANTONY.	Octavius, lead your battle softly on,
	Upon the left hand of the even field.
OCTAVIUS.	Upon the right hand, I; keep thou the left.
ANTONY.	Why do you cross me in this exigent?
OCTAVIUS.	I do not cross you; but I will do so.

He is quite civil about it; but he means to have his way, his

---

[8] *Julius Cæsar* begins the cycle of Shakespeare's greater plays, and *Antony and Cleopatra* ends it. The later relations of Octavius and Antony are implicit in this little scene. The realist, losing grip, will find himself "out-realized" by his pupil.

chosen place in the battle and chief credit for the victory. And Antony does not argue the point. When the opponents in the coming battle are face to face, Cassius and Antony and even Brutus may outscold each the other for past offences. The practical Octavius, with a mind to the present and to his own future, is impatient of such childishness.

> Come, come, the cause: if arguing make us sweat,
> The proof of it will turn to redder drops.
> Look, I draw sword against conspirators;
> When think you that the sword goes up again?
> Never, till Cæsar's three-and-thirty wounds
> Be well aveng'd; or till another Cæsar
> Have added slaughter to the sword of traitors.

This is the first time he has spoken out, and he speaks to some purpose. Nor does he give place to Antony again. When we see them together for the last time in victorious procession, Octavius has the lead.

> All that serv'd Brutus, I will entertain them

"I", not "we". And Shakespeare gives him the play's last word.

CÆSAR

What now of the great shadow of Cæsar which looms over the whole? Let us admit that, even while he lives and speaks, it is more shadow than substance. Is it too harsh a comment that Cæsar is in the play merely to be assassinated? But to have done better by him would have meant, would it not, doing worse by the play as it is planned? Certainly to centre every effort – and it could hardly be done with less – upon presenting to us

> the foremost man of all this world . . .

and then to remove him at the beginning of Act III would

208

leave a gap which no new interest could fill. But there are innate difficulties in the putting of any great historical figure upon the stage: and these, as it happens, would have pressed hard upon Shakespeare just at this stage of his development. He had left behind him the writing of that formal rhetoric which was the accepted dramatic full dress for the great man. He was moulding his verse to the expressing of individual emotion, fitting his whole method to the showing of intimate human conflict. Now a great man's greatness seldom exists in his personal relations. To depict it, then, the dramatist will be thrown back on description, or narrative, or on the effect of the greatness upon the characters around. The last expedient may shift our interest to the surrounding characters themselves. Narrative soon becomes tiresome. And as to description; the great man himself, in the person of his actor, is too apt to belie it. Keep him immobile and taciturn, and the play will halt. But if he talks of his own achievements he will seem a boaster. And if he is always seen in action we can have no picture of the inner man. The convention of Greek drama offers some escape from these dilemmas; for there the man is, so to speak, made in his greatness a symbol of himself, and in a symbol one may sum up a truth. Shakespeare had, certainly, the refuge of soliloquy. Show us the heart of a Cæsar, though, by that means, and where will our interest in the self-revealings of a Brutus be? And it is, we have argued, upon Brutus' spiritual tragedy that Shakespeare's best thoughts are fixed. He comes, therefore, to showing us a Cæsar seen somewhat from Brutus' point of view; a noble figure and eloquent, but our knowledge of him stays skin-deep. It is historically possible, of course, that the virtue had gone out of Cæsar, that no more was left now than this façade of a great man. But we need not credit Shakespeare with the theory. Quite certainly he wishes to show us the accepted Cæsar of history. The innate difficulty of doing so may defeat him; the limitations of the play, as he has planned it, must. And if he has to choose, and it becomes a question of his play's safety, Cæsar will count no more with him than any other character.

But it follows that, as he cannot attempt to do Cæsar dramatic justice, the more we see of him the worse it is. For the devices by which his supremacy can be made effective are soon exhausted and do not bear repetition. The start is excellent. What could be more impressive than that first procession across the stage? Here Shakespeare tries the taciturn-immobile method, and couples it with a strict simplicity of speech; all one can call a trick is the repetition of the name, and Cæsar's own use of it, and even this is legitimate enough. While, for a finish, the confronting of the Soothsayer:

CASSIUS.   Fellow, come from the throng; look upon
            Cæsar.
CÆSAR.   What say'st thou to me now? Speak once
            again.
SOOTHSAYER. Beware the Ides of March.
CÆSAR.   He is a dreamer; let us leave him: pass.

Here is the great man; assuming no attitude, explaining nothing, indifferent to seeming trifles. What could be better? The last line is pure gold.

The episode of the returning procession is as good. That sidelong perceptive survey of Cassius with its deep-biting humour:

Let me have men about me that are fat,
Sleek-headed men, and such as sleep a-nights.
Yond Cassius had a lean and hungry look;
He thinks too much: such men are dangerous.

The yet deeper-bitten realism of

He reads much;
He is a great observer, and he looks
Quite through the deeds of men; he loves no plays,
As thou dost, Antony; he hears no music;
Seldom he smiles, and smiles in such a sort
As if he mock'd himself, and scorn'd his spirit

210

35 The murder of Caesar. Caesar, Charles Fulton; Brutus, Lewis Waller

BEERBOHM TREE'S PRODUCTION OF JULIUS CAESAR; HER MAJESTY'S, 1898

36 Antony's Oration. Antony, Beerbohm Tree

37   The Forum (showing the set's basic structure)

LEWIS CASSON'S PRODUCTION OF JULIUS CAESAR; GAIETY THEATRE, MANCHESTER, 1913

(A single, built set, capable of instant scene changes, providing
for "absolute continuity of voice and action throughout")

38   The Senate House (arches closed by curtains, steps re-set)

**39–40 JULIUS CAESAR, DESIGNED AND PRODUCED BY W. BRIDGES-ADAMS
AT THE OLD THEATRE, STRATFORD-UPON-AVON, 1919
(Reproduced from his own drawings)**

Full sets, with high cyclorama. "The producer's aim was to combine
the spaciousness, intimacy and continuity of action of the Elizabethan
stage with as much scenic effect as seemed desirable. As a rule,
changes were made by the opening or closing of a pair of traverses."

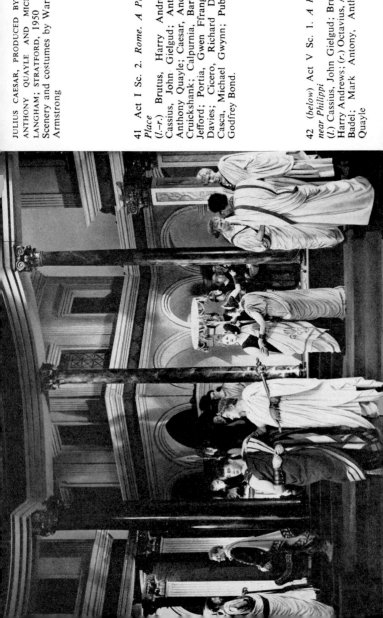

JULIUS CAESAR, PRODUCED BY
ANTHONY QUAYLE AND MICHAEL
LANGHAM; STRATFORD, 1950
Scenery and costumes by Warwick
Armstrong

41 Act I Sc. 2. *Rome. A Public
Place*
(*l.-r.*) Brutus, Harry Andrews;
Cassius, John Gielgud; Antony,
Anthony Quayle; Caesar, Andrew
Cruickshank; Calpurnia, Barbara
Jefford; Portia, Gwen Ffrangcon
Davies; Cicero, Richard Dare;
Casca, Michael Gwynn; Publius,
Godfrey Bond.

42 (*below*) Act V Sc. 1. *A Plain
near Philippi*
(*l.*) Cassius, John Gielgud; Brutus,
Harry Andrews; (*r.*) Octavius, Alan
Badel; Mark Antony, Anthony
Quayle

"Shakespeare, by convention, dressed his Romans more or less in Elizabethan clothes." (Barker's *Preface*, 1925)

43–45 AN EXPERIMENT IN ELIZABETHANISM AT THE OLD VIC, 1953
Hugh Hunt's production of *Julius Caesar*

43 (*above*) The Conspirators   44 (*below*) Before the murder of Caesar

no other characters reach primary im-
effective rather than important, and the
t him is of the break from prose to verse
Scenes ii and iii), which points a kindred
able break in the composition of the char-
l very well to say with Dowden that Casca
rm with his "superficial garb of cynicism
while dramatic consistency may be a virtue,
gives us an instance of "a piece of higher
inconsistency of his characters". If it were
ld still be very clumsily done. What means
h of showing that this is a dramatic inconsist-
r see one flutter of that superficial garb of
Casca remains hereafter the commonplace
rm-scene; the humorous blunt fellow seems
Certainly we have had Cassius' apology for

puts on this tardy form . . .

age in which that occurs is itself weak and
nd it might arguably have been written in to
msiness of the change. The actor must do what
ld the two halves of the man together; but it is
ether he can make this "piece of higher art"

ucer must remember that nine-tenths of the play
eak, orchestrated for men only; the greater the
casting of the parts to set them in due contrast
other. The sort of acting a part needs is usually
enough; if not by some reference, acting itself
is. For instance, if nothing definitely directs us to
Flavius and Marullus of the first scene a mild mar
sterfully noisy one, yet in the acting they will be
answer effectively to that difference. For the cast
cero, on the other hand, we have definite, if mainl
facto, direction; his elderly dry irony is set, whe

212

"We cannot escape from this invented world of Renaissance-Romanism that
Shakespeare uses." (Hugh Hunt: *Old Vic Prefaces*, 1954)
45 The quarrel scene: Brutus, William Devlin: Cassius, Paul Rogers

46 JULIUS CAESAR IN THE CLASSICAL MANNER, STRATFORD ONTARIO FESTIVAL, 1955
Directed by Michael Langham; designed by Tanya Moiseiwitsch

47 JULIUS CAESAR, PRODUCED BY JOHN WYSE, STRATFORD-UPON-AVON, 1936, COSTUMES, BARBARA CURTIS; SCENES, J. WYSE, WITH JAMES COX
Peter Glenville as Mark Antony

That co
Such me
Whiles th
And there

The precise sim
raised above his

    I rather
    Than wh

But it is from this
Cæsar turns to talk
the living man is lost
only to be lost again

    Cæsar should
    If he should s
    No, Cæsar shal
    That Cæsar is
    We are two lion
    And I the elder a
    And Cæsar shall

– while the Olympian speed
a little surprised that a mon
to flow from him. Shakespea
merely into this queer *oratio*
carded rhetoric for its own s
characters round Cæsar stays
actor must effect what sort of
this simulacrum of greatness a
To think of Cæsar as now no
reverberating hollowly, the life
is one way. It must weaken the p
desperate an enterprise to consp
Or is such a frigid tyranny the m
But the supersubtlety of that interpr

211

C A

Among the men
portance. Casca is
only question abou
(as between Act I,
but hardly warrant
acter itself. It is a
appears in the st
dropt", and that,
Shakespeare here
art, the dramatic
so the thing wou
is the actor giver
ency? We neve
cynicism again
Casca of the s
forgotten quite
him, that he

But the pass
mechanical, a
excuse the cl
he can to we
doubtful wh
very valid.
The prod
is, so to sp
need in the
with each
made plain
will test th
make the
and a ma
found to
ing of Ci
ex post

the two meet, in strong contrast with the new ebullient Casca. It is to be noted, by the way, that Shakespeare, history apart, thinks of the conspirators as fairly young men. By theatrical tradition Caius Ligarius is made old as well as ill, but there is nothing to warrant this (for an ague does not warrant it), nor any dramatic gain in it.

Cinna the poet is specified plainly enough in the dandification of

> What is my name? Wither am I going? Where do I dwell? Am I a married man or a bachelor? Then, to answer every man directly and briefly, wisely and truly; wisely I say, I am a bachelor.

The nameless poet of Act IV must be even more eccentric if his flying visit is to be made effective. Cassius calls him a cynic. He is, one supposes, a shabby, ballad-mongering fellow; his modern instance shuffles through the *cafés* of Montmartre today. Shakespeare, rapt in this world of great doings, is a little hard on poets – as some poets are apt to be.

The soldiers that belong to the play's last phase, Messala, Lucilius, Titinius, young Cato, Pindarus, Volumnius, Strato and the rest, can all be known for what they are by considering what they do. In no play, I think, does Shakespeare provide, in such a necessarily small space, for such a vivid array. As parts of a battlepiece, the unity of the subject harmonizes them, but within that harmony each is very definitely and effectively himself.

CALPURNIA AND PORTIA

The boy Lucius has sometimes been played by a woman. This is an abomination. Let us not forget, on the other hand, that Calpurnia was written to be played by a boy. Producers are inclined to make a fine figure of her, to give her (there being but two women in the play) weight and importance, to fix on some well-proportioned lady, who will wear the purple with an air. But Shakespeare's intention is as plain as daylight; and in a part of twenty-six lines there can be no compromise, it must be hit or miss. Calpurnia is a nervous, fear-haunted creature. Nor does she, like Portia, make any attempt to conceal her fears. She is desperate and helpless. Portia, with her watchful constancy, can win Brutus' secret from him. Cæsar treats Calpurnia like a child. Her pleading with him is a frightened child's pleading. Her silence when Decius and the rest come to fetch him to the Senate House is as pathetic in its helplessness. She stands isolated and tremulous, watching him go in to taste wine with these good friends. Failing the right sort of Calpurnia, the dramatic value of her share in the scene will be lost.

A quiet beauty is the note of Portia, and Shakespeare sounds it at once. Her appearance is admirably contrived. The conspirators have gone, Brutus is alone again, and the night's deep stillness is recalled.

> Boy! Lucius! Fast asleep? It is no matter;
> Enjoy the honey-heavy dew of slumber:
> Thou hast no figures nor no fantasies
> Which busy care draws in the brains of men;
> Therefore thou sleep'st so sound.

But so softly she comes, that for all the stillness he is unaware of her, until the soft voice, barely breaking it, says,

> Brutus, my lord!

Portia is a portrait in miniature. But how suited the character itself is to such treatment, and how Shakespeare subdues his power to its delicacy! The whole play is remarkable for simplicity and directness of speech; nothing could exemplify her better. For she is seen not as a clever woman, nor is she witty, and she speaks without coquetry of her "once-commended beauty". She is homekeeping and content; she is yielding, but from good sense, which she does not fear will seem weakness. She has dignity and perfect courage.

Note how everything in the scene – not the words and their meaning only – contributes to build up this Portia. The quiet

entrance, the collected thought and sustained rhythm of her
unchecked speech, the homely talk of supper-time and of
the impatient Brutus scratching his head and stamping, and
of the risk he is running now of catching cold; nothing more
wonderful than this is the foundation for the appeal to

> that great vow
> Which did incorporate and make us one . . .

Nor does the appeal at its very height disturb the even music
of the verse. For with her such feelings do not ebb and flow;
they lie deep down, they are a faith. She is, as we should
say, all of a piece; and her very gentleness, her very reason-
ableness is her strength. Even her pride has its modesty.

> I grant I am a woman, but, withal,
> A woman that Lord Brutus took to wife;
> I grant I am a woman; but, withal,
> A woman well-reputed, Cato's daughter;
> Think you I am no stronger than my sex,
> Being so father'd and so husbanded?

The repeated phrase and the stressed consonants give the
verse a sudden vigour; they contrast with the drop back to
simplicity of

> Tell me your counsels, I will not disclose 'em.
> I have made strong proof of my constancy,
> Giving myself a voluntary wound
> Here, in the thigh: can I bear that with patience
> And not my husband's secrets?

To this, with imperceptibly accumulating force, with that one
flash of pride for warning, the whole scene has led. A single
stroke, powerful in its reticence, as fine in itself as it is true
to Portia.

Then, lest she should seem too good to be true, Shakespeare adds a scene of anticlimax; of a Portia confessing to

weakness, all nerves, miserably conscious that her page's sharp young eyes are fixed on her; outfacing, though, the old Soothsayer, and, with a final effort, spiritedly herself again. While, for one more touch of truth, he gives us,

> O Brutus!
> The heavens speed thee in thine enterprise.

Murder is the enterprise, and Cato's daughter knows it. But he is her Brutus, so may the heavens speed him even in this.

The Play's Structure

There is a powerful ease in the construction of *Julius Cæsar* which shows us a Shakespeare master of his means, and it is the play in which the boundaries of his art begin so markedly to widen. We find in it, therefore, a stagecraft, not of a too accustomed perfection, but bold and free. The theme calls forth all his resources and inspires their fresh and vigorous use; yet it does not strain them, as some later and, if greater, less accommodating themes are to do. We may here study Elizabethan stagecraft, as such, almost if not quite at its best; and a close analysis of the play's action, the effects in it and the way they are gained – a task for the producer in any case – will have this further interest.

Plutarch was a godsend to Shakespeare. Rome, Cæsar and high heroic verse, one knows what such a mixture may amount to in the theatre; though we may suppose that, with his lively mind, he would never have touched the subject had he not found that admirable historian, who, with happy familiarity, tucks an arm in ours, so to speak, and leads us his observant, anecdotic way, humanizing history, yet never diminishing its magnificence. Plutarch's genius, in fact, is closely allied to Shakespeare's own, with its power to make, by a touch or so of nature, great men and simple, present and past, the real and the mimic world, one kin. And this particular power was in the ascendant with Shakespeare now.

He redraws the outline of the story more simply, but he cannot resist crowding characters in. What wonder, when they are all so striking, and he knows he can make a living man out of a dozen lines of dialogue? The fifth act is a galaxy of such creations. And if, on the other hand, Artemidorus and the Soothsayer have little or no life of their own, while the poet of Act IV is a mere irruption into the play, a species of human ordnance shot off, their momentarily important part in the action lends them reflected life enough. But much of the play's virtue lies in the continual invention and abundant vitality of these incidental figures by which the rarer life, so to call it, of the chief characters is at intervals nourished. And as there is no formal mechanism of plot, it is largely with their aid that the action moves forward with such a varied rhythm, upon an ebb and flow of minor event that is most lifelike. The whole play is alive; it is alive in every line.

Elizabethan stagecraft, with its time-freedom and space-freedom, gives the playwright great scope for manœuvering minor character and incident. He may conjure a character into sudden prominence, and be done with it as suddenly. He has not, as in the modern "realistic" theatre, to relate it to the likelihoods of hard-and-fast time and place. The modern dramatist plans his play by large divisons, even as the Greek dramatist did. Time and place must suit the need of his chief characters; if minor ones can't be accommodating they can't be accommodated, that's all. The Elizabethan dramatist has his story to tell, and the fate of the chief figures in it to determine. But, as long as the march of the story is not stayed, he may do pretty well what he likes by the way. The modern dramatist thinks of his play constructively in acts; and the scenes must accommodate themselves to the act, as the acts to the play as a whole. The Elizabethan would instinctively do the contrary. This is not to say that a play did not commonly move to some larger rhythm than the incidental. Every playwright, every sort of artist indeed, feels for the form which will best accommodate his idea, and will come to prefer the comprehensive form. But whether this rhythm with Shakespeare resolved itself into acts is another matter; and that it would resolve itself into the five acts of the editors is more than doubtful.

The larger rhythm of *Julius Cæsar* can be variously interpreted. The action moves by one impetus, in a barely checked crescendo, to the end of Act III. Cæsar's murder is the theme; the mob provides a recurrent chorus of confusion, and ends, as it has begun, this part of the story. Acts IV and V are given to the murder's retribution; this unifies them. They are martial, more ordered, and, for all the fighting at the end, consistently pitched in a lower key. The five-act divison can, however, be defended dramatically; and, if it is valid, it shows us some interesting points of Elizabethan stagecraft. Act I is preparatory and leads up to the conspirators' winning of Brutus, though this itself is kept for the start of Act II. Modern practice would dictate a divison after Act I, Sc. ii; for here is a time interval and a change from day to night. But to Shakespeare – or his editor – it would be more important to begin a new act upon a new note, and with the dominant figure of Brutus to impress us. And this we find: each act of the five has a significant and striking beginning, while the ends of the first four all tail away. Act III begins with the ominous

> CÆSAR.   The Ides of March are come.
> SOOTHSAYER. Ay, Cæsar, but not gone.

Act IV with the sinister

> ANTONY.   These many then shall die; their names are
>   pricked.

Act V with the triumphant

> OCTAVIUS.   Now, Antony, our hopes are answered.

It is easy to see why the beginning of an Elizabethan "act" had to be striking.[9] There was no lowering of the lights, no music, no warning raps, while eyes "in front" concentrated

---

[9] But this might often be as true, if in another degree, of the individual scene.

upon an enigmatic curtain. The actors had to walk on and command the unprepared attention of a probably restless audience, and they needed appropriate material. Equally, to whatever crisis of emotion a scene might mount, they would have to walk off again. Therefore neither acts nor scenes, as a rule, end upon a crisis.

The play is too strenuous, if not too long, to be acted without at least one pause. It must occur, of course, at the end of Act III. This one should, I personally think, be enough; if pauses are to mean long intervals of talk and distraction, it certainly would be. But if a producer thinks more relief from the strain upon the audience is advisable (his actors do not need it), there is the breathing-space at the end of Act II – better not make more of it – and, if that will not suffice, he can pause at the end of Act I. He will be unwise, though, to divide Acts IV and V.

But the form of the play should first be studied in relation to its minor rhythms, for it is in these, in the setting of them one against the other, in their adjustment to the larger rhythm of the main theme, that the liveliness of Shakespeare's stage-craft is to be seen.

The action begins with the entry of the two Tribunes . . . *and certain commoners over the stage*. The Roman populace is to play an important part; we have now but a minute's glimpse of it, and in harmless holiday mood.

> Hence! home, you idle creatures, get you home:
> Is this a holiday?

The first lines spoken are a stage direction for the temper of the scene. It may be that the Globe Theatre "crowd" was not much of a crowd, was liable to be unrehearsed and inexact. Line after line scattered through the scene is contrived to describe indirectly how they should look and what they should be expressing. No audience but will accept the suggestion, though the crowd itself be a bit behindhand. Nor need a producer, here or elsewhere, strive to provide a realistically howling mob. The fugleman convention is a part of

219

the convention of the play; reason enough for abiding in it.

Note before we leave this scene how its first full-bodied speech has Pompey for a theme, and what emphasis is given to the first sound of his name. After the chattering prose of the cobbler comes Marullus'

> Wherefore rejoice? What conquest brings he home?
> What tributaries follow him to Rome
> To grace in captive bonds his chariot wheels?
> You blocks, you stones, you worse than senseless things!
> O you hard hearts, you cruel men of Rome,
> Knew you not Pompey?

For Pompey dead is to Cæsar something of what Cæsar dead is to be Brutus and the rest. And – though Shakespeare naturally does not prejudice an important effect by anticipating it and elaborating its parallel – the name's reiteration throughout the first part of the play has purpose.

A unity is given to these first three acts by the populace; by keeping them constantly in our minds. They are easily persuaded now, controlled and brought to silence:

> They vanish tongue-tied in their guiltiness.

The devastation of the third act's end has this mild beginning.

Against the disorder and inconsequence, Cæsar's processional entrance tells with doubled effect. We are given but a short sight of him, our impression is that he barely pauses on his way. His dominance is affimed by the simplest means. We hear the name sounded – sounded rather than spoken – seven times in twenty-four lines. The very name is to dominate. It is the cue for Cassius' later outburst:

> Brutus and Cæsar: what should be in that "Cæsar"?
> Why should that name be sounded more than yours?
> Write them together, yours is as fair a name;
> Sound them, it doth become the mouth as well;
> Weigh them, it is as heavy; conjure with 'em,

"Brutus" will start a spirit as soon as "Cæsar".

The procession passes. And now that these opposites, the many headed and the one, the mob and its moment's idol, have been set in clear contrast before us, the main action may begin.

It is Cassius' passion that chiefly gives tone and colour to the ensuing long duologue. He sets it a swift pace too, which is only checked by Brutus' slow responses; Brutus, lending one ear to his vehement friend, the other keen for the meaning of the distant shouts. Yet, in a sense, it is Cæsar who still holds the stage; in Cassius' rhetoric, in the shouting, in Brutus' strained attention. With his re-entrance, then, there need be no impression given of a fresh beginning, for the tension created by that first passage across the stage should hardly have been relaxed. It now increases, that is all. Cæsar pauses a little longer on his way, and with purpose. It is like the passing of a thundercloud; presage, in another sort, of the storm by which Nature is to mark his end. To the stately words and trumpet music the procession moves on; and we are left, with the proper shock of contrast, to Casca's acrid and irreverent prose. Now the tension does relax. Then Casca goes, and Brutus and Cassius part with but brief comment on him, without attempting to restore the broken harmony of their thoughts; and Cassius' closing soliloquy, as we have seen, is little more than a perfunctory forwarding of the story.

Thunder and lightning . . .

This, the stage empty, would emphasize well enough for the Elizabethans some break of time and place, and a few claps and flashes more might suffice to put a whole storm on record. It does not now suffice Shakespeare. He sets out upon a hundred and sixty-five lines of elaborate verbal scene-painting; in the economy of the plot they really stand for little more. It is not, of course, merely a passing pictorial effect that he is branding on his audience's imagination. Consider this passage in connection with those appeals of the Chorus in *Henry V*:

221

Think when we talk of horses that you see them
Printing their proud hoofs i' the receiving earth;
For 'tis your thoughts that now must deck our kings . . .

O! do but think
You stand upon the rivage and behold
A city on the inconstant billows dancing;
For so appears this fleet majestical,
Holding due course to Harfleur.

All that the listeners were to do for themselves, since the
dramatist could not even attempt to do it for them. Here
Shakespeare is certainly concerned to picture Rome under
the portentous storm, but it is upon the personal episodes he
fixes – upon the slave with his burning hand, the

hundred ghastly women,
Transformed with their fear, who swore they saw
Men all in fire walk up and down the streets . . .

upon the marvel of the lion that "glar'd upon" Casca and
"went surly by". And their value to him lies chiefly in their
effect upon the emotions of his characters; this is his path
to an effect upon ours. He has discovered, in fact, the one
dramatic use to which the picturesque can be put in his
theatre, and the one and only way of using it. It was not, of
course, a discovery sought and made all complete for the
occasion. But this is, I think, the first time he brings Nature
under such serious contribution. Make another comparison,
with the storm-scenes in *King Lear*. Set this scene beside
those, with their perfect fusion of character and surroundings
and their use to the play, and its method seems arbitrary
and crude enough. It takes the plot little further. And Cicero
is a walking shadow, Cinna a mere convenience; Casca, un-
nerved and eloquent, is unrecognizable as the Casca of the
previous scene, is turned to a convenience for picturing the
storm; while Cassius only repeats himself, and his rhetoric,
dramatically justified before, grows rodomontade. By the end

of the hundred and sixty-five lines we have learned that Cicero is cautious, Casca ripe, that things are moving fast with Cinna and the rest, that Brutus must be won. At his best Shakespeare could have achieved this in fifty lines or less and given us the storm into the bargain.

The contrasting calm of the next act's beginning is an appropriate setting for Brutus, the stoic, the man of conscience and gentle mind. The play's scheme now opens out and grows clear, for Brutus takes his allotted and fatal place among his fellows as moral dictator. To his dominance is due the scene's coldness and rigidity, though the unity of tone gives it dignity and its circumstance alone would make effective drama. Incidental things give it vitality and such colour as it needs; the coming and going of the sleepy boy, the knocking without, the striking of the clock followed by those three short echoing speeches. It all stays to the end rather static than dynamic; for high-mindedly as Brutus may harangue his "gentle friends", fervently as they may admire him, there is never, now or later, the spontaneous sympathy between them that alone gives life to a cause. The ultimate as well as the immediate tragedy is in the making.

The scene with Portia is the due sequel. Even from her he holds aloof. He loves her; but the more he loves her the less he can confide in her. Even the avowal of his love is wrung from him in a sort of agony. And Portia's own tragedy is in the making here. In her spent patience with his silence we might well divine the impatience at his absence which was to be her death. We may question why, after a vibrant climax, Shakespeare so lowers the tension for the scene's end. Caius Ligarius' coming will surely thrust Portia and this more intimate Brutus to the background of our remembrance. There are two answers at least. The play's main action must not only be carried on, but it must seem now to be hurried on, and Brutus, his philosophic reserve once broken, must be shown precipitate.[10] For another answer; the Caius Ligarius

[10] Here, incidentally, is an instance of an effect made for its own sake and in the confidence that no awkward questions will be asked. The immediate suggestion is that Brutus and Ligarius go straight to the conspirators, thence with them to Cæsar and the Senate House. It is

episode keeps the scenes between Brutus and Portia, Cæsar and Calpurnia apart. It would discount the second to bring it on the heels of the first.

Thunder and lightning herald the next scene's beginning; the purpose of its repetition is plain enough. The mood wrought in us by the storm must be restored; and in a moment comes Calpurnia's speech, which is a very echo of Casca's description of the signs and portents. Cæsar, rocklike at first against the pleadings of his wife, wavers from his love for her and yields to Decius' friendliness and flattery, reinforced by the thronging-in of the rest, looking, as Brutus bid them look, so "fresh and merrily'. It is good preparation for the catastrophe, the sudden livening of the scene with this group of resolute, cheerful men. Besides, might not the slim Decius have overreached himself but for their coming? Cæsar was no fool, and Calpurnia would be apt to every sort of suspicion. But the friendly faces disperse the last clouds of the ominous night. Cassius is not here. It is Brutus, the irreproachable Brutus, who gives tone to the proceeding. Does he, even at this moment, feel himself

arm'd so strong in honesty . . .

that he can meet Cæsar's magnanimity without flinching? Is it only ague that makes Caius Ligarius shake as Cæsar presses his hand? And that nothing of tragic irony may be wanting –

Good friends, go in, and taste some wine with me,
And we, like friends, will straightway go together.

The sacrament of hospitality and trust! It is a supreme effect, economized in words, fully effective only in action. And for an instance of Shakespeare's dramatic judgement, of his

left mere suggestion and not further defined, for Portia has to be told of the conspiracy "by and by", and, when we next see her, the suggestion – still mere suggestion – is that she has been told. But Shakespeare knows that no questions will be asked as long as the effects are spaced out, if distractions intervene and positive contradiction is avoided.

sense of balance between an immediate effect and the play's continuing purpose, of his power, in striking one note, to strike the ruthlessly right one, take the two lines with which Brutus, lagging back, ends the scene:

> That every like is not the same, O Cæsar!
> The heart of Brutus yearns to think upon.

Not that a pun or a quibble upon words necessarily struck an Elizabethan as a trifling thing. But it takes a Brutus to find refuge in a quibbling thought at such a moment, and in his own grief for his victim.

Cæsar is now ringed by the conspirators, the daggers are ready, and the two scenes that follow are to hold and prolong the suspense till they strike.[11] Artemidorus, with his paper and its comment, may seem unduly dry and detached. But the solitary anonymous figure comes as a relief and contrast to that significant group, and against that wrought emotion his very detachment tells. It contrasts too with Portia's tremulous intimate concern. The act's end here – if it is to mean a short empty pause while the audience stay seated and expectant, not an interval of talk and movement – will have value. The blow is about to fall, and in silence suspense is greatest. We draw breath for the two long scenes that form the centre section of the play.

Trumpets sound, the stage fills. Cæsar comes again as we saw him go, still circled by these friends, confident, outwardly serene. The trumpets silent, we hear another prelude, of two voices, the one ringing clear, the other pallidly echoing:

> CÆSAR.   The Ides of March are come.
> SOOTHSAYER. Ay, Cæsar, but not gone.

Then follows a little scuffle of voices, a quick shifting and elbowing in the group round Cæsar as the petitions are thrust

---

[11] Unless every clearance of the stage is to mark a division of scenes, they are, of course, but one. No particular change of location is implied. Upon the question of the act-division here, see also page 121.

forward and aside, and once again that fivefold iteration of the potent name. Despite the ceremony, nerves are on edge. Cæsar goes forward to be greeted by the Senators and to mount his state. Now comes a passage of eighteen lines. Toneless it has to be, that the speakers betray not their feelings. In the group of them there is hardly a movement; they must measure even their glances. Popilius Lena's threading his way through them is startling in itself. Yet on this monotone the whole gamut of the conspiracy's doubts, fears and desperation is run. Its midway sentence is the steely

> Cassius, be constant . . .

with which Brutus marks his mastery of the rest. Cæsar is seated. His

> Are we all ready?

turns the whole concourse to him. Some few of them are ready indeed. And now, in terms of deliberate rhetoric, Shakespeare once more erects before us the Colossus that is to be overthrown. Then in a flash the blow falls. Butchered by Casca, sacrificed by Brutus – these two doings of the same deed are marked and kept apart – Cæsar lies dead.

Remark that we are now only a quarter of the way through the scene; further, that the play's whole action so far has been a preparation for this crisis. Yet, with dead Cæsar lying there, Shakespeare will contrive to give us such fresh interest in the living that, with no belittling of the catastrophe, no damping-down nor desecration of our emotions, our minds will be turned forward still. This is a great technical achievement. He might well have shirked the full attempt and have wound up the scene with its next seventy lines or so. But then could the play ever have recovered strength and impetus? As it is, by the long scene's end our concern for Cæsar is lost in our expectations of the Forum. The producer must note carefully how this is brought about, lest even the minor means to it miscarry.

The mainspring of the renewed action will lie, of course,

in the creation of Antony. We may call it so; for, as we saw, he has been cunningly kept, in person and by reference, an ineffectual figure so far. But now both in person and by reference, by preparation, by contrast, Shakespeare brings him to a sudden overwhelming importance.

We have the helter-skelter of the moment after Cæsar's fall; Brutus is the only figure of authority and calm. Old Publius stands trembling and dumb; Antony, that slight man, has fled, and the conspirators seem confounded by their very success. Before, then, they face the Rome they have saved from tyranny, let them make themselves one again, not in false courage – if Rome is ungrateful they must die – but in high principle that fears not death. Let them sign themselves ritual brothers – and in whose blood but Cæsar's?

> Stoop, Romans, stoop,
> And let us bathe our hands in Cæsar's blood
> Up to the elbows, and besmear our swords:
> Then walk we forth, even to the market place,
> And, waving our red weapons o'er our heads,
> Let's all cry, "Peace, freedom, and liberty!"

We need not doubt Brutus' deep sincerity for a moment.

> Fates, we will know your pleasures.
> That we shall die, we know; 'tis but the time
> And drawing days out, that men stand upon.

This is the man of principle at his noblest. But what else than savage mockery is Casca's

> Why, he that cuts off twenty years of life
> Cuts off so many years of fearing death.

And does Brutus, the rapt ideologue, perceive it? Into the sophistical trap he walks:

> Grant that, and then is death a benefit:

227

> So are we Cæsar's friends, that have abridg'd
> His time of fearing death.

And he anoints himself devotedly. Then Cassius, febrile infatuate:

> Stoop, then, and wash. How many ages hence
> Shall this our lofty scene be acted o'er,
> In states unborn and accents yet unknown!

Brutus echoes him as well. And by this last daring and doubly dramatic stroke, Shakespeare reminds us that we are ideal spectators of these men and the event, having vision and prevision too. Comment is forbidden the playwright, but here is the effect of it contrived. For as we look and listen we hear the verdict of the ages echoing. In this imperfect world, it would seem, one can be too high-minded, too patriotic, too virtuous altogether. And then the commonest thing, if it be rooted firm, may trip a man to his ruin. So these exalted gentlemen, led by their philosophic patriot, are stopped on their way – by the arrival of a servant.[12]

This is the play's turning point. And, if but pictorially, could a better be contrived? On the one side the group of triumphant and powerful men; on the other, suddenly appearing, a humble, anonymous messenger.

> Thus, Brutus, did my master bid me kneel;
> Thus did Mark Antony bid me fall down;
> And, being prostrate, thus he bade me say . . .

And so aptly and literally does he represent his master that Brutus, with this chance to test the smooth words apart from their deviser, might, we should suppose, take warning. But it is Brutus who is infatuate now. It is not, as with

---

12 For an excellent analysis of this passage see MacCullum's *Shakespeare's Roman Plays*, quoted by Furness. And for the effect of the servant's entrance see, as before noted, R. G. Moulton's *Shakespeare as Dramatic Artist.*

Cassius, passions that blind him, but principles. He has done murder for an ideal. Not to credit his adversaries, in turn, with the highest motives would be unworthy, would seem sheer hypocrisy. And Antony's message is baited with an uncanny knowledge of the man.

> Brutus is noble, wise, valiant, and honest;
> Cæsar was mighty, bold, royal, and loving:
> Say I love Brutus, and I honour him;
> Say I fear'd Cæsar, honour'd him, and lov'd him.

Wisdom and honesty, valour and love, honour and again honour; Brutus will harp on the very words in his own apology. It is Cassius, with his vengeance fulfilled and his passions gratified, who now sees clear, knowing his Antony as truly as Antony knows his Brutus. His

> misgiving still
> Falls shrewdly to the purpose.

But he lacks authority to lead.

Then follows the revelation of Antony, in his verbal duel with the conspirators; his devoted rhapsody over Cæsar's body; and the swift foresight of the passage with Octavius' servant. It is to be noted that the beginning of the scene in the Forum tags dramatically not to the end of this but to the earlier departure of Brutus and the others. Hence, perhaps, the short opening in verse and Brutus' echoing of his last spoken line,

> Prepare the body, then, and follow us

with

> Then follow me, and give me audience, friends.

Once he is in the pulpit we have a sharp change to prose.

Editor after editor has condemned Brutus' speech as poor

and ineffective, and most of them have then proceeded to justify Shakespeare for making it so. It is certainly not meant to be ineffective, for it attains its end in convincing the crowd. Whether it is poor oratory must be to some extent a matter of taste. Personally, accepting its form as one accepts the musical convention of a fugue, I find that it stirs me deeply. I prefer it to Antony's. It wears better. It is very noble prose. But we must, of course, consider it first as a part of the setting-out of Brutus' character. Nothing – if the speech itself does not – suggests him to us as a poor speaker; nor, at this moment of all others, would he fail himself. But we know the sort of appeal he would, deliberately if not temperamentally, avoid. Shakespeare has been accused, too, of bias against the populace. But is it so? He had no illusion about them. As a popular dramatist he faced their inconstant verdict day by day, and came to write for a better audience than he had. He allows Brutus no illusions, certainly.

> Only be patient till we have appeas'd
> The multitude, beside themselves with fear. . . .

This is the authentic voice of your republican aristocrat, who is at no pains, either, to disguise his disdain.

> Be patient till the last.
> Romans, countrymen and lovers! hear me for my cause; and be silent, that you may hear. . . .

For the tone belies the words; nor is such a rapping on the desk for "Quiet, please" the obvious way into the affections of the heady crowd. He concedes nothing to their simplicity.

> Censure me in your wisdom, and awake your senses, that you may be the better judge.

But the compliment, one fears, is paid less to them than to his own intellectual pride. It is wasted in any case, if we may judge by the Third and Fourth Citizens:

Let him be Cæsar.

Cæsar's better parts
Shall be crown'd in Brutus.

He has won them; not by what he has said, in spite of it, rather; but by what he is. The dramatic intention, and the part the crowd plays in it, is surely plain. Men in the mass do not think, they feel. They are as biddable as children, and as sensitive to suggestion. Mark Antony is to make it plainer.

Antony has entered, and stands all friendless by Cæsar's bier. Brutus descends, the dialogue shifting from prose to easy verse as he shakes free of the enthusiasm, and departs alone. His austere renouncing of advantage should show us how truly alone.

Antony makes no glib beginning; he protests, indeed, that he has nothing to say. He tries this opening and that, is deprecatory, apologetic.

The noble Brutus
Hath told you Cæsar was ambitious;
If it were so, it was a grievous fault,
And grievously hath Cæsar answered it.

But he is deftly feeling his way by help of a few platitudes to his true opening, and alert for a first response. He senses one, possibly, upon his

He was my friend, faithful and just to me

– for that was a human appeal. But he knows better than to presume on a success; he returns to his praise of the well-bepraised Brutus. He embellishes his tune with two grace notes, one appealing to sentiment, the other to greed. More praise of Brutus, and yet more! But the irony of this will out, and he checks himself. Irony is a tricky weapon with an audience uncertain still. Nor will too much nice talk about honour serve him; that sort of thing leaves men cold. A quick

231

turn gives us

> I speak not to disprove what Brutus spoke,
> But here I am to speak what I do know

and, to judge by the hammering monosyllables of the last line, he is warming to his work, and feels his hearers warming to him.

One may so analyse the speech throughout and find it a triumph of effective cleverness. The cheapening of the truth, the appeals to passion, the perfect carillon of flattery, cajolery, mockery and pathos, swinging to a magnificent tune, all serve to make it a model of what popular oratory should be. In a school for demagogues its critical analysis might well be an item in every examination paper. That is one view of it. By another, there is nothing in it calculated or false. Antony feels like this; and, on these occasions, he never lets his thoughts belie his feelings, that is all. And he knows, without stopping to think, what the common thought and feeling will be, where reason and sentiment will touch bottom – and if it be a muddy bottom, what matter! – because he is himself, as we said, the common man raised to the highest power. So, once in touch with his audience, he can hardly go wrong.

How easy he makes things for them! No abstract arguments:

> But here's a parchment with the seal of Cæsar;
> I found it in his closet, 'tis his will.[13]

We pass now, however, to a less ingenuous, more ingenious, phase of the achievement. Those – it is strange there should be any – who range themselves with the mob and will see in Antony no more than the plain blunt man of his own painting, have still to account for this slim manipulator of Cæsar's will that Shakespeare paints. It is tempting, no doubt, to make men dance to your tune when the thing is

13 And later, he will propose to his colleagues Octavius and Lepidus that they all three consider

How to cut off some charge in legacies.

done so easily. When they stand, open-eared and open-mouthed, how resist stuffing them with any folly that comes handy? And as there is no limit, it would seem, to their folly and credulity, greed and baseness, why not turn it all to good account – one's own account? Antony is not the man, at any rate, to turn aside from such temptation. Is he less of a demagogue that Cæsar's murder is his theme, and vengeance for it his cause? Does poetic eloquence make demagogy less vicious – or, by chance, more? Shakespeare's Antony would not be complete without this juggling with Cæsar's will.

What so impresses the unlearned as the sight of some document? He does not mean to read it. They are Cæsar's heirs. There, he never meant to let that slip! Trick after trick of the oratorical trade follows. The provocative appeal to the seething crowd's self-control tagged to the flattery of their generous hearts, the play with the mantle, which they "all do know", that soft touch of the "summer's evening" when Cæsar first put it on! Self-interest well salted with sentiment, what better bait can there be? Much may be done with a blood-stained bit of cloth!

> Through this the well-beloved Brutus stabbed
> And as he pluck'd his cursèd steel away,
> Mark how the blood of Cæsar followed it,
> As rushing out of doors, to be resolved
> If Brutus so unkindly knocked, or no. . . .

If our blood were still cold the simile might sound ridiculous, but it thrills us now.

> This was the most unkindest cut of all;
> For when the noble Cæsar saw him stab,
> Ingratitude, more strong than traitors' arms,
> Quite vanquished him: then burst his mighty heart;
> And, in his mantle muffling up his face,
> Even at the base of Pompey's statua,
> Which all the while ran blood, great Cæsar fell.

How fine it sounds! How true, therefore, by the standards of popular oratory, it is! There is poetic truth, certainly, in that ingratitude; and as for Pompey's statue, if it did not actually run blood, it might well have done.

> O! what a fall was there, my countrymen;
> Then, I and you, and all of us fell down,
> Whilst bloody treason flourished over us.
> O! now you weep, and I perceive you feel
> The dint of pity. . . .

What were Brutus' tributes to their wisdom compared to this? Antony has won their tears, and has but to seal his success by showing them the very body of Cæsar, and to endorse it with

> Good friends, sweet friends, let me not stir you up
> To such a sudden flood of mutiny.
> They that have done this deed are honourable. . . .

for irony is a potent weapon now; and to forbid mutiny is only to encourage it, the word of itself will do so.

The peroration is masterly, a compendium of excitement. We have again the false restraint from passion, the now triumphant mockery of those honourable men, of their wisdom, their good reasons and their private grief; again, the plain blunt man's warning against such oratorical snares as the subtle Brutus set; and it is all rounded off with magnificent rhythm, the recurrent thought and word flung like a stone from a sling.

> . . . but were I Brutus,
> And Brutus Antony, there were an Antony
> Would ruffle up your spirits, and put a tongue
> In every wound of Cæsar that should move
> The stones of Rome to rise and mutiny.

And to what end? To the routing of the conspirators from Rome, truly. A good counterstroke. But the first victim of

Antony's eloquence, as Shakespeare takes care to show us, is the wretched Cinna the poet, who has had nothing to do with Cæsar's murder at all.[14] The mob tear him limb from limb, as children tear a rag doll. Nor does knowledge of his innocence hinder them.

> Truly, my name is Cinna.
> Tear him to pieces, he's a conspirator.
> I am Cinna, the poet, I am Cinna the poet.
> Tear him for his bad verses, tear him for his bad verses.
> I am not Cinna the conspirator.
> It is no matter, his name's Cinna; pluck but his name out of his heart, and turn him going.

Well, we have had Antony's fine oratory; and we may have been, and should have been, stirred by it. But if we have not at the same time watched him, and ourselves, with a discerning eye, and listened as well with a keener ear, the fault is none of Shakespeare's. He draws no moral, does not wordily balance the merits of this cause against that. He is content to compose for the core of his play, with an artist's enjoyment, with an artist's conscience, in getting the balance true, this ironic picture; and, finally, to set against the high tragedy of the murder of Cæsar a poor poetaster's wanton slaughter.

The beginning of the fourth act sets against the calculations of the conspirators the arithmetic of the new masters of Rome.

> These many then shall die; their names are pricked.

It is an admirably done scene, of but fifty lines all told, giving an actor, with just twenty-two words, material for Lepidus (the feat would seem impossible, but Shakespeare manages it; and so can an actor, rightly chosen and given scope), giving us Octavius, showing us yet another Antony, and outlining the complete gospel of political success. Brutus

14 A scene which the average modern producer takes great care to cut.

and Cassius, its finish informs us, are levying powers. We are shown them straightway at the next scene's beginning, and from now to the play's end its action runs a straight road.

Drum. Enter Brutus ...

The philospher has turned general. He is graver, more austere than ever.

> Your master, Pindarus,
> In his own change, or by ill officers,
> Hath given me some worthy cause to wish
> Things done undone. . . .

But he says it as one who would say that nothing, be it big or little, can ever be undone. We hear a *Low march within,* congruous accompaniment to the sombre voice. It heralds Cassius.

Enter Cassius and his Powers

CASSIUS.	Stand, ho!
BRUTUS.	Stand, ho!
1ST SOLDIER.	Stand!
2ND SOLDIER.	Stand!
3RD SOLDIER.	Stand!

The voices echo back, the drumbeats cease, the armed men face each other, silent a moment.[15]

This long scene – the play's longest – thus begun, is dominated by Brutus and attuned in the main to his mood. Now the mood of the good man in adversity may well make for monotony and gloom; but Shakespeare is alert to avoid this, and so must producer and actors be. We have the emotional elaboration of the quarrel, the eccentric interlude of the poet as preparation for the sudden drop to the deep still note struck by the revelation of Portia's death; next comes the

[15] The Chorus in *Henry V* could not apologize enough for the theatre's failure to show armies in being. But by a little music, this cunning of speech and action, and a bold acceptance of convention, these "ciphers to this great account" can be made to work well enough upon the "imaginary forces" of the audience.

steady talk of fighting plans (note the smooth verse), then the little stir with which the council breaks up and the simple preparations for the night. Varro and Claudius are brought in, so that their sleep, as well as the boy's, may throw the calm, wakeful figure of Brutus into relief. The tune and its lapsing brings a hush, we can almost hear the leaves of the book rustle as they are turned. Then the ghost appears; the tense few moments of its presence have been well prepared. The scene's swift ending is good stagecraft too. Lucius' protesting treble, the deeper voices of the soldiers all confused with sleep, the dissonance and sharp interchange break and disperse the ominous spell for Brutus and for us. And the last words look forward.[16]

The last act of *Julius Cæsar* has been most inconsiderately depreciated. Nothing, certainly, will make it effective upon the modern "realistic" stage, but we can hardly blame Shakespeare for that. He writes within the conventions of his own theatre, and he here takes the fullest advantage of them. He begins by bringing the rival armies, led by their generals, face to face.

> *Enter Octavius, Antony and their army . . .*
> *Drum. Enter Brutus, Cassius and their army.*

BRUTUS.   They stand, and would have parley.
CASSIUS.   Stand fast, Titinius; we must out and talk.
OCTAVIUS.   Mark Antony, shall we give sign of battle?
ANTONY.   No, Cæsar, we will answer on their charge.
　　　　　　 Make forth; the generals would have some
　　　　　　 words.

16 "Sleep again, Lucius", would point, if nothing else did, to the drawing-together of the curtains of the inner stage upon the scene. Where Varro and Claudius have been lying is a question. They enter, of course, upon the main stage. Brutus apparently points to the inner stage with "Lie in my tent and sleep". They offer to keep watch where they are, *i.e.* by the door. I am inclined to think that they lie down there, too. This would not only make the business with the ghost better, but it would bring the scene's final piece of action upon the centre stage and give it breadth and importance.

This to the Elizabethans was a commonplace of stagecraft. Before scenery which paints realistically some defined locality, it must needs look absurd. But, the simpler convention accepted, Shakespeare sets for his audience a wider and more significant scene than any the scenic theatre can compass. And, confronting the fighters, he states the theme, so to speak, of the play's last event, and gives it value, importance and dignity.

The whole act is constructed with great skill, each detail has its purpose and effect. But we must dismiss, even from our memories if possible, the *Scene ii, The same, the Field of Battle;* and *Scene iii, Another Part of the Field,* of the editors. What happens to begin with is this. Antony, Octavius and their powers departed, the talk between Brutus and Cassius over – it is (for us) their third and last, and a chill quiet talk; they feel they are under the shadow of defeat – the stage is left empty. Then the silence is broken by the clattering *Alarum,* the symbol of a battle begun. Then back comes Brutus, but a very different Brutus.

> Ride, ride, Messala, ride, and give these bills
> Unto the legions on the other side.

Now a *Loud alarum,* which his voice must drown.

> Let them set on at once, for I perceive
> But cold demeanour in Octavius' wing,
> And sudden push gives them the overthrow.
> Ride, ride, Messala: let them all come down.

And he is gone as he came. In its sharp contrast it is a stirring passage, which restores to Brutus whatever dominance he may have lost. But it cannot be achieved if tension is relaxed and attention dissipated by the shifting of scenery, or by any superfluous embroidering of the action.

Remark further that to follow the course of the battle an audience must listen keenly, and they must be able to concentrate their minds on the speakers. When the defeat of

Cassius is imminent, when Titinius tells him:

> O Cassius! Brutus gave the word too early;
> Who, having some advantage on Octavius,
> Took it too eagerly: his soldiers fell to spoil,
> Whilst we by Antony are all enclos'd

the situation is made clear enough. But if we do not master it at this moment, the rest of the scene and its drama will go for next to nothing.

Now we have Cassius grasping the ensign he has seized from the coward who was running away with it (and, being Cassius, not content with that, he has killed the man), the very ensign the birds of ill omen had hovered over; and he makes as if to plant it defiantly, conspicuously in the ground.

> This hill is far enough.

His death is of a piece with his whole reckless life. He kills himself because he will not wait another minute to verify the tale his bondman tells him of Titinius' capture. He ends passionately and desperately – but still grasping his standard. Even at this moment he is as harsh to Pindarus as Brutus is gentle to his boy Lucius and the bondman who serves him:

> Come hither, sirrah:
> In Parthia did I take thee prisoner;
> And then I swore thee, saving of thy life,
> That whatsoever I did bid thee do,
> Thou shouldst attempt it.

His last words are as bare and ruthless.

> Cæsar, thou art reveng'd,
> Even with the sword that kill'd thee.

Pindarus' four lines that follow may seem frigid and formal. But we need a breathing-space before we face the tragically ironic return of Titinius radiant with good news. The stage-craft of this entrance, as of others like it, belongs, we must (yet again) remember, to the Elizabethan theatre, with its doors at the back, and its distance for an actor to advance, attention full on him. Entrance from the wing of a conventional scenic stage will be quite another matter.

MESSALA.	It is but change, Titinius; for Octavius Is overthrown by noble Brutus' power, As Cassius' legions are by Antony.
TITINIUS.	These tidings will well comfort Cassius.
MESSALA.	Where did you leave him?
TITINIUS.	All disconsolate, With Pindarus his bondman, on this hill.
MESSALA.	Is that not he that lies along the ground?
TITINIUS.	He lies not like the living. O my heart!
MESSALA.	Is not that he?
TITINIUS.	No, this was he, Messala, But Cassius is no more.

Stage direction is embodied in dialogue. We have the decelerated arrival telling of relief from strain, the glance around the seemingly empty place; then the sudden swift single-syllabled line and its repetition, Titinius' dart forward, Messala's graver question, the dire finality of the answer.

We come to Titinius' death; and it is a legitimate query why, with two suicides to provide for, Shakespeare burdened himself with this third. The episode itself may have attracted him; the soldier crowning his dead chief with the garland of victory; then, as the innocent cause of his death, set not to survive it.[17] The death speech is fine, and the questioning sentences that begin it whip it to great poignancy. But neither here nor anywhere, we must admit, does Shakespeare show full understanding of the "Roman's part" and the strange faith that let him play it. His Romans go to their deaths stoically enough, but a little stockily too. Hamlet, later, will

[17] Shakespeare finds this more clearly put in Plutarch than he leaves it in the play.

find the question arguable, and Macbeth will think a man a fool not to die fighting. Brutus and Cassius and Titinus, it is true, could hardly be made to argue the point here. But there is an abruptness and a sameness, and a certain emptiness, in the manner of these endings.

Another and technically a stronger reason for adding Titinuis to the suicides, is that it is above all important Brutus' death should not come as an anticlimax to Cassius'. This episode helps provide against that danger, and the next scene makes escape from it sure.

The bodies are carried out in procession with due dignity, and again the effect of the empty stage keys us to expectancy. Then

Alarum. Enter Brutus, Messala, Cato, Lucilius, and Flavius.
Enter soldiers and fight.

It is a noisy melee; so confused that, though we hear the voices of the leaders from its midst, Brutus disappears unnoticed. The scene has its touch of romance in young Cato's death, its dash of intrigue in Lucilius' trick. If these things are given value in performance, they knot up effectively the weakening continuity of theme, which, by its slacking, would leave the death of Brutus and the play's end a fag end instead of a full close.

Yet the effects of the last scene are in themselves most carefully elaborated. Hard upon the clattering excitement of the fight, and the flattering magnanimity of the triumphant Antony, comes into sight this little group of beaten and exhausted men, the torchlight flickering on their faces.[18]

BRUTUS.   Come, poor remains of friends, rest on this rock.
CLITUS.   Statilius show'd the torch-light; but, my lord,
          He came not back: he is or ta'en or slain.
BRUTUS.   Sit thee down, Clitus: slaying is the word;
          It is a deed in fashion. . . .

[18] It has been held (I do not stress the point) that Elizabethan outdoor performances were timed to end near twilight. In that case the torchlight would prove doubly effective here.

They throw themselves down hopelessly; to wait – for what! – and to brood in a silence which Brutus hardly breaks by his whisper, first to Clitus, next to Dardanius. Then he paces apart while the two watch him and themselves whisper of the dreadful demand he made. He calls on Volumnius next, to find in him, not hope, only the instinctive human reluctance to admit an end. But his own end – and he knows and desires it – is here. Threatening low alarums vibrate beneath his calm, colourless speech. His followers cry to him to save himself, and a like cry from far off pierces that still insistent alarum, and they echo it again. Well, these men have life and purpose left in them; let them go. He praises and humours their loyalty. But, at his command, they leave him. The end is very near.

But Shakespeare himself is not yet at the end of his resources, nor of his constant care to weave the action in a living texture, to give the least of its figures life. What, till this moment, do we know about Strato? He makes his first appearance in the battle; he is Brutus' body-servant, it seems. A thick-skinned sort of fellow; while the others counted the cost of their ruin, he had fallen asleep. Twelve lines or so (he himself speaks just seven) not only make a living figure of him but keep Brutus self-enlightening to the last. For the very last note struck out of this stoic, whose high principles could not stop short of murder, is one of gentleness.

BRUTUS.   I prithee, Strato, stay thou by thy lord:
                    Thou art a fellow of a good respect;
                    Thy life hath had some smatch of honour in it:
                    Hold then my sword, and turn away thy face,
                    While I do run upon it. Wilt thou, Strato?
STRATO.   Give me your hand first: fare you well, my lord.
BRUTUS.   Farewell, good Strato. . . .

The man's demand for a handshake, the master's response to it; – how much of Shakespeare's greatness lies in these little things, and in the love of his art that never found them too little for his care! Then Brutus closes his account.

> Cæsar, now be still:
> I kill'd not thee with half so good a will.

In silence on both sides the thing is done. Nor does Strato stir while the loud alarum and retreat are sounded; he does not even turn at the conquerors' approach – Antony, Octavius and the already reconciled Messala and Lucilius, who only see by the light of the torches this solitary figure standing there.

Nor have we even yet reached the play's formal close, the ceremonial lifting of the body, the apostrophe to the dead, and that turning towards the living future which the conditions of the Elizabethan stage inevitably and happily prescribed. Chief place is given here, as we have noted, to Octavius, Cæsar's heir and – if Shakespeare may have had it in mind – the conqueror-to-be of his fellow-conqueror. But we have first a bitter-sweet exchange between Strato and Messala. They – and they know it – are commoner clay than their master who lies here; no vain heroism for them. Next Antony speaks, and makes sportsmanlike amends to his dead enemy.

The play is a masterpiece of Elizabethan stagecraft, and the last act, from this point of view, especially remarkable; but only by close analysis can its technical virtues be made plain. Within the powerful ease of its larger rhythm, the constant, varied ebb and flow and interplay of purpose, character and event give it richness of dramatic life, and us the sense of its lifelikeness.

Staging and Costume

No difficulties arise – why should they? – in fitting the play to such a stage as we suppose Shakespeare's at the Globe to have been; at most a few questions must be answered as to the use of the inner stage for this scene or that. Further, the resources of this stage, its adapting of space and time to the playwright's convenience, are so fully exploited that the producer who means to use another had better be very careful he does not lose more than he gains.

Act I can be played wholly on the main stage.

Act II. *Enter Brutus in his Orchard,* says the Folio. This looks like a discovery upon the inner stage. There will certainly be the dramatic effect of contrast, after the feverish excursions through the night of storm, in our seeing Brutus, a chief subject of them, sitting in the contained quiet of his garden. The opening speech, by which, as a rule, Shakespeare paints us the aspect of his scene if he wants to, gives it its tone and in its interspersed silences both the solitary man and the stillness after the storm:

> What, Lucius! ho!
> I cannot, by the progress of the stars,
> Give guess how near to day. Lucius, I say!
> I would it were my fault to sleep so soundly.
> When, Lucius, when! Awake, I say! what, Lucius!

Lucius may enter directly upon the inner stage. Brutus might speak his first soliloquy still sitting there. It is possible that at the Globe he did not, the actor there may have needed a better point of vantage for such an intimately reflective passage.[19] The knocking would almost certainly be heard beyond one of the main-stage doors, through which the conspirators would come, for the scene's general action must be upon the main stage without a doubt. For the scene which follows the traverse must, one would suppose, be closed, to hide whatever properties suggested Brutus' garden. But *Enter Cæsar in his nightgown,* even though he enter upon the main stage, will sufficiently suggest an interior. And the main stage will serve for the rest of the second act.

We should note the space-freedom Shakespeare assumes. "Here will I stand," says Artemidorus, "till Cæsar pass along"; but, speaking five lines more, he goes off, to reappear with the crowd that follows Cæsar. And Act III begins with a most significant instance of it. The inner stage is disclosed and

---

[19] I write this very much under correction. But I believe that only experiment will tell us what could and could not be made effective upon the inner and upper stages at the Globe.

Cæsar's "state" is set there. Cæsar, the conspirators, the Senators and the populace enter upon the main stage. Cassius speaks to Artemidorus:

> What! urge you your petitions in the street?
> Come to the Capitol.

Eighteen lines later we have

CÆSAR.   Are we all ready? what is now amiss
             That Cæsar and his Senate must redress?
METELLUS. Most high, most mighty, and most puissant
             Cæsar,
             Metellus Cimber throws before thy seat
             An humble heart –

Nothing more complicated has occurred than Cæsar and the Senators taking their places, while the crowd disperses and the conspirators regroup themselves, so that the "state" becomes the centre of attraction – and we are in the Senate House. Later, Cæsar must fall and lie dead in a most conspicuous position upon the main stage; still later provision must be made – as it is – for removing the body.

For the following scene the traverse is closed and the upper stage is used for the pulpit. Moreover, the dialogue tells us, to a second or so, the time it takes to ascend and come down.

The first scene of Act IV might, but need not, be played in relation to the inner stage.[20] The second and third scenes,

---

[20] I think that scenes were more often played "in relation to" the inner stage than consistently within its boundaries; that is to say, the actors, having gained the effect of a discovery, would be apt to advance upon the main stage, where their movements would be less cramped, where they would be in closer touch with the audience and certainly in a better position to hold an unruly audience. I see this happening in the scene in Brutus' garden, and possibly in this scene. There are signs of such a treatment, too, of the scene in Brutus' tent. When he asks Lucius, "Where is thy instrument?" "Here in the tent" is the answer, not a simple "I have it here". When he calls in Varro and Claudius, he says, "I pray you, sirs, lie in my tent and sleep". It sounds very much like people upon the main stage indicating the inner stage with a gesture. Certain things, the study of the map, the playing of the lute,

which are not divided in the Folio – which are indeed conspicuously left undivided there – presents us with another significant instance of space-freedom, and of Shakespeare's ready use of the conventions which belong to it.[21] We have

> *Enter Brutus, Lucilius and the Army. . . .*

The editors cannot leave this alone. *"The Army"* becomes *"and soldiers".*[22] This falsifies Shakespeare's intention. By *"the Army"* he does not mean a few casual soldiers, he means the integral group of followers, in some uniform possibly, and with banner, drum and trumpet, which in Elizabethan stage convention personified and symbolized an army entire. Later, after a *Low march within* comes

> *Enter Cassius and his Powers.*

And much the same thing is meant. The effect to be gained is of the spaciousness and order of armies in the field in contrast with that chaos of the market place; and it is as important as an explanatory scene would be.

And what really occurs where modern editors mark a change of scene?

BRUTUS.   Let us not wrangle: bid them move away;

the reading by the taper's light, show, of course, the use of furniture. This would probably be set and left upon the inner stage, though it would be advantageous to have it placed as near the traverse-line as possible, and actors, using it, would be constantly passing the line. And, speaking generally, one need not suppose that the Elizabethan actor ever saw the division between inner stage and main stage as a fixed boundary, nor that the Elizabethan audience had cultivated such a sense of locality that they questioned its crossing and recrossing or even asked themselves at certain ambiguous moments where exactly the characters were meant to be. The main effect and its dramatic purpose were reckoned with; whatever assisted this was allowed.

21 The play in the Folio (and there are no Quartos) is one of those which start bravely with *Actus Primus, Scæna Prima* and then pay no further attention to scene-division at all. I refer in my enumeration of scenes to the current modern editions, which are, however, in this particular most misleading to the student of the Elizabethan stage and of Shakespeare the dramatist.

22 Capel did no worse than change it to *"Forces"*.

> Then in my tent, Cassius, enlarge your griefs,
> And I will give you audience.

CASSIUS.   Pindarus,
> Bid our commanders lead their charges off
> A little from this ground.

BRUTUS.   Lucius, do you the like; and let no man
> Come to our tent till we have done our conference.

Exeunt. Manet Brutus and Cassius.

Then, without more ado, with no slackening of tension nor waste of this excellently ominous preparation, the intimate wrangle begins. The stagecraft is plain enough. The symbolized armies, with their banners and drums, go off; and either the traverse is now drawn, disclosing the tent furniture, in which case Brutus and Cassius have but to place themselves in relation to it for the scene to be effectively changed; or it is as possible that the traverse has been open from the beginning and that the removal of the "armies" and the reorientation of the chief actors were felt to be change enough. This would repeat the mechanics of the Senate House scene (but it would, of course, forbid an immediately previous use of the inner stage for Antony and Octavius).

We come to Act V, which must be envisaged as a whole. The locality is a battlefield. We have still the symbolical armies. The scenes are divided by alarums. The conventions, in fact, are all accepted. The upper stage is used, for a moment, as the high point of a hill.

> Go, Pindarus, get higher on that hill,

says Cassius, and six lines later the direction reads:

> *Pindarus above.*

The only sign of use of the inner stage is for the scene beginning,

BRUTUS.   Come, poor remains of friends, rest on this rock.

Brutus and his friends may need something better to sit upon than the floor. It need be no realistic rock, for a while back when Cassius said,

> This hill is far enough

there certainly was no hill. On the other hand, if you require some things to sit on it is as easy to make them look like rocks as anything else. The rock or rocks, in that case, would have to be set upon the inner stage. A further indication of its use is the mention of torches, for these would show up better in its comparative shade.

The question of costume raises difficulties. Shakespeare, by convention, dressed his Romans more or less in Elizabethan clothes. To those of the chief characters (for whom this could be afforded) some definitely exotic touches have been added.[23] Nationality, we know, was, at times, pointed by costume. So, possibly, was period; but not, one suspects, with any consistency, not, for a certainty, with any historical accuracy. In this text, at any rate, while there are no direct indications of "Roman habitings", there are a round dozen of references to the Elizabethan. Therefore we cannot simply ignore Shakespeare's convention in favour of our own, which pictures the ancient Roman, bare-headed, clean-shaven and wrapped in a toga.[24] But then, neither can we very easily and altogether ignore our own. The questions of costume and scenery differ in this: whatever the background, if one is kept conscious of it once the play's acting is under way, it is a bad background; but the look of the actors is of constant importance. We are in this dilemma, then. Cæsar, we, hear, plucks ope his doublet; the conspirators' hats are plucked about their ears; Brutus walks unbraced and turns down the leaf of a book which he keeps in the pocket of his gown. Do these seem trivial things? Nothing in a play is trivial which bears upon

23 See the Henry Peacham illustration to *Titus Andronicus*, reproduced in Chambers' *Shakespearean Gleanings* and elsewhere.
24 Whether our picture is a true one is beside the point. Quite possibly the Roman Senate assembled did *not* look like the cooling-room of a Turkish bath.

the immediate credibility of the action. The theatre is a game of make-believe, and the rules of any game may be varied by use and acceptance, but mere contrariness is tiresome. An actor may point into vacancy and fill it by description, and we shall be at one with him; but to wear a toga, and call it a doublet, will be distracting. And, apart from direct verbal contradictions, there are passages enough whose full effect must remain one with the picture Shakespeare made of them. The boy Lucius asleep over his lute; who ever can have realized that episode in its exact and delicate detail and want to transform and botch it? Yet it must be confessed that a Cæsar in doublet and hose may offend and will undoubtedly distract us.

The difficulty must, I suggest, be met by compromise, in which we can find some positive advantage too. We are not concerned with the accuracy of our own picturing of Rome, but to reconcile two dramatic conventions. It goes without saying that the nearer we can in general come to Shakespeare's point of view the better. But for a particular gain, has not the vulgar modern conception of Rome, nourished on Latin lessons and the classic school of painting, become rather frigid? Are not our noble Romans, flinging their togas gracefully about them, slow-moving, consciously dignified, speaking with studied oratory and all past middle age, rather too like a schoolboy's vision of a congress of headmasters? Compare them with the high-mettled, quick-tongued crew of politicians and fighters that Shakespeare imagines; and if it comes to accuracy, has he not more the right of it than we, even though his Cæsar be dressed in doublet and hose? So let the designer at least provide an escape from this cold classicism, which belongs neither to the true Rome nor to the play he has to interpret. His way can be the way of all compromise. What need each side insist on? The figure of Brutus must not make a modern audience think all the time of Shakespeare himself, but where the gain to Shakespeare that it should? On the other hand, whatever has been woven, even casually, into the fabric of the play, we must somehow manage to respect. If we change, we must not falsify.

The methods of the Masque and the way of Renaissance painters with classical subjects give us the hint we need. Whether from taste or lack of information, when it came to picturing Greeks and Romans they were for fancy dress; a mixture, as a rule, of helmet, cuirass, trunk hose, stockings and sandals, like nothing that ever was worn, but very wearable and delightful to look at. Women's dresses seem to have been manipulated less easily; perhaps the wearers were not so amenable, or so tolerant of the outrage upon fashion.[25] But even here something of the sort is managed. And something of the sort, with emphasis upon this period or that, according to his judgment, will get our designer out of his difficulty. Shakespeare's own consent, so to speak, to such a compromise can be determined, for the tests are all to hand before ever the play is acted. Upon the tacit consent of an audience one can only speculate. But the problem with an audience in this as in other things is less to satisfy their opinion, if they have one, than to release them from its burden for the fuller, the unself-conscious, enjoyment of the play. *Julius Cæsar*! They may come expecting the familiarized figures set against some popular picture-book background of Rome. For good reasons given they cannot have this. The designer must overreach them. He must appeal, that is to say, past expectation and opinion, to their readiness to be pleased and convinced; and there are no rules by which that can be forecast. But this much law can be laid down. He must first be sure that this work will fuse with Shakespeare's. What Shakespeare's purposes will not accept, he must reject. For the rest, he may be bold or cautious as it suits him. He had better be simple. If he can so picture the play to himself that nothing in the picture raises any thought but of the play, he will probably not go far wrong.

The Music

Only one difficulty presents itself; we are given no text for the *Music and a Song* of Act IV, Scene iii. Custom prescribes

25 Women appeared in the Masques, though not in the publicly given plays.

the use of

> Orpheus with his lute made trees. . . .

from *Henry VIII*, and this may well be allowed. Mr Richmond Noble in his *Shakespeare's Use of Song* suggests that the stage direction in the Folio may be a later interpolation and that no song is called for, only the playing of an air. This he would presumably justify by Brutus'

> Canst thou hold up thy heavy eyes awhile,
> And touch thy instrument a strain or two?

But a song would be more usual, a lute solo not very audible in a public theatre, and the evidence of the Folio is not negligible.[26] This apart, we have only to give careful attention to the sennets, flourishes, drums, and marches, alarums, low alarums and retreats, which find place throughout the play, for they have each a particular purpose.

A Stumbling Block in the Text

The text, as the first Folio gives it us, is an exceptionally clean one and I do not examine its few minor difficulties here. There is, however, one serious stumbling block in Act IV. What are we to make of the duplicate revelation of Portia's death? The question has, of course, been argued high and low and round about, and weighty opinion will be found set out in the Furness Variorum. The weightier the worse, one is driven to complain. For surely it is clear that a mere corruption of text is involved, not the degeneracy of Brutus' character. Shakespeare may have fumbled a little at this point. But that his final intention was to give us a Brutus wantonly "showing off" to Messala or indulging at this moment in a supersubtle defence of his grief, I would take

---

[26] Mr Richmond Noble also says that he has recommended the use of "Weep ye no more, sad fountains", from Dowland's *Third Book of Airs*. It is difficult not to recommend such an entirely beautiful song when any opportunity occurs. But the words of "Orpheus with his lute" are very appropriate; they could, indeed, be made a pertinent enough illustration of Shakespeare's use of song.

leave to dispute against the weightiest opinion in the world. One must, however, suggest some explanation; and here is mine. It is not provably correct, but I suggest that corrections of text are not provable. The vagaries of a playwright's mind may be guessed at, they can never be brought within the four corners of a system and so tested.

My guess is that Shakespeare originally wrote this, or something like it:

> BRUTUS. Lucius, a bowl of wine.
> CASSIUS. I did not think you could have been so angry.[27]
>
> *Enter boy with wine, and tapers.*
>
> BRUTUS. In this I bury all unkindness, Cassius. . . .

And so on as the text now stands, omitting, however, both

> CASSIUS. Portia, art thou gone?
> BRUTUS. No more, I pray you

and (possibly)

> CASSIUS. Cicero one?
> MESSALA. Cicero is dead, and by that order of proscription.

These have something the air of additions, designed to keep Cassius active in the scene; and the first, of course, involves his knowledge of Portia's death. By this text Brutus first hears the news from Messala, and he exhibits a correct stoicism.[28] Then Shakespeare found that this made his hero not so much stoical as wooden, so he threw the disclosure back into closer conjunction with the quarrel and made it an immediate, and sharply contrasted, sequel to the eccentric-

---

27 This line of Cassius might be a later addition.
28 Cassius' "I have as much of this in art as you" does not tell against this, for "art" does not of course mean anything like "artfulness".

comic interruption by the poet. The passage here has all the air of a thing done at a breath, and by a man who had taken a fresh breath for it too. Whether or no thereafter he cut Messala's disclosure I do not feel positive.[29] He may have thought there was now a double effect to be gained (the original one had not been perhaps so bad, it had only not been good enough); and, in performance, there is an arbitrary sort of effect in the passage as it stands. It is quite likely that, patching at the thing, he did not see to what subtle reflections upon Brutus' character the new combination would give rise (so seldom apparently did he consider the troubles of his future editors!). I hope that he made the cut. I think on the whole that he did. I am sure that he should have done; and I recommend the producer of today to make it, and by no means to involve his Brutus in that incidental lie, nor his character in the even more objectionable subtleties of an escape from it.

[29] I now feel positive that he did (1945).

1–2. Garrick followed his predecessors and always omitted the Fool, who had been removed by Nahum Tate in his 1681 rewriting of the play (cf. 22), and was not restored until 1838 when Macready cast a woman for the part. By all accounts Lear was Garrick's finest performance, in spite of the debased version he played, with its happy ending. The lightning featured in this and 2 and 22 was a favourite stage-effect from Restoration times. *The Illustrated London News* praised the "clouds and electric fluid travelling rapidly across the sky in the distance" in Charles Kean's production (2) as "grandly terrific". In Macready's 1838 production, "forked lightnings now vividly illume the broad horizon, now faintly coruscating in small and serpent folds, play in the distance." *(John Bull)*

3. Drawing by George Scharf (cf. Vol. I, Note 12).

4. Water-colour; design probably by T. Grieve, who did the finished sketch. Victoria and Albert Museum.

6–7. The "Souvenir" of the play, from which these drawings by Bernard Partridge are taken, contains nine other scenes and two other portraits.

8 and 19. See under Notes 13–15.

10. The permanent set, composed entirely of steps, was originally designed by Komisarjevsky for the 1927 O.U.D.S. production of the play at Oxford. It was used at Stratford in 1936 and 1937.

11. Reproduced in colour in *Settings and Costumes of the Modern Stage*, The Studio Winter Number, 1935. Other illustrations of Bel Geddes' Project for *King Lear* will be found in *Twentieth Century Stage Decoration* by W. R. Fuerst and S. J. Hume, (1929).

12. "What the very first three minutes manage marvellously to convey is the whole history of the man that has led up to them; so that we are dropped immediately not into a beginning but into a climax. His passionate, wilful, gusty king has reached just exactly that crisis of old age when anything, however wrongheaded, may be expected of him. Second childhood, like first, demands that every whim be translated into immediate action, here, now, on the spot. An unbridled authority has bred in him an unquestioning expectation of immediate indulgence. It is this especially – this violence of the arbitrary will – that Mr Wolfit places at the centre of his minutely observed portrait of age. His old king may have begun in moments of repose to mutter to himself: he cannot all the time keep his head or his hands quite motionless, but he still commands a demoniac rage at being crossed, a passion for imposing his authority in gross and detail alike. So absolutely to this pitch has Mr Wolfit tautened up his character that he somehow carries into his delineation of this moment the years' long process that has led him there. So quickly and surely is this established that whereas other actors begin to tap our tears in the storm scene, Mr Wolfit has them pricking at the eyelids long before."

(T. C. Worsley in *The New Statesman*, 1949)

13–15. John Gielgud's first Lear at the Old Vic in 1931 was produced by Harcourt Williams who had worked for Barker and followed his methods. It was a fine performance, and a most remarkable achievement for a young man of 27: Gordon Bottomley, the poet, wrote to him, "I cannot believe that I shall ever see it more worthily done." His second Lear, in 1940, again at the Old Vic, was produced by Lewis Casson, with ten rehearsals taken by Granville-Barker. No one in the English theatre, therefore, can ever have approached to anything like the same intimate knowledge of how Barker the producer interpreted in the theatre this most stupendous of the tragedies, for which he had written what is generally considered the finest of his *Prefaces*. Gielgud kept to this same interpretation in his 1950 Stratford production and in his recital from the last scene, first given in this country in 1959 at the Queen's Theatre. In the interview with *The Times,* quoted in the caption of 13, he gives an all-too-brief glimpse of Barker at rehearsal. "When I was monotonous, he would say: 'You've *done* that!' Again, of tone and inflexion, 'The scaffolding must be firm. That will always hold you up, if the pinnacles are wobbly'." In *John Gielgud: An Actor's Biography in Pictures*, compiled by Hallam Fordham, (1952), there are eight action-snapshots of this production taken during performance. Audrey Williamson's comments upon the opening scene fit this fine portrait-study very well:

> Barker's stage blazed colour, but with darkness beyond. The glowing satins and jewelled earrings bespoke a Court decked in splendour, a living witness to the King's passion for pomp and power. Lear himself on his first entrance was no senile uncombed chieftain dressed in a nondescript nightgown (a not unusual stage presentation of the character), but a great King still proud in person and mind, robed in blue satin and rich furs and with white hair and curled beard carefully trimmed. The emphasis, therefore, was on an active octogenarian rashly dividing his kingdom and divesting himself of cares of State before he was, in physique and temper, ready to relinquish authority: an interpretation that threw the real nature of the scene, and the inevitability of the later tragedy, into sharp relief. Gielgud himself, tall enough to convey royalty and putting on an additional weight of virile majesty, reinforced this first impression magnificently in his performance. One felt the force of his presence almost before he appeared, and at his thumped sceptre the Court held its breath in fear. The superb head, with its high-marked cheekbones and forcible nose, had the regal poise of one accustomed to rule without question, and the voice held possibilities of thunder.   *(Old Vic Drama,* 1948)

Her account of the whole performance preserves much detail that is particularly illuminating. She describes Stephen Haggard's Fool, (14) as "queer and disconcerting at first, but found it 'grew' on one the more one saw the play." He was "a strange, frail creature with restless eyes, a cracked wandering song, an odd grotesque mixture of 'natural' and jester." He himself described the exhilaration of being rehearsed by Barker for "nine ecstatic days", when he "drew us all out, broke us down, filled us and built us up again, and made us all feel we were having the experience of our lives." To his father he wrote,

> He has taken the whole dead thing and made it sit up and look at you. He has changed my part from the sort of thing one felt one ought to apologize for doing and has turned me into a graceful, dancing, mad, and (I hope) amusing harlequinade (perhaps I should have spelt it Harleyquinade). He's an object of reverent admiration for the whole cast (and that's a feat in itself). I think he's fairly pleased with me: at least he's continually asking new things of me, as of all of us – which is a good sign.

His friend and biographer, Christopher Hassall, who was puzzled, like many of the critics, by the 'grotesque' element in his performance, notes that

> Only when he sat on the ground and listened (so intently, as was his wont whether on or off the stage), with the bauble of his office dangling at his side, was his human comeliness apparent and his natural place among the other human creatures on the scene an easy thing to accept. *(The Timeless Quest)*

The 1950 production, "With acknowledgments to the late Harley Granville-Barker" formally made by the programme, had not come together on the opening night, and in consequence was somewhat coolly received, so that the notices in general yield a quite inadequate idea of what became later in the season a fine production, with as fine a rendering of Lear as Gielgud has ever given. He has certainly never made the awakening and the reunion with Cordelia more exquisitely moving, nor could anything have matched it more perfectly than Peggy Ashcroft's playing. T. C. Worsley wrote at the time that his performance

> trembled all the time on the brink of greatness but, except perhaps at the very end, kept all the time just short of it. Yet a strong conviction that this was an accident of the night rather than a fault inherent in the conception persuaded me to stay for the second performance. And I was rewarded by seeing the perfection come right through. (*New Statesman*)

He accepted him as "the great tragic actor *par excellence* of our generation . . . by virtue of his ability to exhibit the particular kind of simplicity that lies at the heart of passion in highly conscious, complicated personalities", and praised in particular the reconciliation and the little scene with the Fool after the cursing of Goneril, "which foreshadows all that is to follow" in the "amazed and frightened half-realization of how far he has exposed himself."

> A projected self-pity makes him gentle with his fool as with a dog. But in these indulgent caresses, the follies of the last few days flash up one after the other, and are held there, each in a half-broken sentence . . . The weight that is put into this short scene carries its echoes right through the play. And to mark it deeper there is a charming little piece of business at the end (Granville Barker's, too, like so much of the rest?). When Lear for the second time asks impatiently if the horses are ready, and at last they are, the fool – to distract him out of his melancholy mood – gently nods out the chucking noise that ostlers make with their tongues, and leads him off to that. And here I should like to congratulate Mr Alan Badel on his haunting, haunted fool, the very embodiment of pathos, loyal as a mongrel, frightened as a lost child.

With certain reservations, he considered the acting of the

whole cast "worthy of the fine central performance", and commented on the admirable contrast between Goneril and Regan, (19), "Miss Audley's icy whiteness freezing the air at the beginning with her 'Not only, sir, this your all licensed fool', and Miss Ffrangcon-Davies' following up with a red ferocity, at its best at the moments of violence, her own death and the putting out of Gloster's eyes."

The following letters, concerning the 1940 production, are printed by kind permission of Sir John Gielgud and the executors of the late Harley Granville-Barker.

The Athenaeum.
Pall Mall, S.W. 1

Sunday morning.
(April 14, 1940)

My dear Gielgud   Lear is in your grasp.

Forget all the things I have bothered you about. Let your own now well self-disciplined instincts carry you along, and up; simply allowing the checks and changes to prevent your being carried *away*. And I prophesy – happily – great things for you.

Yrs.
H.G.B.

April 29, 1940
18, Place des Etats-Unis.

My dear Gielgud   Did we ever agree as to the precise mo- at which Lear goes off his head?

I believe that Poor Tom's appearance from the hovel marks it. The "grumbling" inside, the Fool's scream of terror, the wild figure suddenly appearing – that combination would be enough to send him over the border-line. Do you mark the moment by doing something quite *new*? Difficult, I know, to find anything new to do at that moment. But something queer and significant of madness, followed (it would help) by a dead silence, before you say (again in a voice you have not used before)

Did'st thou give all . . .

I don't doubt you have devised something. But thinking over the scene this struck me – ought to have struck me before; perhaps we *did* agree to it – so I drop you this line.

You're having an interesting, if exhausting, time, I am sure, and I fancy a most successful one. Congratulations.

Yrs.

H.G.B.

April 30 morning.

I think I have it: – see next sheet

. . . show the heavens more just.

Lear remain on knees at end of prayer, head buried in hands

Edg: Father. . . poor Tom.

make much of this; don't hurry it; give it a "Banshee" effect, lilt and rhythm. At the sound Lear lifts his head. Face seen through his outspread fingers (suggestion of madman looking through bars)
The Fool screams and runs on: business as at present. This gets Lear to his feet. He turns towards the hovel watching intently for what will emerge.

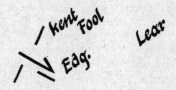

Dialogue as at present.
Edgar's entrance and speech Away . . . warm thee: *much as now. And Lear immensely struck by it. c.f. Hamlet-Ghost. Just as it is finishing (Edgar not to hurry it) stalk him to present position for* Didst-thou . . .

*and as he turns for the speech at B. we see that he is now
quite off his head.*

*N.B. Once Edgar is on he, Kent and Fool must keep dead-
ly still so that these movements of Lear may have their
effect. Translate the Hamlet-Ghost business into terms
of Lear and it will about give you the effect.*

I believe this may be right. Worth trying anyhow.

May 6th 1940
18, Place des Etats-Unis.

My dear Gielgud   Your letter of the 2nd arrived this morning. I'll take thought and answer it tomorrow.

Meanwhile here's a trifling point:
In the last scene Lear quite ignores (as you now do) the "Tis
noble Kent, your friend" and merely gives a general answer
"A plague upon you, murderers, traitors all". And later when
he looks at him and says "Are you not Kent?" it should clearly
be in a highly indignant "How-dare-you-enter-our-presence-
after-I-have-banished-you" tone. And when Kent answers "The
same, your servant Kent", before he can go on to the rest of the
line, the old gentleman should repeat, rather feebly, the magnificent "out of my sight" gesture with which in the first scene
he banished him. "*He's* a good fellow – *He*'ll strike . . ." clearly
refers to the Caius impersonation and the tripping up and
beating of Oswald. Perhaps we did work this out.

Yrs.
H.G.B.

16.   (see also 21). This production would have pleased Barker, in that it had only one interval and that one in the right place, after Act III, (see p. 12), – still all too rare an occurrence in the theatre. Where the actor and the producer disagreed with Barker was in the handling of the play's opening. The 'megalithic grandeur' was realised in the setting and in our first glimpses of Lear enthroned (21); but the interpretation of the scene explicitly denied the 'sustained magnificence' he stresses at pp. 12, 23, 26–27. It is no exaggeration to say that Barker's *Preface* restored *Lear* to our theatre's repertoire and has dominated our acting tradition for thirty years; and by disappointing common expectation of this usual 'magnificent portent' opening, Laughton and Byam Shaw took a no-doubt-calculated risk, which was brilliantly justified in the upshot, (see the present writer's "*King Lear* at Stratford-on-Avon, 1959," *Shakespeare Quarterly*, XI, 2, 1960).

The upper stage was never seen in any detail nor did it call attention to itself except when lighted for upper stage action. It was used for Edgar's hiding place before his flight and for the 'shelter' to which Gloucester brings Lear before the flight to Dover. This scene is usually played as far down-stage as possible and it was a bold experiment to set it upstage and also 'above', in view of the attitude taken by the theatre about inner and upper stage remoteness (cf. Foreword, Vol. I). It reminded Harold Hobson (*Sunday Times*) "of Renoir and the New Testament". It reminded me of sixteenth century Flemish paintings, and its situation lent credibility to Gloucester's swift comings and goings. As a practicable equivalent for Elizabethan upper-stage facilities it was a legitimate and economical contrivance within the natural architectural plan of the castle-courtyard set, in which it functioned as an outer gatehouse. The photograph shows the structure of the set, not the effect of this particular scene when lighted.

l.–r.   The Fool, Ian Holm; Lear, Charles Laughton; Cornwall, Paul Hardwick; Regan, Angela Baddeley; Gloucester, Cyril Luckham; Lear's Knight, Michael Blakemore; Kent, Anthony Nicholls.

17.   Lear calls down vengeance on his daughters before rush-
ing rushing out into the gathering storm. *l.–r.* Cornwall,
Harry Andrews; Gloucester, George Relph; Regan, Margaret
Leighton; the Fool, Alec Guinness; Kent, Nicholas Hannen;
Goneril, Pamela Brown. Audrey Williamson, in *Old Vic
Drama* (1948) considers Olivier's

> greatest moment was in Lear's distraction before the
> storm, when, baited to a fury in which Heaven and Hell
> were inextricably mixed, his mind rocked and cracked
> under the strain of giving utterance to his grief –
>> I will have such revenges on you both
>> That all the world shall –I will do such things, –
>> What they are yet I know not; but they shall be
>> The terrors of the earth.
>
> Olivier's 'terrors of the earth' was Aeschylean; the sheer
> torrential sound of it swept across the senses like Niagara,
> but in all this raving music one could still hear the tor-
> tured cry of a drowning man. The sudden drop of the
> voice at 'O Fool, I shall go mad', the clutching at the
> jester for support and wild, broken flight from the scene
> wrung the heart as no other Lear at this moment has
> succeeded in doing. Olivier made his chief note of coming
> madness here, just as Gielgud selected the earlier 'O let
> me not be mad, not mad, sweet heaven'.

She found his kneeling in prayer at this line "less moving
than Gielgud's simple gesture of lifting his hand to his temple", but praises his mastery, throughout the scene, of every
shift of mood.

> One felt the blinding echo of that rage with which Lear
> in the first scene had flung the coronet to the floor for
> Cornwall and Albany to part between them. His groping
> towards Regan had, in contrast, a melting beauty, and
> there was real effort, here, to subdue his rash impatience,
> to make concessions, to try and understand. But always

the rage could be lashed at a touch; Lear's temperance in adversity was still to come, and his cry at the renewed sight of Kent in the stocks – "Death on my state! Wherefore should he sit here!" – was like unleashed thunder.

The Times critic noted that "when he threatens the terrors of the earth, the roof rings with the controlled resonance of his full-toned utterance"; and Una Ellis-Fermor, in a masterly appreciation in *Theatre Today* (Winter, 1946) praised the "full force of a great actor's inspiration" which led "directly into the emotions of the storm scene", while deploring the "shocking miscalculation in elementary crowd psychology" which placed an interval between this and Act III Sc. ii, so that when he came on again he "had to lift the action by a superb effort of genius, and start, at the height of passion, out of nothing", letting "this reservoir of emotion" run to waste and having to "start the heath scenes with the audience's imaginations cold." With Audrey Williamson's, her review recreates most vividly a performance of genius which "challenged superlatives", in spite of shortcomings in certain aspects of the production. "The progress of the mind of Lear was deeply and continuously imagined – and no greater tribute can be paid to an actor than this."

18.   Lear, wandering in his madness in the fields near Dover, encounters the blinded Gloucester, led by Edgar (Michael Warre). For sheer power, unfalteringly sustained throughout every phase of the action, Olivier's Lear and his Titus, both created when he had come to full maturity as an actor, represent the top of his Shakespearian achievement. In Lear, as W. A. Darlington wrote, "He was never less than first-rate, and again and again he touched magnificence." Like most of the critics he was deeply impressed by the way in which the power to dominate in the storm scene was equalled by an exquisitely sensitive command of the pathos of the scene with Gloucester at Dover and the concluding scenes.

20.   The actual production – setting, costumes, music – is discussed in great detail and illustrated with the two very good photographs in W. M. Merchant's *Shakespeare and the Artist,* 1959, pp. 152–57. In its union of "sight and sound, of the arts of acting, design, and music", he considers it "the finest post-war presentation of Shakespeare in this country." The more general opinion, expressed by Richard Findlater, was that the actor was "ill-served by the décor", the "aggressively noisy music, the clumsily picturesque costumes that seemed to be animated dress-designs not clothes for actors, and the fussy modernity of the set with its multi-purpose pillar and its sombre monotony of space". (*Michael Redgrave, Actor,* 1956).

22–23.   For Rowe's frontispieces see *Notes*, vol. I, 1, and cf. Barker, Vol. IV, p. 66 fn.   On Rowe as editor see Barker, this volume, pp. 115, 117; Vol. III, pp. 9, 14–15, 17–18 and Vol. IV, pp. 49, 134.

27–28.   In his notice of the Lyceum production of *Cymbeline* Shaw, for once, has high praise for Irving. His Iachimo is "a new and independent creation ... no bagful of 'points', but a true impersonation, unbroken in its life-current from end to end, varied on the surface with the finest comedy, and without a single lapse in the sustained beauty of its execution." Of Imogen he writes: "do, please, remember that there are two Imogens. One is a solemn and elaborate example of what, in Shakespeare's opinion, a real lady ought to be. With this unspeakable person virtuous indignation is chronic. Her object in life is to vindicate her own propriety and to suspect everybody else's, especially her husband's ... But this Imogen has another one tied to her with ropes of blank verse (which can fortunately be cut) – the Imogen of Shakespeare's genius, an enchanting person of the most delicate sensitiveness, full of sudden transitions from ecstasies of tenderness to transports of childish rage, and reckless of consequences in both, instantly hurt and instantly appeased, and of the highest breeding and courage ... There is one scene in *Cymbeline*, the one in which Imogen receives the summons to 'that same blessed Milford', which might have been written for Miss Terry, so perfectly does its innocent rapture and frank gladness fit into her hand. Her repulse of Iachimo brought down the house as a matter of course . . . Miss Terry had evidently cut her own part; at all events the odious Mrs. Grundyish Imogen had been dissected out of it so skilfully that it went without a single jar." (cf. Barker, p. 172, fn.)

31–32. The combination of masque scenes and Jacobean costuming with masquing elaborations suits the play well, and ruffs and paned hose combine as happily with the buskins and helms and loricas of *costume à la romaine* as they did in the time of Inigo Jones. "Look at those drawings", says Barker, (p. 107) and "then read some of the more decorative passages . . . there is a common fancy in both." Gower Parks's costumes and his set, with its varying levels, its central discovery space, its pillars and arches with windows above, backed with curtains when required, (as in the *Julius Cæsar* set shown in 37 and 38), made imaginative and intelligent use of all Barker's comments on the style of the play and the necessity for reflecting it in the *décor*. The complete set of ten changes, and four scenes from the acted play, are included in the Arts Council *Shakespearian Production* exhibition (see *Acknowledgments* in Vol. I.). Much the same basic design of pillars and arches, but with the addition of a gallery above the central recess, was used by Nugent Monck at Stratford in 1946.

35–36. Scenes by Joseph Harker and Walter Hann: scenery and costumes under the supervision of Alma-Tadema. Barker's comments on the insufficiency of the Alma-Tadema tradition for the costuming of Shakespeare's "high-mettled, quick-tongued crew of politicians" (p. 249) are dramatically and theatrically perceptive. It *is* "rather frigid", and his plea that the designer should "at least provide an escape from this cold classicism" is justly urged. In most modern productions it is done by getting plenty of colour in the opening scene, and sometimes by using coloured togas for the conspirators – Brutus, for example, in blue, in the 1957 Stratford production.

Tree's production, nevertheless, was very fine, and the play remained, with *Twelfth Night*, the most popular item in his repertoire. It was revived in 1900, 1905, 1906, 1907, 1909, 1910, 1911, and 1913. All the notices stress the archaeological interest and the splendour of what Dr. Percy Simpson describes as "this exquisite picture of vanished Rome". It was superbly theatrical, in that it gave back to its contemporary audience their own pictorial imaginings, only bigger and better, and surgingly alive with people and colour and movement. The workmen in tunics and short, hooded mantles, in sober tints, set off the bright dresses of rich bystanders and the pomp of the imperial procession in the opening scene, in which Cæsar, in claret-red silk with an amethyst toga and a laurel wreath, was brought in with the full pageantry of a Roman triumph, (cf. 46). In the Senate scene (35), the senators took their places at the sides, with archivists above in the balcony, and Cæsar entered in procession escorted by the conspirators, who joined the senators and then rose, one by one, to kneel before him, each man moving nearer as he urged his support of Cimber. When Casca struck the first blow, Cæsar sprang to his feet, and half-defending himself rushed down the steps, being stabbed by each of the conspirators as he passed, to meet, with outstretched hands as shown in the photograph, Brutus waiting for him at the foot. "Those not in the secret fled with a cry of horror", which was succeeded by a deadly hush, followed by the rising murmur of the crowd outside.

The second act opened with the Forum scene (36), with the rostrum in front of the Temple of Concord, facing the Temple of Saturn. Dr. Simpson notes particularly the impression of an enormous space that was given to the scene by the height and grandeur of the buildings in the distance and the "vast surging crowd". At "We'll mutiny!" it surged up the terraced steps to the rear. Opposite the rostrum there was a shattered pedestal inscribed "Cæsar", upon which Antony sprang to get their attention and recall them for the reading of the will. At "fetch fire" some of the crowd hurried off and then returned with flaming torches to head the general rush off stage.

Dr Simpson's description, from which these extracts have been taken, is printed in Sir Mark Hunter's edition and in the New Variorum Shakespeare. It is long and very detailed, and notes such things as Calpurnia's robe of pale blue, worn with a sapphire blue palla patterned with gold lilies, and the "lovely glimpse of garden seen from the end of a pillared court" which was Brutus's orchard. He also comments on the acting and notes "the quieter tone of dramatic elocution to-day", as contrasted with the "sound and fury" of the past, when speaking of Lewis Waller's delivery as Brutus.

37–38. There is a full account of this early, simplified setting in *The Stage Year Book 1914*, p. 45. It illustrates another aspect of that carry-over into the commercial theatre of William Poel's ideas and principles for which Barker, Lewis Casson and Barry Jackson were first responsible. Both the Gaiety and the Birmingham Repertory Theatre had apron stages, for which "daring innovation" at Manchester Sir Lewis says he was "soundly rated by Miss Horniman."

In the opening scene the centre arch (37) was closed by grey velvet curtains, and represented the entry to the circus. For the night scene (I iii) a cloth of a wall of great squared stones, painted without perspective, was dropped behind the small permanent P. and O.P. arches, clearly shown in 38. The centre arch, (a truck), was run down to stage left and set diagonally for the entrance to Brutus's house in the orchard scene, and a few dark, profiled tree-wings were silhouetted upstage right by the single shaft of light which was the only illumination, falling from the flies on to the steps of the arch. Cæsar's house (II ii) was a front scene, played as in the Barker productions on the forestage area, before a draped, old-gold curtain, with a bold, blue stencilled border. It was again used, with other furniture and different lighting, for the house of Lepidus (IV i). After the Senate scene (38), a black drapery was dropped behind Antony, and during his "Havoc" speech and the scene with Octavius's servant the set behind him was converted to 37. The murder of Cinna the poet was played on the fore-stage in front of the stage curtain, as were a few other short scenes. For the last part of the play, a simple open-air scene with backcloth, ground rows and some silhouetted tree-cut-outs were used for the Plains of Philippi. For the Tent scene, the panorama curtains were closed. These were the curtains used to close the arches in 38.

39–40.   To the information he gives in the caption Bridges Adams adds the following notes on his general practice: "Small truck stages were often used, and, in the new theatre (1932–34) full-size moving stages which could raise or roll an entire scene into view and permitted the construction of scenes more than twice the width of the proscenium opening, any portion of which could be exhibited, according to the action."

Bridges Adams had stage-managed for Poel in 1910, had had considerable acting experience in the provinces and London, and in 1916–17 had produced at the Liverpool Repertory, now the Playhouse. He was thirty when he became Director at Stratford in 1919. With the help of W. H. Savery, formerly Benson's manager, he recruited a company mainly of old Bensonians, among them Arthur Whitby, H. O. Nicholson, Basil Rathbone, Murray Carrington, Andrew Leigh; and in his first one month's summer season put on *The Merry Wives, Winter's Tale, Midsummer Night's Dream, Tempest, Romeo and Juliet* and *Julius Cæsar*. It is worth noting that Nicholson had played the Old Shepherd, Fabian and Starveling in the three Savoy productions and Whitby had played Autolycus, Sir Toby Belch and Quince.

41–42   This was a very spirited production which had a bad first night reception because the second half of the play was so darkly lit that no one could see properly, and the mob, though smaller than usual, drowned the orations with their yells and shouting and distracted attention from the author's intentions with too much meaningless leaping and rushing about. As too often happens, even when the mob is properly co-ordinated, the crucial "Let him be Cæsar!" was totally lost in the general uproar, and remained so, though the lighting trouble was remedied and the mob movements and noise brought under better control during the run. (cf. *Notes*, 46).

The semi-permanent set for the first part of the play was admirably conceived, and came in for some quite unmerited and indeed stupid criticism, partly, perhaps, because the darkness of the second part and the noisy confusion of the forum scene stunned first nighters' faculties and put them 'agin' the show'. It suffered, for example, from such frivolous complaints as that there was no realistic, pictorial orchard for Brutus to walk in. As 41 shows, it was a handsome formal setting, composed of cyclorama, varying levels and easily-adjusted architectural units – classical columns, cornices and arcading – which could be instantly re-combined for the several different localities without any loss of continuity. It seemed to me at the time to be another forward move in design towards a practical and pleasing convention for the classic scene, dignified and well-calculated for interesting and effective movement and grouping, and setting off the figures of the actors extremely well. Like the 1946 *Antony and Cleopatra* design, (see *Introduction to the Illustrations*), though avoiding actual theatrical miscalculations, it was probably rather ahead of its time, as when Hugh Hunt produced his 1953 *Cæsar* nobody was complaining about the similar lack of a realistic orchard for Brutus, (43).

The acting, individually and as team-work, was excellent. Gielgud as Cassius and Harry Andrews as Brutus were finely matched and I have never known a more poignant and moving tent scene in consequence. Cassius is one of Gielgud's most dynamic creations – a man of passionate, fanatic conviction, intense, vibrant, sympathetic, and rightly meriting Cæsar's description of "dangerous". Cæsar himself was deliberately played as unsympathetic and bombastic. A production loses by this misunderstanding and denial of the Tudor values intended by the author, as was magnificently demonstrated by the Cæsar of Stratford's next production in 1957. Alan Badel was an outstanding Octavius, of whom Barker says, "he appears three times, speaks some thirty lines, and not one of them is wasted." In the modern phrase, he can 'play it cool', and this performance was positively spine-chilling.

43–45.   Of this *Julius Cæsar*, his last production as director of the Old Vic, where it had not been staged for 18 years, Hugh Hunt says in his *Old Vic Prefaces*, "It is because Shakespeare was bound to see the Romans through the eyes of an Elizabethan that the costumes designed for this production show a hint of the Renaissance below the Roman togas, for we cannot escape from this invented world of Renaissance-Romanism that Shakespeare uses." Barker recommends the designer to seek the way of compromise, with "a mixture of helmet, cuirass, trunk hose, stockings and sandals, like nothing that ever was worn, but very wearable and delightful to look at." (p. 250, and cf. Vol. I pp. 20–22). Alan Tagg's designs made just such a compromise as Barker envisaged. These players were Elizabethan Romans (cf. Ernst Stern's designs, Vol. III, 6 and 13). The production was one of the successes of the season, with excellent and sympathetic portraits of Cassius and Brutus from Paul Rogers and William Devlin. In the last Old Vic production, in 1935, Devlin had been an outstanding Cassius, and in 1955, in its next *Cæsar*, Rogers played Brutus. In both instances each actor received the greater praise for his Cassius.

43.   The Conspirators meet at the house of Brutus: Casca, William Squire; Trebonius, Patrick Wymark; Cassius, Paul Rogers; Brutus, William Devlin; Decius Brutus, John Warner; Metellus Cimber, Daniel Thorndike; Cinna, James Maxwell.

44.   Cæsar, Douglas Campbell.

In 1952 the Cambridge Marlowe Society staged at the Arts Theatre a *Julius Cæsar* completely Elizabethan in speech and Romano–Elizabethan in costume. It has been staged a number of times in modern dress, in the professional theatre and by schools and amateurs.

272

46. Cæsar's entry, Act. I. Cæsar, Robert Christie; Antony, Donald Davis; Brutus, Lorne Greene; Cassius, Lloyd Bochner; Casca, Douglas Campbell; Calpurnia, Eleanor Stuart.

Tanya Moiseiwitsch's costume designs, with three in colour, have been reproduced in *Thrice the Brinded Cat hath Mew'd* (1955), – the record of the third Stratford Ontario Festival. Robertson Davies comments on the way the colour and richness of the costumes and appurtenances helped to create the impression of Imperial Rome, and mentions particularly

> a great golden spreadeagle mounted on a pole; a ponderous standard with the *Senatus Populusque Romanus* symbol; golden wreaths and sheaves of wheat borne in procession; the splendid sceptre of Cæsar himself, and the handsome chair in which he was carried; the banners topped with busts; the armour and weapons of the soldiers.

The suggestion of "pompous wealth" given by the portable properties was "finely effective", but he wondered if at times "too much was not being done to suggest the location of a scene", as "some of the more solid decoration, such as the tent and the shattered statue of Pompey, were more trouble than they were worth." The tent was done with "drapery somewhat laboriously hung from the permanent balcony" and it was "precisely to escape from such encumbrances that the Stratford stage was devised". (cf. *Note* to 9–10, Vol. I). While warmly praising the excitement generated by the crowd scenes, when the players "ranged over the theatre until the stage seemed to include the whole of the auditorium", he also notes the risk of doing too much of this kind of thing: "there were times when we wished that the Crowd would be still, and let us see and hear the chief actors".

Bibliographical Note

Between 1923 and 1927 Ernest Benn published the first seven volumes of a handsomely printed, *de luxe* edition called *The Players' Shakespeare*, each volume illustrated by some eminent contemporary artist or stage-designer, with a general introduction and a preface to each play by Granville-Barker. When this project was abandoned Barker included five of these prefaces, to some extent re-arranged or revised, in his *Prefaces to Shakespeare*, First to Fifth Series, which were published by Sidgwick and Jackson between 1927 and 1947. In describing the nature and extent of his revision Barker states that the *Prefaces* to *Love's Labour's Lost* and *Julius Caesar* have been "largely rewritten" and that the *Introduction* is "practically new"; and in the 1930 volume that *The Merchant of Venice* and *Cymbeline Prefaces* "bear small relation" to the originals. He says nothing of any revision of the *Lear Preface* until, in 1936, a footnote to a long extract published in *Shakespeare Criticism 1919–1935* (World's Classics) states that this portion "was revised in 1935 for the present collection". In May 1945, for the first American edition, he stated that in preparing it he had "made only a few changes (there are some of comparative importance in *King Lear* and one in *Julius Caesar*)." The 1947 note to Volume II made this last reference more explicit by adding that the author had "reworked" his analysis of the character of Cassius.

The second impression of the *Hamlet* Preface (April 1937) was described as "revised", and Barker's own copy, now in the British Museum, contains extensive revisions, including the cancellation of 28 of the 40 pages dealing with Hamlet's character. He was apparently still dissatisfied with it, as no final revision was ever published. *Coriolanus* was passed for press by the author a few months before his death in 1946, and published the next year. In the original five-volume *Series*, all except the first and last carried brief prefatory notes in which Barker referred to helpful criticisms and added some useful comments on his aims and methods. The critical portions of these notes have been reprinted in this edition.